HANDBOOK FOR COLLEGE TEACHING

W.R. Miller, Ed. D.
The University of Missouri-
Columbia

Marie F. Miller, Ph.D.
Auburn University
Auburn, AL

PineCrest Publications
P.O. Box 71
Sautee-Nacoochee, GA 30571

Preface

T his handbook is designed for individuals with limited teaching experience at the post-secondary level. The primary premise for effective instruction is that the instructor must have a thorough knowledge and understanding of the subject matter to be taught. To paraphrase Will Rogers, "You can't teach what you don't know no more than you can come back from where you ain't been." Knowledge of subject matter is essential to effective instruction. However, knowledge of subject matter alone is an insufficient base for effective instruction. Effective instructors must understand the principles of learning and the pedagogy that relate to instructional planning, instructional delivery, and instructional evaluation.

The HANDBOOK FOR COLLEGE TEACHING provides basic information of practical value to instructors of adults at the post-secondary school level (e.g., community college instructors, graduate instructors, teaching assistants, and new Ph.D.s). The initial chapter defines and describes the role of the instructor in the post-secondary setting. Chapters that follow focus on the *learning process*, the *identification of content* to be taught, *specifying learner expectations, planning for instruction, instructional strategies, instructional technology,* and the *evaluation of student achievement*. Each chapter concludes with a list of references.

The HANDBOOK FOR COLLEGE TEACHING is based upon field tested research in the domain of teaching and learning. However, the handbook focuses upon the every day challenges faced by instructors who want to facilitate learning and growth on the part of their students. Much of the research evidence upon which the *Handbook* is based is referenced in the extensive list of publications at the end of each chapter. These reference lists will provide direction for those who have a special interest in the "why" as well as the "how" of the teaching/learning process.

About the Authors

Dr. W. R. Miller is a native of Missouri and a graduate of the University of Missouri-Columbia where he received his baccalaureate, masters, and doctoral degrees.

After teaching in the Hazelwood School District in suburban St. Louis and the University Laboratory School in Columbia, Missouri, W.R. taught at Purdue University in West Lafayette, Indiana. In 1963, Dr. Miller returned to the University of Missouri-Columbia where he moved through the ranks from Assistant to Full Professor in the College of Education. Through the years he served as a Department Chair, as Associate Dean, and as Dean of the College of Education.

Dr. Miller authored or co-authored three professional books, edited an industrial arts series, and contributed more than 40 articles in professional journals, monographs, and yearbook chapters. The focus of W.R.'s research, teaching, and scholarship has been on the professional development of the technical specialist as a teacher. His book, Instructors and Their Jobs, is a classic in the field of technical teacher education.

Dr. Marie F. Miller is a native of Pensacola, Florida. She received her baccaluareate degree from the University of Wisconsin-Stevens Point, her masters degree from the University of Wisconsin-Stout, and her Doctor of Philosophy from the University of Missouri-Columbia.

Dr. Miller is currently on the faculty at Auburn University, Auburn, Alabama. Prior to joining the Auburn faculty, Marie was an instructor of communications at Mid-State Technical Institute in Wisconsin Rapids, Wisconsin; an Assistant Professor at Dalton Junior College, Dalton, Georgia and at Mississippi State University in Starkville, Mississippi.

Dr. Marie F. Miller has authored a textbook on communication skills and more than 35 articles in refereed journals. Marie's teaching, research and scholarship has focused on self-concept, work values, program planning, curriculum design, evaluation and the teaching of adults.

Both authors have served as teaching/learning consultants to business, industry and proprietary schools. They have conducted new instructor workshops and seminars for post-secondary proprietary schools as well as community colleges and technical institutes. Much of the pedagogical body of knowledge is generalizable and transportable to a variety of educational settings. Their experience base is extensive, and they have made every effort to share the results of their experience in *The Handbook for College Teaching*.

In full recognition that there is also a companion body of pedagogical knowledge that is field specific, the authors have exercised care in selecting concepts and processes that have stood the test of time and application in a variety of education settings. It is their hope that this handbook will serve as a foundation upon which you will build professional competence through further study and experience.

Acknowledgements

W hen one engages in a project of this magnitude, the time and talent of many individuals are involved. First and foremost we acknowledge the positive contributions that were made to our professional development by a long line of talented college professors with whom we studied. In addition our students and colleagues at Dalton Junior College, GA,MidState Technical Institute, Wisconsin Rapids, WI, University of Wisconsin-Stout, Mississippi State University, Auburn University, AL, Purdue University, IN, and the University of Missouri provided a context for our college teaching experience. In addition, we are appreciative of the opportunities we have had to conduct new instructor orientation workshops and seminars for post-secondary proprietary schools. These experiences enriched our backgrounds and added depth to our understanding of the needs of post-secondary instructors. We acknowledge the support of a host of proprietary school leaders and especially the management of DeVry, Inc. with whom we worked for the past fifteen years.

The supportive role of the University of Missouri-Columbia in general and the Provost Dr. Gerald Brouder in particular is acknowledged with gratitude. His support and encouragement during the manuscript preparation stage of this project were essential to the successful conclusion of the effort.

The prior work that culminated in the book INSTRUCTORS AND THEIR JOBS, written by Dr. W. R. Miller and published by American Technical Publications, Inc., provided a conceptual framework for the HANDBOOK FOR COLLEGE TEACHING. We are grateful to the President of American Technical Publishers, Inc., Mr. Thomas E. Proctor, for permission to use appropriate descriptions, figures and passages from INSTRUCTORS AND THEIR JOBS.

We acknowledge with sincere appreciation the work of the staff of the University of Missouri word processing unit of the College of Education as coordinated by Ms. Judy Diehl, and finally, the technical assistance and graphic design contributions of Amy Hess and Lamar Henderson of the Center for Educational Assessment at the University of Missouri-Columbia.

Contents

3   Human Learning: Facilitated or Impeded 53

THE ROLE AND RESPONSIBILITY OF THE INSTRUCTOR

T he instructor's role, stated simply, is to facilitate learning. It may be somewhat humbling; however, if the learner does not learn, the teacher has not taught. The instructor's role cannot be limited to that of dispensing information. There are many more efficient and effective ways of dispensing and acquiring information than "the oral transmission of information from the notebook of the lecturer to that of the student without going through the mind of either."

The facilitation of learning imposes a wide array of responsibilities upon the instructor. The most fundamental responsibility is to be well prepared in one's discipline, field, and specialty. The course(s) to be taught must be well conceptualized in terms of its position within the body of knowledge. There must be carefully stated objectives to guide the selection of content and learning experiences. The instructor has the responsibility to assess the extent to which the student has achieved the course objectives. Finally, the instructor must assume responsibility for securing student input about the course and instructional process in a never ending quest for improvement. Facilities, instructional materials, and equipment designed to meet student needs are basic requirements for educational programs. However, effective instructors are indispensable to successful educational programs. Without instructors fully competent in their subject and the teaching process, no educational program can be completely successful.

At any level and in any setting, the key variable in effective educational programs is the instructional leader—the instructor. This book focuses on professional competency, which is the knowledge and skills essential for instructors to perform their instructional tasks effectively.

Two other competency areas equally important to the teaching/learning equation are technical or subject matter competency and personal competency. These two competency areas plus professional competency provide the balance and harmony required for effective instruction. All three are essential, like the three legs of a stool.

The objectives of this book are to (a) summarize systematically the existing body of knowledge related to the theory and practice of teaching and learning; (b) present these concepts, principles, and practices in a straightforward manner; (c) show the range of applications of instructional theory and practice; and (d) encourage the formulation of new instructional strategies.

While the applications of the theory and practice related to teaching and learning presented in this book are designed for post-secondary instructors, the principles of instructional planning, delivery, and evaluation are universal. Teaching is an incredibly complex task requiring numerous decisions before and during each class session. Instructors are successful only to the extent that they enable their students to learn at the right time, rapidly, and well. The measure of the instructor's success is the learning that results from instruction. Student learning is a direct result of the quality of the instructor's decisions as instruction is planned, delivered, and evaluated.

With this concept in mind, educational researchers and scholars examine the personal qualities and professional practices that contribute to instructional effectiveness. Through systematic observation of skilled instructors in action and an analysis of their techniques, a body of knowledge emerges, which can be used for self-evaluation and professional development. This body of knowledge can guide those who select, develop, and supervise instructors.

Personal qualities desirable in instructors may be identified in several ways. Long lists have been prepared that include such hints as "stand on both feet," "look at the class," and "keep shoes shined." Little is gained by listing such items that vary from person to person and are accepted by students as part of the instructor's total personality. Many of these variables have little impact on learners. Most personal qualities and mannerisms become important only in extreme cases.

Competency areas that determine the effectiveness of instructors are (a) *technical competency* (the knowledge and skills to be taught), (b) *professional competency* (knowledge of instructional planning, delivery, and evaluation), and (c) *personal competency* (personal characteristics and behaviors that impact the teaching/learning process).

SUBJECT MATTER COMPETENCY

Knowledge of the subject matter to be taught and the skills involved in its application are the key ingredients to effective teaching. To paraphrase Will Rogers, You can't teach something you don't know any more than you can come back from a place you haven't been.

Benefits

Instructional effectiveness is a unique blend of scientific knowledge and artistic expression. There are many variables involving the subject matter, environment, instructor, and learner. Therefore, it is difficult to make absolute statements about the impact of these interacting variables on learner behavior. However, there is no substitute for knowledge and skill in the subject being taught. Knowledge and skill can be acquired in a variety of ways, and the value of certain types and amounts of experience can be debated. What is not debatable is the need for basic competence. Learners should never need to ask, "Is the instructor competent in the subject matter?"

An instructor's level of education and experience affect credibility. Experience can provide examples that can be used to make instruction interesting and meaningful. Additionally, instructors' knowledge of and experience in their subject matter create a level of confidence that contributes to instructional effectiveness. The nature and extent of an instructor's background provide an additional level of credibility that leads to student respect. However, if that experience is not backed up with evident knowledge and skill, the advantage will be lost. Even the beginning instructor, with experience to support detailed knowledge and skill in the subject, is typically more at ease with students than an instructor with limited experience related to the subject matter.

Limitations

The instructor's skill and knowledge of the subject to be taught are important, but such skill and knowledge alone are not sufficient. Many people who have substantial depth of knowledge as well as a high degree of technical skill are not effective in the instructional role. The instructor's role requires the acquisition of knowledge and skills by the learner. The instructor's knowledge and skills are of limited value if the instructor does not have the ability or patience to assist a beginner. Instructors must analyze their competencies and structure the subject matter so that learners can develop their own competency in the subject. Often basic performance elements are so well-integrated into the total movement pattern of a highly skilled performer that basic steps may be difficult to recognize for instructional purposes. When this occurs, the instructor's high level of competence in the subject may interfere with instructional effectiveness rather than contribute to it.

Instructors must make a continuing effort to maintain a high level of competence through additional study and experience with the subject matter. This is particularly true for those students being prepared for positions involving specific and specialized tasks. Students are alert and capable in appraising the competence of their instructors. The competent instructor earns their respect.

Students are quick to spot bluffing or faking and are likely to become suspicious even in those aspects of the subject in which the instructor is well-prepared. The instructor who attempts to bluff when uncertain of what to say or do is not respected by students. No instructor can know everything about the subject. It must be expected that students may ask questions that the instructor cannot answer. When this happens the instructor should not feel threatened and display, either through verbal tone or expression, disgust, frustration, or irritation that might prevent further questions. Respect and credibility are important elements. They can be earned by instructors who are competent in their field. The instructor should compliment students for raising the questions and proceed as follows:

SITUATION	PROPER TECHNIQUE
Information that should be known and taught in the lesson.	Offer to find out. Keep the promise, and relate information back to the class.
Material of interest to advanced students but beyond the scope of the course.	Identify source of information and help locate.
Something for which there is no exact information known.	Inform the class that the facts are not known. Discuss work that has been completed in this area.
Material that is too advanced or complicated for the students at this time.	Briefly describe the technique or process, and indicate its complexity. Suggest that the question be asked again in a later lesson or course. If appropriate, make a note to include it later.

SITUATION	PROPER TECHNIQUE
Material that is not related to the topic being studied.	Indicate that the question is outside the scope of the course. Offer to help the questioner to locate information after class.

PROFESSIONAL COMPETENCY

Professional competency may be conceptualized in a variety of ways. However, this handbook focuses on three major areas of the instructor's professional role (i.e., instructional planning, instructional delivery, and instructional evaluation). The instructor's effectiveness related to these three major areas of professional responsibility will be determined in large measure by his/her knowledge and understanding of the theory and practice of the teaching/learning process.

Instructional Planning

The essential element of instructional planning is the content of the instructional process. Identification of the skills and knowledge to be acquired by the learner cannot be taken for granted or passed over lightly. Systematic procedures have been developed by educational researchers and scholars that can answer the fundamental question: "Have the appropriate knowledge elements or skills been identified for inclusion in an instructional program?" Most instructors, especially new ones, are not involved in the content identification process as this is typically accomplished when the curriculum for the program or school is established. However, instructors are frequently involved in updating and verifying the content, especially in content areas that are subject to rapid change.

After the subject area has been analyzed and the inherent skills and knowledge have been identified, the portion of that knowledge to be included in a given course must be selected. The selection process involves a number of factors such as objectives to be met at a given level and the background and experience of the learners.

After selecting the content to be included in a given program or course, the instructional planner focuses more directly on units and lessons to be experienced by students. The instructor makes decisions regarding specific objectives to be met during a specified time period, learning activities that lead to achievement of the objectives, and evaluation procedures that assess the extent to which students have mastered the objectives.

Instructional Delivery

After the instructor has planned the course of instruction and made detailed plans for specific lessons, the plan must be delivered. The fundamental task is facilitating student learning. This may involve direct presentations of content through such general methods as lecture, demonstration, or assigned readings. It may involve the supervision of students as they conduct a laboratory exercise, watch a film, prepare a diagram, or engage in other activities designed to help them develop competencies specified in the instructional plan. Many different instructional materials, techniques, and aids are available for use as the instructor guides the learning process. As emphasized by McKeachie, college teaching has many important goals, not the least of which is to increase the student's motivation and ability to continue learning after leaving college.

Instructional Evaluation

Instructional evaluation is typically viewed as a systematic means of assessing the extent to which a student meets specified objectives. Instructional evaluation is also an indirect assessment of the instructional process itself.

Evaluation can be conducted in a variety of ways. Competent instructors select the appropriate evaluation procedure for a given group of learners at specific points in the instructional process. Some procedures are precise and objective while others are based on the instructor's observational and judgmental abilities. Regardless of the specific procedures used, the process is continuous as it provides information about student achievement and the effectiveness of instruction. Instructors must be sensitive to student responses. A continuing effort, both informal and formal, is required to assess student progress. In formal evaluation, examination questions are used to determine whether or not students have met specific objectives. Students must demonstrate the level of skill, knowledge, or attitude for which the instructional program was designed. In informal evaluation, the instructor may read the facial expressions of students and listen to their questions to determine the extent to which they have assimilated a particular idea, process, or skill.

The primary purpose of student evaluation is to monitor the amount or quality of learning, not to rate or grade the student. The process of thinking through the material and helping students organize it in their own way is of tremendous value in fixing the important ideas and relationships in the students' memory. Examples of this strategy include the review preceding an examination or the discussion following an examination.

PERSONAL COMPETENCY

People have different characteristics and learned behaviors. No two people are alike. The diverse characteristics of instructors and students and the absence of absolutes or predictable outcomes make the educational process challenging, complex, and interesting. Instructors possess certain characteristics and behavior patterns that influence their performance and the performance of their students.

Personal Characteristics

An individual's personal characteristics determine the way that person is perceived by others. Physical characteristics are obvious, but there is very little relationship between an instructor's height, weight, color, or sex and instructional effectiveness. Psychological and emotional characteristics influence instructional effectiveness more directly, yet there is a broad range of variability within which little difference in effectiveness is noted.

Attitudes. An instructor possesses both general and specific opinions or feelings about people, things, and events. A person's behavior and comments often reveal either a positive or negative attitude. Attitudes, often reflected through behavior, typically result from life experiences and interaction with others. By the time a person reaches adulthood, changes in attitude are difficult to achieve.

People with positive attitudes are generally more effective instructors than those whose general outlook is negative. Specific examples of attitudes that impact on instructional effectiveness are the instructor's feelings toward students and the learning process. Instructors who use their position to gain attention or impress their students have ego needs that interfere with their instructional effectiveness. An attitude of caring must be projected to students. Students are more motivated to learn under the direction of an instructor interested in students as individuals and in the particular subject.

The instructor with a positive attitude toward teaching sends a reinforcing message to the student, which has a positive impact upon learning. Encouragement and expectation are factors that enhance learning. The instructor behaves in ways that make student development a self-fulfilling prophesy. Students think, "I believe I can because you believe I can." "I kept trying until I did it because you convinced me that I could do it."

Instructors who do not like their jobs or the organizations in which they work, frequently project a negative attitude in their classrooms. Their attitudes have a significant impact on the learning environment, which affects student learning and student attitudes as well. The role of the instructor demands involvement with students. It is a contradiction for instructors to say they like teaching but are unwilling to assist students in the learning and development process.

Intellectual abilities. An instructor must read, write, reason, synthesize, solve problems, compute, formulate and express ideas, and make decisions with a reasonably high level of competency. These are tasks of the mind that require facility with the symbols used to communicate about ideas, people, and things.

Good communication is essential for an effective instructor. Individuals wishing to teach must have above-average cognitive abilities. Various terms such as intelligence, cognition, and perception, are used to indicate the mental abilities essential to an effective instructor. In conjunction with the ability to speak clearly and distinctly, instructors must possess the intellectual abilities that provide the substance for oral expression.

Creativity. While current research and theory contend that creativity is a part of intellectual functioning, it does deserve some separate attention as it relates to the role of the instructor. Creativity and resourcefulness are qualities that tend to distinguish outstanding instructors from average instructors. Creativity produces the novel idea, strategy, or approach that gets the job done. A creative instructor thinks of ways to describe or illustrate subject matter so that it comes alive for the learner.

Poor instructors often use the same method of presentation regardless of the topic However, the method that works well for one individual, one class, or one lesson may not be satisfactory in another situation. Effective instructors are alert to the slightest evidence of confusion, misunderstanding, or lack of interest among the students, and they are able to adjust the presentation to correct the difficulty.

A primary reason for varying instructional procedures with different classes or students is that individuals differ in native capacity, experience, and learning style. The rapidity with which students learn a particular subject depends to a large extent on their ability to adapt their learning pattern to the instructor's teaching method. This instructor-student relationship should work both ways, and the effective instructor must be quick to modify instructional procedures so that learning is aided. Understanding the principles of learning allows the creative, resourceful instructor to design a new instructional aid to illustrate a principle, use a current event to emphasize a concept, or develop more effective methods of measuring the progress of each student.

Interpersonal skills. The ability to interact with students, administrators, parents, employers, and community leaders is vital to the effective instructor. It is often said that educators are in the *people development* business. While good interpersonal skills do not ensure learning, the research evidence is quite convincing that students' learning is adversely affected by negative feelings toward the instructor. A student who is afraid, angry, or worried does not learn effectively.

A central factor affecting the learning environment is the instructor's self-concept and confidence. People's personalities are the total of their personal, social, and emotional traits. Some of these personality factors are inherited, while others result from environmental conditioning and experiences over a lifetime. As adults, instructors can anticipate little change in personality. However, awareness of characteristics and behavior that have an adverse effect on learning can be helpful. Negative feelings about self are often reflected through sarcasm, defensiveness, insults, hostility, aloofness, and overreaction to student behavior. These negative instructor behaviors interfere with the development of good personal relationships with students.

Although a clear understanding of the instructor's role is necessary to establish a professional distinction between instructor and student, this professional distance must not be viewed as uncaring, uninterested, or a distinction based on human value. An important line exists between a close friendship or social relationship and a professional relationship based on the mutual respect and concern of individuals engaged in the teaching/learning process. The instructor must maintain a positive relationship with students that contributes to rather than detracts from the primary goal of learning.

The instructor must work in harmony with fellow instructors and supervisors. Willingness to do more than is required helps earn the respect of one's associates and superiors, unless this willingness is accompanied by aggressiveness or lack of consideration. Interpersonal skills are important in the classroom and in all areas of the educational enterprise.

Behavior. Personality, which is largely determined by the time one reaches adulthood, is the primary variable in establishing relationships with others.

This complex integration of characteristics is largely responsible for presenting the instructor to others. Some of the ways one presents oneself and is perceived by others occurs naturally without any conscious decision making. Nevertheless, much of the instructor's impact on learning is a result of behavior, both word and deed. Obviously, instructor behavior that is consistent with one's feelings and value system seems most believable to students. However, appropriate behavior depends upon the time and conditions and cannot be predetermined by someone else. This is a part of the complex decision making process that happens continuously in any teaching/learning environment. General principles of behavior are applicable and appropriate in most situations.

Considerate. Consider the feelings of others. Since one cannot know how others feel about many things, instructors should be cautious in situations that may possibly be embarrassing. Dogmatic statements about such issues as politics, racial, or cultural differences, or the value of one school subject over another are best avoided.

Controversial matters can be discussed, but instructors' behaviors should be tactful and considerate. Instructors should react to ideas or statements in a manner that is not demeaning to the person. Think first and talk second is good advice since meaningful discussions are difficult if the instructor is perceived to be unreasonable or opinionated. Honesty with students and colleagues is most appreciated when one seems willing to listen and consider other points of view.

When students present an incorrect response, the instructor should avoid demeaning them. Whenever possible, build on a portion of the incorrect response. For example, "Joe, I believe you may be on the right track, but there are some problems with your response. Jane, what can you add?" or "Joe, elaborate a bit more. Why do you believe this to be true?" Short responses like, "No, you are dead wrong." or "Joe, how could you possibly think that way?" or "Jane, where were you when we talked about this yesterday?" can embarrass students and may be perceived as demeaning. Sarcasm and ridicule have no place in teaching. They have a negative impact on learning and often result in undesirable behavior as the student tries to save face.

Cooperative. Instructors should be sensitive to the total school program and keep their own teaching responsibilities in perspective. Other activities in the school and in the lives of students may be more important than a given class period in a particular course. The understanding instructor should avoid being dogmatic and inflexible in these situations.

It is essential for instructors to cooperate as they work together for the benefit of students. The instructor should discuss noninstructional responsibilities with the administration to understand clearly the expected role. An instructor who carries out this role in a friendly, cooperative manner develops a positive reputation and can expect a high degree of cooperation from others.

Complimentary. A significant factor in human achievement is positive reinforcement. Compliments spur people to increased productivity and satisfaction. Showing interest in a student's or a colleague's accomplishment is a form of compliment. Instructors who achieve unusual success with a class or a particular approach to a student's problem should be complimented sincerely. Avoid excessive flattery and too frequent compliments about inconsequential matters.

Friendly. The instructor who meets both students and associates with a smile and a word of greeting finds it easier to work with them. A free and natural relationship should be maintained with fellow instructors as well as with students. The age old advice to new teachers, "Be fair, be firm, and be friendly," is still relevant today. It is important for students to perceive their instructors as approachable and pleasant. Positive rapport is built on a number of factors including a smile, an exchange of greeting, and acknowledgement of another's worth.

An instructor may establish a reputation for being tough by any of the following methods (a) using aggressive behavior, (b) speaking in a commanding tone of voice, (c) frowning constantly, (d) displaying an inflexible attitude, (e) bragging or threatening that few A's are given, (f) stating that extraordinary effort is required to pass the course, (g) refusing to repeat instructions or questions, (h) acting as though students must be driven rather than led, and (i) showing little consideration for students.

Instructors who use these tactics seem to believe that students can be bullied into learning. Such techniques discourage students from cooperating with the instructor and fill them with fear or disgust. Little learning occurs when the student feels fear, disgust, or resentment. The effective instructor develops patience, tact, and self-control while exhibiting maturity to facilitate learning.

Involved. The instructor should be involved in the total school program. Interest in and attendance at school functions develop rapport with students and colleagues. Participation in appropriate recreational and social activities better acquaints the instructor with other faculty and administrators. The instructor need not have social contacts with fellow staff members but should interact with them to develop a congenial, informal relationship within the group.

Professional. Professional instructors take pride in their role and are highly ethical in dealing with others. They also take pride in being competent and in using that competency to help students become competent. As a professional educator, an instructor values education and reinforces all parts of the curriculum. For example, the teacher of computing must recognize and reinforce the value of correct English usage, good communication skills, and other elements of the total educational program. According to the Carnegie Foundation for the Advancement of Teaching, the educated person is intellectually curious, thinks critically, weighs evidence dispassionately, is tolerant, temperate, mature, is not intellectually lazy, and does not permit rational processes to be at the mercy of fears and prejudices.

To paraphrase a familiar advertising jingle, the professional instructor needs to look sharp, feel sharp, and be sharp. A clean, neat appearance is an asset in any job, but an instructor is in a position to be observed closely, and poor grooming can have an adverse influence on students and colleagues alike. Associates gain their first impression from general appearance. Such impressions are very strong.

TEACHING AND SCHOLARSHIP

There should be no conflict between the role of teaching and scholarship in higher education. Teaching is informed and enhanced through the scholarly efforts of the instructor. The general public often perceive college teaching somewhat like an actor or performer onstage dispensing bits of wisdom to expectant students sitting passively in a huge auditorium. While this scenario certainly occurs, it is a relatively minor part of the instructor's role. In fact, effective instructors realize that passive students are not effective learners. Learning requires involvement and participation by the learner. Learners must assume ownership of their education to maximize the schooling process.

According to Dr. Dennis P. Jones, President of the National Center for Higher Education Management Systems (NCHEMS) there is a disturbing failure to distinguish between the concepts of research and scholarship in many U.S. universities. The term "research" refers to a strategy of inquiry through a variety of activities designed to expand the knowledge base of a discipline. The term "scholarship" is a broader concept which refers to those activities that are intended to synthesize the most recent knowledge in a field and organize it in a way that provides new insights and enhances the ability of the faculty member to present information to students in the classroom. Given these distinctions, it is important for all college faculty to be scholars. They must be current with the developments in their disciplines and continually strive to find ways to help their students acquire this knowledge. However, all faculty members need not be researchers. Relatively few institutions have the resources to support research faculty in ways necessary to make significant contributions to the furtherance of their discipline. (As Dr. Jones suggests, there are relatively few faculty members who have the capacity to make truly significant contributions to their field. Many engage in research activities but relatively few generate significant research outcomes.)

Unfortunately, the reward structure in higher education has become skewed so that it overemphasizes research. The tenure and promotion policies at true research universities have become examples copied by institutions that cannot claim distinction in research. This over-emphasis on research in the reward system for individual faculty members closely associated with notions of institutional status— the more research done at the institution, the higher the institutional status is not always valid. This combination of factors has led to two unfortunate consequences. First, it creates an unfulfillable desire on the part of all institutions that they become research institutions. Some faculty members downgrade teaching, pedagogical scholarship, and service and emphasize research whenever they can. As a consequence, there is much relatively meaningless research published in obscure journals with too little attention given to excellence in teaching. Too many faculty members have lost pride in being participants in institutions that emphasize quality of undergraduate education.

The second consequence is that it becomes particularly difficult to separate the notions of research and scholarship in those institutions where research is a legitimate part of the mission. Even in these institutions not all faculty members in all disciplines should strive to be full-time researchers. Only a few can be full-time researchers and rewarded for excellence only in research endeavors. Many (perhaps most) will find it impossible for one reason or another to engage in major research efforts. These individuals should pursue (and be recognized for pursuing) worthwhile scholarship related to their teaching and service activities.

A report from the Carnegie Foundation suggests replacing the oft suggested dichotomy between researchers and teachers with a modern view of scholarship that includes discovery, integration, application, and teaching as a better model for higher education.

DIVERSITY IN THE CLASSROOM

Too frequently instructors behave in ways that ignore the diversity of gender, race, ethnicity, social class, age, religion and experience. Higher education mirrors the pluralistic nature of the society of which it is a part; however, instructional practices are rooted in European traditions. The term "multicultrualism" is often used to encompass the diversity that exists within the classroom although some of the elements of diversity such as gender and age are not generally associated with cultural components.

Sensitivity to the differences among learners is the first and easiest step in the establishment of a multicultural learning environment. However, it is even more important for instructors to accomodate these differences through their instructional practices and behavior. The higher education experience of most college instructors is often considered to be culturally neutral, nevertheless, a closer look suggests academic traditions that are both masculine and rooted in the European derived belief that higher education provides a means to economic and social advancement. Other examples such as competitive or assertive behavior, "talking out" or "speaking up" in class, and acceptance of grading curves by which one person gains at the expense of another suggest that the mores of academe reflect the traditionally dominant culture. It is difficult for faculty to see beyond their own acculturation and to visualize alternative strategies and behaviors that would not be at conflict with the mores and values of students with non-traditional orientations whether they be older students, Afro-American, Asian-American, Native American, foreign born, or some other form of diversity. It is important that college faculty become aware of the ways in which the traditional classroom culture excludes or constrains learning for some students.

While it is easy to over simplify and make sweeping generalizations, the effective instructor needs to be aware of the research cited by Border and Van Note Chism which suggests that the instructor use a variety of participatory learning strategies to accomodate ethnic cultural differences as well as gender differences. The research literature further suggests that women profit from shared classroom authority versus the instructor dominated classroom. Women students may need (1) special challenges to establish and defend their own view points, (2) reinforcement of independent thinking, (3) creative uses of peer learning groups, (4) carefully designed collaborative efforts and (5) emphasis on the use of discussion methodology.

Individuals vary in terms of their learning styles. This variance from individual to individual occurs within cultural groups; therefore, it is inappropriate to generalize that all black students, Asian students, white students learn best from any given approach. A varied repertoire of teaching strategies permits all students to experience a variety of cultural styles rather than to expect all students to give way or adapt to the dominate cultural mode.

In addition to a knowledge of learning styles as they impact on the teaching/learning interface for all students, the effective instructor needs to be especially sensitive to the impact of cultural differences on learning styles of each individual. A knowledge of cultural mores and values allows instructors to modify their behavior to create a more effective learning environment.

While there is insufficient time or space in this handbook to provide you with even an adequate sample of the characteristics of the various groups which comprise diversity in the college classroom, it is important for the college teacher to recognize that groups of students enter college with variations in (1) motivation styles, (2) learning styles and strategies, (3) information processing skills and preferences, (4) social relations skills and values, and (5) communication patterns.

THE INSTITUTIONAL CULTURE

While most aspects of the instructor's role are "culture free" or constant irrespective of the type of institution in which they are employed, the nature of the institution and the "cultural" norms and expectations cannot be ignored. For example, the course is scheduled in a given place, for a given time, specified days of the week, with a beginning and ending date. Instructors are expected to give examinations, perhaps at specified times, and assign course grades. They may or may not be expected to keep attendance. However, if you believe participation is essential to learning you must expect students to attend class. Regulations are a part of the system in which one is employed, and they provide the parameters for actions. Likewise, institutional mores affect students' expectations for the teaching/learning process. The typical class in a given institutional setting may rely heavily on one or more methods (e.g., lecture, question and answer, discussion, group activity). There may or may not be extensive use of written reviews, case studies, research papers, or other supplemental learning activities. Also there may be norms with regard to the type of test used, frequency of testing, and methods of grading. These norms do not need to hamper the innovative instructor; however, sensitivity to expectations and mores suggest that deviant procedures need careful consideration and explanation to students. Instructors must learn to operate within the parameters of institutional regulations as well as within the informal mores of the institutional culture.

CONCLUSION

An instructor's effectiveness is determined in large measure by technical or subject matter competency, professional competency, and personal competency. Inadequacy in any one of these areas will have an adverse impact on student learning. A professional instructor's responsibility is to facilitate student learning. Investment through participation by students and instructors in a cooperative enterprise facilitates learning.

An instructor's role is a challenging one that demands a lifetime commitment to learning. However, there are rewards that justify the effort. One of the most satisfying experiences instructors have is knowing that through their efforts someone has become more competent, more confident, a better human being, and a more productive citizen. Through the application of good teaching skills, an instructor brings new opportunities to others. Good instructors discover dormant talents in students. To motivate students, develop their skills, and see the pleasure that results from newfound competencies is a reward unique to teaching.

Contacts made with students often develop into strong, lifelong friendships because of the mutual respect and understanding gained through working and learning together. Instructors also enjoy exchanging ideas with fellow instructors and developing new ideas and interests.

It has been said that the only way to really know something is to teach it. Since this is at least partly true, instructors often find themselves studying the things students must learn from a new, more analytical point of view. Such study adds to an instructor's knowledge of the subject.

REFERENCES _____ **1**

Allen, R. R. & Rueter, T. (1990). Teaching assistant strategies: an introduction to college teaching. Dubuque, Iowa: Kendall/Hunt.

Border, Laura & Van Note Chism, Nancy (Ed) (1992). Teaching for diversity. San Francisco: Jossey-Bass.

Boyer, Ernest L. (1990). In search of community. Carnegie Foundation for the Advancement of Teaching, American Council on Education, Washington, D.C.

Bruner, J. (1966). Toward a theory of instruction. Cambridge: Harvard University Press.

Eble, K. E. (1988). The craft of teaching (2nd ed.). San Francisco: Jossey-Bass.

Ericksen, S. C. (1985). The essence of good teaching. San Francisco: Jossey-Bass.

Ericksen, S. C. (1974). Motivation for learning: a guide for the teacher of the young adult. Ann Arbor, Mich.: The University of Michigan Press.

Fuhrmann, B. S. & Grasha, A. F. (1983). A practical handbook for college teachers. Boston: Little, Brown and Co.

Good, T., & Brophy, J. (1986). Educational psychology: A realistic approach. New York: Longman, Inc.

Gliesman, David H. (1981). Learning how to teach. Washington, D.C.: ERIC Clearinghouse on Teacher Education.

Greive, Donald (Ed.) (1989). Teaching in college: A resource for college teachers. Cleveland: Info-Tec, Inc.

Gullette, M. M. (Ed.) (1982). The art and craft of teaching. Cambridge, Mass.: Harvard-Danforth Center for Teaching and Learning.

Johnson, Glenn Ross (1988). Taking teaching seriously: A faculty handbook. College Station, TX: The Center for Teaching Excellence.

Lee, Calvin B. (Ed.) (1967). Improving college teaching. Washington, D.C.: American Council on Education.

Lowman, J. (1984). Mastering the techniques of teaching. San Francisco: Jossey-Bass.

McKeachie, W. J. (1986). Teaching tips: a guidebook for the beginning college teacher. Lexington, Mass,: D. C. Heath and Company.

Neff, Rose Ann & Weimer, Maryellen (Ed.) (1990). Teaching college: Collected readings for the new instructor. Madison: Magna Publications, Inc.

Schwartz, Joel J. (1988). Teaching at Carolina. Durham, N.C.: Center for Teaching and Learning at the University of North Carolina.

2

PLANNING AND GETTING STARTED

The essential elements of an effective educational program are instructional planning, instructional execution, and evaluation. Instructional planning is the base or foundation upon which the other two elements are built. Any human enterprise requires planning. The complexity of the enterprise or undertaking determines the magnitude of the planning needed. One does not invest much time in planning a trip to the local restaurant. However, a ten day 3000 mile vacation trip requires a considerable amount of planning time. The time and energy invested in planning pays dividends in terms of increased efficiency and quality of a product or service resulting from the enterprise or activity. The benefits of planning are no less true for an educational enterprise. The professional instructor knows that the time spent in planning is an investment that pays dividends. The dividends of planning are (1) increased learning, (2) more efficient use of class time, (3) fewer discipline problems, (4) incremental improvement in instruction, and (5) a more relaxed pace and emotional feeling of the instructor "who has planned the work and who can work the plan."

This section covers planning at the macro level, which might include an entire program or sequence of courses, and the micro level, which would involve the planning of a unit of instruction such as a course, lesson, or even a ten minute presentation. It is recognized that your teaching assignment may be for a course that has already been planned. However, additional planning on your part will be required for each class session and the attendant assignments to students. Obviously, if you are given the entire responsibility for a course, your responsibility for planning and organizing prior to the beginning of class will be much more extensive than if you had been hired to teach or assist with one section of a multi-section course for which others have major planning responsibilities. Nevertheless, it is important for you to understand the planning process as well as the rationale for the decisions that have been made related to the selection and organization of course content.

As planning is discussed, reference will be made to instructional objectives, instructional strategies, and evaluation. Details of these important aspects of the instructional process will be included in separate chapters. It is important for you to recognize the sequencing of these components even though you may not have sufficient background at this point to understand them fully. Do not let this concern you since they will be covered adequately in subsequent chapters.

INSTRUCTIONAL PLANNING

Whether planning is applied to the entire post-secondary program or to a ten minute demonstration, it is still planning, and it is important.

At the macro level, the planning effort is typically referred to as curriculum design. After a content analysis has been conducted, major decisions have to be made regarding the packaging and sequencing of educational experiences that will enable learners to acquire the identified competencies (knowledge and/or skills). The curriculum design process typically involves committees of instructors, administrators and staff specialists who work together to determine the courses to be taken by students in a given program, the content of the courses, and the sequence in which the courses are taken. Consistent with this process, the term curriculum is defined as "a series of planned experiences which are designed to assist learners in the achievement of major goals."

At the micro level, the planning effort is typically the full responsibility of the instructor. At this level, the instructor must plan the course to be taught. There is considerable variation among organizations with regard to the decisions for which the instructor is responsible. For example, the instructor may be provided with a course title, a topical outline and told that a given textbook has been adopted. In another situation, the course may be well structured with performance objectives for the several units of the course, and a topical outline for each unit and lesson plans. The first example, which would involve the instructor in much more decision making and planning, is probably more typical than the second. Technical educators, industrial trainers and military instructors have long recognized the value of well planned programs of instruction. As a result, they have been increasingly willing to provide the staff resources necessary to do both macro and micro planning. This resource investment permits instructors to devote more time to lesson planning, execution and evaluation of instruction. Unfortunately, too few colleges and universities have invested the necessary institutional resources to facilitate a comprehensive planning effort.

SYSTEMS APPROACH

The word system is a generic term that is applied to everything from the "home entertainment system" to the missile detection or "early warning system." However, the context within which the term is used in instructional design refers to *general systems theory*. In this context, a "system" is a way of thinking about a phenomenon or event whereby a set of objects, principles or facts are arranged in a form which reveals their regular interaction as a rational or coherent whole. The most common graphic representation of a system is shown in Figure 2-1. The basic structure of a system will include at least the following elements: (1) INPUT (anything taken into the system, (2) OUTPUT (anything that is generated outward from the system), (3) PROCESSOR (mechanisms that convert input into output—procedures, policies, materials, decisions, etc.), (4) FEEDBACK (output resulting from past processing that is used as input at any stage), and (5) ENVIRONMENT (external circumstances which can influence inputs, the process, outputs or the feedback loop.)

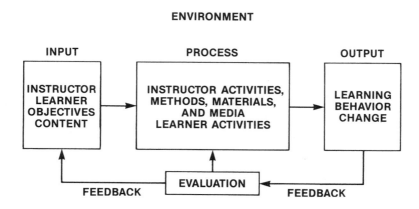

Figure 2-1. Application of general systems theory to instruction reveals the interrelationships among elements of the teaching-learning process.

The instructional designer or planner can utilize the general systems approach to reveal or depict the interrelationships of all elements involved in the teaching/learning enterprise.

COURSE PLANNING

As one moves from the macro level of planning to course planning the focus shifts to the means for achieving the desired end of competence. Figure 2-2 provides a graphical representation of the process by which the educational planner might think through the process and arrive at decisions regarding the general structure of courses within the curriculum. Assuming that the rectangle in Figure 2-2 represents all the content that is in a given subject area (the theoretical body of knowledge), the analysis process

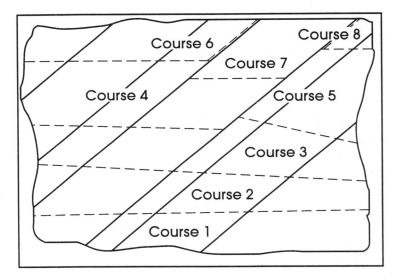

Figure 2-2. The body of knowledge is analyzed and organized into major divisions and courses.

would identify a portion of the whole. In the diagram, the irregular figure within the rectangle symbolically encompasses the content identified through the analysis procedures. The content thus identified is categorized into major divisions represented by space between diagonal lines. The next step in the process involves dividing the total content into manageable components which are typically called courses. In the diagram these are illustrated by the dashed lines cutting across several major divisions of content. Each course, thus identified, must be planned.

COURSES OF STUDY

The document containing the results of the instructor's planning efforts for a course is referred to as a course of study. A course of study should consider:

1. relationship of the course to the entire educational program,

2. objectives of the course,

3. needs of the student,

4. content to be taught,

5. specialized equipment and facilities

6. appropriate methods of instruction,

7. student learning activities,

8. resource materials, and

9. procedures and instruments for evaluation.

The following paragraphs describe the components of a course of study.

Course Title. The instructor should select an appropriate, descriptive course title, one that is as specific as possible. The course title should indicate content covered and type and level of instruction. Examples include:

1. Fundamentals of Geology,

2. Architectual Design,

3. Descriptive Geometry,

4. American Literature,

5. Southern American History,

6. Watercolor Fundamentals,

7. Principles of Economics,

8. Computer Programming-Fortran,

9. Learning Theories,

10. Residential Landscape Design, and

11. Teaching and Learning Strategies.

Introductory Statement. After choosing an appropriate title, the instructor should prepare an introductory statement that defines the level at which the course is appropriate. Prerequisites and information about the length and nature of the course should also be specified.

Course Objectives. Objectives should specify the information to be learned and the skills and affective behaviors to be developed by the learner. The following performance objectives might be written for a course in beginning photography. The conditions and criteria of the performance objectives have been omitted.

The student will:

1. describe the relationship between lens size and speed of exposure,

2. describe the measurement and control of light and the chemistry of development,

3. mix photographic chemicals to develop black-and-white film,

4. develop contact prints and enlargements, and

5. identify good composition and technical quality in photography.

Objectives should be realistic. Always consider the facilities and amount of class time available, as well as the educational level and interests of the students. If objectives are realistic and instruction is effective, nearly every student should be able to exhibit the specified performance.

Determining Content. With course objectives in mind, instructors should select the knowing (cognitive) and doing (psychomotor) elements of content that they wish to teach. Instructors should select elements that best meet their objectives and can be included within the time limits of the course.

After tentatively selecting knowing and doing elements consistent with course objectives and time limitations, instructors may find it beneficial to seek the opinions of other instructors and administrators.

Content identified through analysis and a statement of behavioral objectives should be the same. Both should state desired student behavior. Through the process of analysis, student behavior is identified, while in an instructional program, student behavior is specified as the desired end result of instruction.

Arranging Content. When possible, the least complex content should be taught first. Also, knowledge-related content must be taught before doing, or performance, content. It is best to teach related knowledge and theory before the student needs it to solve practical problems. If possible, information should be taught in small segments throughout the course.

Instructional Materials. The selection or preparation of visual aids, textbooks, and other instructional materials should follow decisions about course content and teaching methods. Instructional materials must be consistent with student ability, emphasize key elements of the course, and present information effectively.

Good textbooks are essential for effective instruction. Textbooks are often written with general objectives in mind and are designed to be used in a variety of situations. As a result, supplemental materials are often required for a specific course.

Selection of films may depend on availability from a film library. Therefore, films should be requested for a specific date as early as possible. Films from business, industry, and trade associations should be used only if they contribute to instructional objectives.

Other instructional aids, including charts, illustrations, and overhead projection transparencies, should be selected or prepared for each lesson. Special equipment and supplies should be ordered early.

Written examinations, performance tests, and assignment sheets should be prepared and reproduced as soon as the objectives, course content, and schedule have been determined. These materials should be reproduced as soon as the objectives, course content, and schedule have been determined. These materials should be ready well in advance of their use. The content of an assignment or test should not come as a surprise to the student.

Learning Activities. The purpose of instructional planning is to facilitate learning. Therefore, the selection of appropriate and effective learning activities is a critical factor in the planning process and the course of study. Learning activities may be as varied and creative as the instructor's imagination. Learning activities may include reading assignments, prepared notebooks, field trips, and other projects.

A project is a learning experience in which students apply skills and knowledge to create a product. A project may be a notebook in a class on education, a set of house plans in architectural drawing, or a garden in agriculture. The order of instruction is influenced by the practical nature of projects. For example, in a photography course, taking pictures would normally precede developing film and making prints.

The fundamental purpose of projects is to provide an opportunity for practical, meaningful application of specific skills as they are learned. When students are required to construct practice pieces that are thrown away, there is usually less motivation to succeed than when the same skills are developed through construction of useful projects. Projects must be designed so the right skills are emphasized. A common failure is to use projects without careful analysis of the skills and knowledge inherent in the activity, or to use projects in which a disproportionate amount of time is spent developing relatively unimportant skills.

In selecting or designing projects for instructional purposes, a number of objectives should be considered:

1. Projects should develop skills specified in the course objectives.

2. Projects should have intrinsic and/or extrinsic value.

3. Projects should use readily available materials where practical.

4. Projects should follow consistent principles and standard practices.

Concepts in mathematics, physics, and chemistry lend themselves to various types of projects. Photography, printing, drafting, painting, and other subjects in which design is important are also taught effectively through the use of projects. A project is a meaningful product for the learner. Laboratory exercises that allow mastery of skills are beneficial for students. Since there is no finished project to grade, the preferred evaluation tool is a performance test that involves systematic observation and rating.

Field trips are very important in allowing students to see beyond the classroom and understand the application outside the classroom. Field trips also help the instructor keep course material up-to-date and interesting. Business and industrial firms are usually pleased to have visitors. Arrangements should be made in advance, and students should be given a thorough briefing. The host should know the students' backgrounds and the types of experiences that will be of particular value during the visit. If possible a schedule of events for the visit should be prearranged.

Students should be given the opportunity to discuss the field trip. It is also appropriate for the teacher to send a letter of appreciation to the host after the visit.

Outside speakers often provide valuable experiences for students. Technical specialists, scientists, authors, designers, and managers are frequently willing to demonstrate or lecture about their fields. These outside speakers can provide motivation for students and add variety and realism to the course. In making arrangements, be sure the demonstration or lecture is consistent with lesson objectives.

Since most potential speakers are busy, every effort should be made to facilitate their participation in the course. Transportation and a time schedule should be arranged carefully. A capable student may be assigned to assist the speaker with preparation details. The instructor and class should find appropriate means of showing their appreciation.

Supplementary reading assignments, in addition to regular assignments, are part of most courses of study. Instructors should make reading materials readily available. An occasional reference to a book, current article, or appropriate movie may urge alert students to expand their interest in the subject.

Teaching Plan. Effective instructors frequently change resource materials, teaching-learning aids, and student activities, even though course objectives and content may be relatively stable. A course of study may be prepared in advance of instruction, but it changes continually because the revision and updating process is never complete.

The teaching plan becomes the instructor's guide as it places instruction in sequence. A teaching plan format involves a series of columns that permit the instructor to list (1) each major subdivision, or unit, and the amount of time to be devoted; (2) student learning activities for the unit; (3) demonstrations to be provided by the instructor; (4) informational content covered in the unit, keyed to textbook or other resource; and (5) supplementary aids or activities, such as field trips or films, as well as evaluative activities such as performance tests, rating scales, and written examinations. See Figure 2-3.

SUGGESTED TEACHING PLAN FORMAT				
MAJOR UNIT	LEARNING ACTIVITY	DEMONSTRATION	INFORMATIONAL TOPIC DISCUSSION, LECTURE, READING	SUPPLEMENTARY AIDS

Figure 2-3. A teaching plan provides a skeletal framework for a course.

The teaching plan provides general information for the course; however, it does not provide enough detail to guide day-to-day instruction. See figure 2-4.

COURSE SYLLABI

It is important for students to know the direction that a given course will take. In fact, one of the dividends cited for the instructor's investment in instructional planning is increased learning. This results from the structure that planning provides as well as the efficiency and direction that accrues from the process. However, these learner-related outcomes of planning will not be maximized unless the results of the instructor's planning efforts are shared with the students.

One of the systematic ways in which the results of planning can be shared with students is through a well-designed course syllabus. The format for a course syllabus may vary from a one to two page topical outline (see Figure 2-5) with test dates noted to a comprehensive document that includes performance objectives and all course handouts provided to students. The suggested format is some place in between these two extremes and contains the following components:

		TEACHING PLAN		
Suggested Activities	Demonstrations	Topics for Class Discussion	Informational Assignments	Other Instructional Aids
FUNDAMENTALS OF ELECTRICITY				
		Increased use and decreasing cost of electricity	1	Film: "What Is Electricity?"
		Nuclear structure and electron theory		
	Solve problems with Ohm's law	Ohm's law		
1. Wire a series circuit	Read an ammeter	Construction, use, and precautions with meters	2	Film: "Series and Parallel Circuits"
	Read a voltmeter	Characteristics of DC series circuits		
	Read an ohmmeter			
	Read a VOM			
2. Use a voltage tester	Wire meters in circuits			
3. Wire a parallel circuit		Characteristics of DC parallel circuits		
4. Calculate electric power	Measure power with wattmeter, voltmeter, and ammeter	Electric power in DC circuits	3	List of power distributors
		Rate structures		
		Power unit coversion efficiency calculation		
5. Operate overcurrent protective devices	Overload a fuse	Overcurrent protective devices	4	File on newspaper clippings dealing with electric shock
		Safety precautions and first aid		
				Demonstration panel with various sizes and types of fuses
		Grounding considerations		
		Open and closed circuits		
				Films: "Electrical Safety in the Home" "How to Do Rescue Breathing"
		Electrical and electronic schematic symbols	5	Chart of symbols
				Architectural plans with wiring diagrams and schematic circuit drawings

Figure 2-4. A teaching plan indicates course planning.

Course Syllabus
Circuit Analysis 101
5 Credit Hours

Circuit Analysis 101 (CA-101) covers basic DC electrical principles. Previous course experience in electricity and algebra is not considered prerequisite to success in CA-101.

I. Course Organization

Content and Scope of the Course

Unit I.	Current and Voltage	4 days
Unit II.	Resistance	3 days
Unit III.	Ohm's Law	2 days
Unit IV.	Power and Energy	4 days
Unit V.	DC Series Circuit	8 days
Unit VI.	DC Parallel Circuits	8 days
Unit VII.	DC Series—Parallel Circuits	8 days
Unit VIII.	DC Methods of Analysis	18 days
Unit IX.	DC Network Theorems	15 days
Review and Final Examination		5 days
		75 days

For each unit there are assignments, references, and study questions. Assignments specify learning activities. Chapters and/or pages of the text to be read are specified. Study questions are designed to present situational problems, which call for acquaintance with and the interpretation of facts, understanding of concepts and principles, as well as formation of judgments.

II. Course Objectives

Through the content selected and the activities planned, students will:

1. Explain the interrelationships among current, voltage, resistance, power and energy.

2. Apply Ohm's law.

3. Analyze linear bilateral DC series, parallel or series—parallel circuits with Ohm's law and the power formulas when one or more quantities are unknown.

III. Basis for Evaluation

A. Examinations	60%
B. Weekly quizzes	15%
C. Written reports	15%
D. Classroom participation	10%

Figure 2-5. A course syllabus indicates the results of course planning.

Cover Page. The only critical elements of this page relate to identification. It should provide the name of the institution, the curriculum in which the course is included, the course title, the length of the course and the year.

Introduction. This statement should place the course in context by indicating its place in the curricular sequence. The general nature of the course should be described. If there is an "official" or catalog description for the course, it might be appropriately included here. Any prerequisites or general expectations should be included in the statement.

Course Organization. Include a section that describes the organizational structure or format of the course. It is here that the major units or blocks of content to be covered in the course are revealed. In a general way, this provides an overview for the student. When the amount of time, e.g., days, weeks, class periods, to be devoted to each major unit or component of the course is indicated, the students have a basis for judging the amount of emphasis or depth of study expected in the various areas included. It is in this section of the syllabus that the selected instructional strategies, e.g., lecture, group discussion, assigned readings, research papers to be utilized in the course are specified.

Course Objectives. The major performance outcomes expected of the students upon completion of the course should be delineated in this section. These course objectives may not be quite as specific and complete, in terms of specified conditions and criteria, as instructional objectives written for the unit or lesson level; however, they should communicate the instructor's expectations with more precision than can be accomplished with course and unit titles alone. The objectives should be written in terms of student performance rather than focusing on the instructor's actions and intent.

Basis for Evaluation. It is important for students to know, in advance, the criteria and guidelines to be used by the instructor in the process of evaluation and the assignment of grades. Much of the anxiety which students experience results from a lack of information about the evaluation process. This information needs to be communicated in a clear and precise manner as early in the course as possible. Dates for examinations need to be set well in advance to permit adequate student preparation and schedule adjustments.

Format for Papers and/or Reports. If the instructor expects students to complete written assignments by using a prescribed format or style, these expectations need to be expressed in a clear and precise manner. Irrespective of the instructor's verbal facility, it is wise to place this detailed expectation in written form with examples where appropriate, e.g., bibliographic citations, reference page format. This process will save class time and provide an information "back up" for the student who is absent or forgets between the time the assignment is made and the time he/she begins to work on the paper or report.

Assignment Sheets. One of the often overlooked aspects of instructional planning relates to the design of learning activities to be completed outside of class and communicating these activities to the learner. Too frequently the instructor makes a hurried assignment of reading or "homework" after the bell rings and students are leaving the classroom. If the assignment of learning activities is important, then it deserves more than "a lick and a promise." One of the most effective ways to make assignments is with an assignment sheet prepared to cover a major unit or block of the course. When this is done, a daily or weekly reminder can be provided in an efficient manner because the details of the assignment are covered in a "hand-

---

ASSIGNMENT SHEET
CURRENT AND VOLTAGE

Introduction

      Content to be covered

      Importance of the unit

Assignment(s) and Due Date(s)

      Readings

      Problems to be solved

      Paper(s) to be written

      Study questions

References

      Complete bibliographic information

Study Question(s)

      1. What are three particles of an atom?

      2.

Figure 2-6. An assignment sheet includes information about assignments, references, and study questions.

out" which may be included in the student's course syllabus. The nature of the assignment sheet can vary considerably depending on the type of course and the resourcefulness of the instructor. Some of the basic elements to be included are described in Figure 2-6.

Handouts and Organization. Written materials distributed to students during the conduct of a course are referred to generically as "hand outs." Presumably, these materials are important as they convey information needed by students to help them achieve certain course, unit or lesson objectives. If this is the case, then the instructor needs to deal with them in a systematic manner and assist students in their retention, review and use. It is not reasonable to distribute all of the course hand outs at the beginning of a course and expect students to retain and use them at the appropriate time.

A loose leaf notebook system for students is recommended because of the sequencing flexibility it provides. The instructor needs to "teach" organization and provide opportunities for students to practice organizing. The notebook system can be facilitated by the instructor who has all handouts prepunched. The syllabus itself is a handout, and as such, it should be prepunched and distributed appropriately. For example, some of the syllabus elements described previously might be distributed at the first class meeting. This could include the assignment sheet for the first unit of work as well as any other handout for the first unit. Other assignment sheets and hand outs could then be prepunched and distributed at appropriate times during the course. The loose leaf notebook system has sufficient flexibility to accommodate student use of spiral notebooks for class notes as well as student prepared papers and reports. This allows all paperwork associated with a given course to be organized in one location.

TRANSLATING CONTENT INTO OBJECTIVES

After the content elements have been identified for the course you have been assigned to teach, they should be transformed into performance objectives. In recent years, most professional educators including trainers in the business, industrial, and military sectors have become "outcome" or performance oriented.

Outcome Based Instruction

There are many labels attached to this orientation that is focused on the bottom line, "Is the individual competent" or "Can the person perform?" Some of the more common labels are:

- Competency Based Instruction
- Criterion Referenced Instruction
- Mastery Learning

- Performance Based Instruction
- Objective Referred Learning
- Systems Based Instruction

While these terms are not synonomous, they are all outcome focused which requires the careful specification of the competency to be acquired and the behavior or performance necessary to demonstrate the required level of competency. In addition, these instructional approaches focus attention on the individual learner and vary the time as well as the learning activities in order that the learner can "master" each task or perform at a predetermined level.

GOALS AND OBJECTIVES

As educational programs are developed, there must be direction and boundaries for the developmental process. Educational goals can be thought of as a sort of guidance system that provides direction for an educational effort. In this regard, they are, by necessity, broad statements of desired end results.

For an instructional program to be designed in a manner that will assure the development of specific competencies, there must be clear and unambiguous statements of instructional intent. These statements of instructional intent are referred to as "objectives."

Within a given course, there may be many short range or enabling objectives which specify behaviors that the learner must exhibit as the learner moves through the process of becoming competent. These specific behaviors which may be called "instructional," "performance" or "behavioral" objectives are derived from the same knowing (cognitive), doing (psychomotor), and attitudinal (affective) content that professionals in the education field have been talking about for years.

Much time and effort is wasted in educational programs because of overlapping of course content, unintentional omissions of important content, and improper emphasis. Since all knowledge has some relationship to performance, the major problem in planning instruction is to identify, select, and teach those elements of content that are most appropriate in terms of specified objectives. Therefore, carefully selected and properly stated objectives become the key to instructional design. If the objectives change, content may need to be added or removed and changes may be needed in methods of instruction as well.

While the value of performance objectives may be obvious in terms of determining whether or not a learner has received the desired benefit from a given educational experience, objectives provide a number of other benefits to the professional instructor as follows:

Instructional objectives are:

1. helpful in lesson planning.

2. useful in the selection of learning aids such as textbooks, films, etc.

3. beneficial in determining appropriate assignments for individual students.

4. valuable in selecting and/or constructing classroom tests.

5. beneficial to the instructor in summarizing and reporting the results of evaluation.

6. helpful to learners in determining where they are going and their progress in the course.

7. valuable to students as they become increasingly independent learners.

ELEMENTS OF PERFORMANCE OBJECTIVES

As indicated previously, "goals" are broad statements of desired educational outcomes while objectives imply more specific statements of instructional intent. The level of specificity can be increased as one moves from the course through unit and lesson levels of educational planning; however, at some point, it is essential to specify the precise performance that is required. These performance objectives are often referred to as "target" or "terminal" objectives. In the preparation of performance objectives the instructor must be knowledgeable of and be able to apply the three basic elements: *Performance, Conditions,* and *Criteria.*

Performance. The heart of an objective is the clear and concise statement of the performance required of the learner. The performance component does not have to include repetitive statements such as "the student should be able to." This kind of lead statement can be placed as the head of a list and assumed to apply to the entire group of objectives. The key word in the performance component is an action verb such as "remove," "clean," "measure," "list," "draw," "prepare," "fasten," "describe." It is important to remember that performance can be related to "knowing" as well as "doing" content. Such action verbs as "define," "illustrate," "compose," "name," "contrast" are appropriate for an objective dealing with the cognitive domain. A comprehensive list of appropriate terms is included in Bloom's Taxonomy of Educational Objectives.

Conditions. A second key element of a performance objective is the conditions (the setting or set of circumstances) within which the learner is to perform or demonstrate competency. The conditions often specify "things" to be used as the learner performs, e.g., given a bunsen burner, a beaker and selected elements. Conditions may describe situations or certain restrictions, e.g., provided with the results of a diagnostic test; without the use of a calculator; or presented with a detailed working drawing. Avoid long lists of materials and equipment or items that can be logically assumed as necessary for performance. For example, the previously stated condition "given a bunsen burner and a beaker" would not be necessary if the course dealt only with labatory experiments involving these pieces of equipment. The conditions can make a difference in an individual's level of performance. Type a manuscript would be a different objective if the conditions varied, e.g., "from a handwritten draft;" from an audio tape;" or "from dictation transcribed from shorthand."

Criteria. The third element of a performance objective indicates the basis upon which the performance is judged. In other words, criteria are used to assess how well the learner must perform to be judged competent. Most criteria are stated within the qualitative dimensions with due recognition that the learner will take more time than a more experienced and competent individual. Examples of criteria are, "with 90 percent accuracy;" "with no errors;" or "all steps performed in the specified sequence." The criteria may relate to either the process or the product.

An example of a performance objective with all three elements is as follows: With the aid of a sales tax chart, compute without error, the sales tax for purchases of $.23, $1.25, $2.79, $51.50 and $103.92. Can you identify the performance statement, the condition(s) and the criteria or criterion?

WRITING OBJECTIVES

There are no shortcuts to well written objectives. The instructor must communicate the performance, the conditions and the criteria with sufficient clarity that someone else who is knowledgeable of the field could teach and/or test from the objective without misinterpreting the instructional intent. There is an old adage, "Objectives are not written, they are rewritten," which emphasizes the necessity to revise and continually seek increased clarity. An important consideration is that students should be able to read and understand the course and lesson objectives. In writing course objectives the choice of action verbs to describe the expected behavior is very important. Many educators use words such as the following that have many interpretations and are difficult to measure.

To know	To understand
To appreciate	To really understand
To develop	To fully appreciate
To believe	To grasp the significance of
To enjoy	To have faith in

It is much better to choose verbs from the following list which are open to fewer interpretations and have measurable qualities. This list is not to be considered all inclusive but rather a collection of usable key words that should prove helpful as you develop your lesson objectives.

COGNITIVE VERBS

KNOWLEDGE (Level 1)	APPLICATION (Level 3)	SYNTHESIS (Level 5)
define	apply	arrange
list	demonstrate	assemble
memorize	dramatize	collect
name	employ	compose
recall	illustrate	construct
record	interpret	create
relate	operate	design
repeat	practice	formulate
	schedule	manage
	sketch	organize
	translate	plan
	use	prepare
		set up

Figure 2–7. When writing objectives, instructors should use specific verbs to specify cognitive behaviors expected of students. *(continued on page 38.)*

COGNITIVE VERBS (continued)

COMPREHENSION (Level 2)	ANALYSIS (Level 4)	EVALUATION (Level 6)
describe	analyze	appraise
discuss	calculate	assess
explain	compare	choose
express	contrast	compare
identify	criticize	estimate
locate	debate	evaluate
recognize	diagram	inspect
report	differentiate	judge
restate	distinguish	rate
review	examine	revise
tell	experiment	score
	inspect	select
	inventory	value
	question	
	relate	
	solve	
	test	

AFFECTIVE VERBS

		PSYCHOMOTOR VERBS	

accept	enrich	advance	heave
admit	excel	anchor	inscribe
advocate	exhibit	assort	inspect
allow	express	build	intersect
aspire	flatter	carry	juggle
assist	fulfill	climb	make
attain	impart	converse	manipulate
belong	impel	convert	observe
commend	imply	demonstrate	operate
compliment	incite	enlarge	perform
concern	induce	enter	practice
concur	invigorate	equip	proceed
confer	kindle	execute	rebuild
congratulate	motivate	fabricate	recast
correspond	oblique	fill	remodel
dedicate	perceive	finish	straighten
deserve	ratify	fix	transfer
engage	reinforce	furnish	transpose
enhance	stimulate	gather	work
enlighten	urge	generate	
enliven		grind	

Figure 2–7. When writing objectives, instructors should use specific verbs to specify affective and psychomotor behaviors expected of students.

The instructor must make numerous decisions as objectives are specified. It may be decided that the terminal performance objective based on the work task is too broad or comprehensive to be used most effectively. Therefore, it is better to divide the task into several sub-parts with an objective for each part. As students meet each of these preliminary or enabling objectives, they are being prepared to meet the terminal objective. In some instances, the sequence of instruction is vital to the eventual performance while in other instances the mastery of one objective is not dependent upon the mastery of another. The instructor must be sensitive to the problems of timing, prerequisites and sequencing if instruction is to be both effective and efficient.

CHECKLIST FOR PERFORMANCE OBJECTIVES

How well do your objectives measure up?

1. PERFORMANCE—Does the performance objective describe what the learner will be doing to demonstrate that the objective has been achieved?

2. CONDITION—Does the performance objective specify the important circumstances under which the learner must demonstrate competence?

3. CRITERION—Does the performance objective describe the standard(s) by which the learner's proficiency can be judged?

4. PRECISION AND CLARITY—Has the performance objective been specified using action words that preclude misinterpretation?

5. SUCCESS EXPECTATION—Has the performance objective been specified in sufficient detail to assure that the expected performance outcome can be recognized?

6. COMPLETENESS, RELEVANCE AND ACHIEVABLE—Has a separate statement been developed for each performance objective?

7. LEARNER CENTERED—Does the objective specify what the learner is to do and not what the teacher is going to do?

The identification of content and the specification of behaviors provide the foundation upon which educational planning efforts are built. If the competencies are not identified carefully, the base upon which an educational program is built will be faulty. It would be of marginal value to do an excellent job of helping an individual develop a skill that is no longer needed. Therefore, the identification of content and the translation of this content into performance objectives is of vital importance in program development. Several of the chapters which follow are designed to assist the instructor as he/she executes instruction and evaluates the results of instruction. To perfrom these tasks effectively, it is important that the instructor be knowledgeable of and, where appropriate, involved in the identification of the content he/she is expected to deliver as well as participate in the translation of competencies into performance objectives.

DESIGNING LESSONS AND LEARNING PACKAGES

Just as each learner brings a unique background and learning style to a learning experience, instructors also bring a background that causes them to view the structure of their discipline or subject matter in a certain framework or context. Likewise, educators develop certain patterns or organizing structures that they believe are most beneficial to both instructors and learners. As a result, there is no single format or pattern of organization that is universally adopted as a planning structure for instructors or delivery mechanism for learners.

The term *lesson plan* is used to describe the structure used by an instructor to organize, in a concise manner, the results of planning and decision making as related to the teaching and learning of selected content. A lesson plan not only includes the results of planning and decision-making, but it also becomes a guide for the teacher's action during one or more class periods required to teach an element of content. Lesson plans are typically prepared for use in group instruction by the instructor of the course although time constraints are such that initial planning is limited and complete lesson plans evolve over time.

A *learning package* contains many of the same components as the lesson plan; however, the learning package is designed primarily to guide an individual's learning of a given element of content. Because the learning package is primarily for individualized instruction, it can be thought of as a well-designed and carefully developed learning aid that gives students detailed instructions to guide them through the learning process. The package provides the learner with appropriate materials at the appropriate time and for the length of time needed by each student to reach mastery of a specified performance objective. Even though learning packages vary from simple to complex in their composition and format, they typically are categorized as *direction sheets, learning guides* or *modules*. Examples of the more sophisticated versions of the latter type would be "programmed instruction" or "learning modules." Since these packages are detailed for self instruction and cover relatively small elements of content, a "team" approach is often taken in their development.

Components

As indicated, there is a substantial amount of variation in the format of lesson plans and learning packages. Nevertheless, there are certain elements or components that need to be included regardless of the terminology employed. These key components are derived from the classic four step method of teaching, i.e., *Preparation, Presentation, Application* and *Evaluation*.

Preparation. Whether one prepares a lesson plan to guide group instruction or a learning package for individualized instruction, there will be a need to "set the stage." This process may be referred to by a variety of terms such as "introduction," "set induction" or "anticipatory set." Nevertheless, the purpose is the same as it seeks to prepare students for the lesson. The introductory statement suggested for the *course syllabus* likewise emphasizes the need to provide reasons for learning and to stimulate or motivate the learner to invest time on the learning task. As a part of this introductory effort, the learner must perceive the learning task. This is best achieved through revealing the performance objective to be achieved and the rationale for establishing the objective.

Presentation. The heart of a lesson or a learning package is the linking of the learner to certain concepts, ideas, information, principles, etc., through which the individual learns and will ultimately be able to demonstrate competence. This linking may be accomplished through the instructor's lecture or demonstration, a reading assignment, viewing a video tape or through any other form of media. Chapters 4 and 5 of this text deal with the methods, techniques and materials that allow this component of the lesson plan and/or learning package to be implemented. This is often referred to as the instructional input phase of a teaching/learning model.

Application. In a well developed lesson plan or a well designed learning package, opportunity must be provided for the learner to apply the newly acquired information, concepts, principles, or motor skills. This phase of the teaching/learning process is not to be confused with evaluation. At this point, the student is still learning and the purpose of application is to provide reinforcement, to identify weaknesses that need to be strengthened, and to provide an opportunity for practice. Additional experiences with the content, regardless of the nature of the experience, contribute to the application phase.

Evaluation. The final step in the four step method which is inherent in effective instruction, regardless of the manner in which instruction is packaged, is *evaluation*. There are many ways in which this step may be carried out, e.g., oral questioning, observation of performance, written tests. However, the principal concept relates to the extent to which the student has achieved a given objective. If the objectives are written properly with a clear statement of (1) the performance, (2) the conditions, and (3) the criteria, the evaluation step can be conducted in a very straightforward manner.

Formats

The manner in which the various instructional components are organized is referred to as a *format*. The format may be relatively simple with typed or printed statements or directions to guide the learner through one or more activities to successful performance. On the other hand, it may be a mediated program with video tape or a series of 35mm slides accompanied by an audio tape.

The sophistication of the packaging may not correlate positively with the achievement of an objective(s) by the learner. The consumer (educator) must not be misled by appearances. It is logical to assume that a carefully packaged learning system would also be a carefully designed system that "really works;" however, the consumer must be wary of exaggerated claims. Systems may have consumer appeal and may be quite expensive, but they may not "deliver" in terms of higher achievement levels or increased efficiency.

When learning packages are designed with media material, simulation and performance appraisal, a substantial investment of resources is required. Normally, this investment must be made by the course coordinator or department chair. Such factors as (1) multiple use over time, (2) volume of usage, (3) cruciality of competency in terms of safety or equipment damage, (4) cost, (5) learning level, and (6) efficiency must be considered as decisions are made regarding investments of this magnitude. Instructors are often involved as members of committees when decisions are made regarding learning packages. However, the instructor's direct involvement in developing learning packages is typically limited to instruction sheets and learning guides.

Lesson planning is typically approached as the instructor's plan for a given instructional session. Although there are notable exceptions, e.g., military, corporate and private school systems with multiple locations, the instructors are generally responsible for developing their own lesson plans.

LESSON PLANNING

A *lesson plan* provides detailed directions for teaching one or more class periods on a given topic or theme. Lessons may be as short as 30 minutes or as long as five hours. The content, age and maturity of the students, and nature of the instructional program(amount of student application) are some of the factors that determine a lesson's length.

It is possible, of course, for a lesson plan to be thought through and carried out without putting it on paper. For most instructors, however, a written plan is necessary if they are to do their best.

Purpose of the Lesson Plan. There are a number of reasons why a lesson plan is necessary. A lesson plan helps the instructor think through the lesson as it will be taught. The lesson plan assists in the organization of the materials needed to carry out the plan. A good lesson plan helps the instructor to:

1. provide needed motivation,

2. properly emphasize various parts of the lesson, including those requiring student activity,

3. ensure that essential information is included,

4. provide for the use of instructional aids,

5. insert questions at the proper time, and

6. stay on schedule.

Skilled instructors write a detailed lesson plan and reduce it to a few notes for use in the classroom. Other instructors prefer to teach from a detailed outline. In any event, the plan should be designed to fit the instructor's needs for the lesson at hand.

Lesson plans prepared by someone else may be of value, but usually need modification. Each instructor needs a customized plan, which may be newly developed or modified from an existing plan.

Key Elements of a Lesson Plan. A lesson plan may be prepared for a single class period, or it may be designed to cover two or more periods. Good lesson plans contain the following elements:

Title - The exact title of a lesson should be given. For example, the title "Micrometer" is not as good as the title "How to Read a Micrometer." The title of a lesson plan usually comes from knowing and doing content identified in the analysis. In addition to the title, a code consisting of course, unit, and lesson numbers may be used to assist in filing.

Objectives - A lesson plan should include objectives. For example, to list and describe types of poetry or to write a poem may be lesson objectives. Objectives should include the expected performance, conditions, and criteria.

Instructional Aids - As the lesson is planned, the instructor should list charts, models, films, and other aids that will facilitate learning. This list serves as an inventory when preparing to teach, and is of great help the next time the lesson is taught.

Texts and References - Be sure to identify specific knowing and doing content from the analysis to be included in the lesson. Reference to texts used to prepare the lesson should also be included. If the plan will be used for some time, space should be left to add new references as they become available. All instruction sheets and text material to be used by students should be listed. Care should be taken to include complete reference citations.

Introduction - A well-planned introduction will develop interest and motivate students to become involved in the subject. A good introduction may include:

1. what the lesson is about,

2. where and when students can use what they learn in the lesson,

3. how the lesson will be taught,

4. what will be expected from students during and after the class, and

5. a review of what was learned in previous lessons.

Repetition is usually necessary for effective instruction. The procedure used, however, should not be repetitious. Essential information may be emphasized in many ways, one of which is reviewing the previous lesson as a part of the introduction to the current lesson.

It may be necessary to think through previous lessons and reinforce key points before the current lesson can proceed smoothly. The review should not be long and involved. The question and answer approach may be the most effective for certain lessons, or the instructor may simply remind students of key points previously discussed.

Presentation - This is the core of the lesson. It contains two interwoven elements: (1) A complete outline revealing exact content and the sequence in which it will be taught, and (2) notes about ways to teach various parts of the lesson. For example, the instructor might include the following notes:

1. Ask the following questions....

2. Through discussion develop the reason for....

3. Introduce the film and run first 11 minutes only, or

4. Discuss the following points before showing the remaining part of the film.

In planning the presentation, refer to the content to be taught, and consider lecturing, discussing, demonstrating, and questioning as ways to teach each part of the lesson. Make sure all parts of the presentation follow in logical order with no awkward gaps, and estimate the time required for each part of the lesson.

Interaction items. Preplanned questions, whether they are rhetorical, instructor answered, or require a student response, provide stimulation and highlight a lesson. These items appropriately interspersed in a presentation stimulate interest. They help to assess the level of understanding, and they focus student attention on a specific concept or principle. Interaction items, as the term implies, provide a basis for class discussion and interaction between instructor and students. Appropriately phrased, these items can lead students to higher levels of cognition, e.g., analysis, synthesis, evaluation, generalization. These items may be coded and noted in pencil on the instructor's presentation outline.

Application and activity. Application occurs whenever, either mentally or both mentally and physically, the student applies the learned content to some type of problem. Application occurs all through the lesson if the student understands and mentally applies the content being presented. Questions, illustrations, problems, examples and exercises, when properly used, cause the student to apply abstract concepts to specific and practical situations. This application is essential for full understanding of basic concepts and for learning to transfer the basic theory to a variety of specific tasks.

In most effective lessons, a part of the time is reserved for application. When good application occurs, it is generally the result of the instructor's planning. The stage must be set and materials must be available. In many situations, assignments to individuals in the group must be made and a schedule may need to be prepared for the use of equipment. Individual instruction sheets and other written materials must be made available when needed. The instructor must be free to observe and guide individuals as they work through a learning activity. Well-planned activities serve many purposes, e.g., change of pace, variety, and additional experience with the subject; however, the primary purpose is that it allows the learner to apply the information or skill being learned.

Evaluation items. As the instructor plans a lesson, it is appropriate to prepare evaluation items. A few minutes invested at this time will pay dividends at the time a test is prepared. The instructor's attention is focused on the specific performance objective(s) to be achieved and the content to be experienced by the learner; therefore, the time is right to prepare appropriate evaluation items for use immediately following a lesson or later in the course. Evaluation items should be designed to measure student achievement of lesson objectives. The objectives will suggest appropriateness of certain types of items, e.g., recall, explain, describe, identify, perform, or draw. Suggestions for writing evaluation items will be found in Chapter 6.

Summarize and test. The lesson may be summarized or culminated in several ways. One good way is to review the main points, to emphasize them, and to help students organize the content in their minds. This is often followed by oral questions to assure that the students can apply the content of the lesson and to check on their understanding.

Using a short test, covering the main points in the lesson, is a valuable teaching strategy because it helps to motivate students to analyze and synthesize the content being learned. Tests can provide valuable feedback to indicate the parts of the lesson that have been taught well and the parts needing clarification or more emphasis. Marks or grades may be given if desired; however, it is more important to use the test as a teaching and learning device than for the purpose of assigning grades.

Assignments. When an assignment for work outside the class period is to be made, it is not enough to say, "For tomorrow, read Chapter 5." It pays to tell the student what to look for, what to read for general understanding, which parts to study for detailed information, and what questions to answer. As suggested in the course syllabi section, written assignment sheets for large units might be prepared to facilitate lesson-by-lesson assignments. A good assignment:

1. is thought out and planned in advance so that when given, it is easy to understand.

2. contains specific instructions regarding the method of approach. Anticipated difficulties and problems should be discussed. Specific problems, questions, and methods should be listed and emphasized.

3. is given slowly so that notes may be taken. This suggests giving the assignment at the beginning of the period when there is less chance of running out of time, unless the students need today's lesson in order to understand tomorrow's assignment.

4. includes questions by the instructor to make sure everyone understands the assignment, and allows time for students to ask questions.

In some cases, the instructor may allow time for students to start the work on the assignment so that misconceptions may be noted and corrected.

CONCLUSION

The activities encompassed by the phrase, "instructional planning," involve everything from the broader curriculum and educational program decisions to those decisions that relate to a demonstration lesson or a homework assignment. Although the instructor is often not involved in macro level planning, it is important for the instructor to be aware of the decision-making process that leads to the specification of courses in the curriculum and the content specified for a given course. As a professional educator, the instructor needs to be knowledgeable of the big picture and understand the conceptual framework involved in curriculum design as well as the detailed planning for courses and lessons.

Any subject matter field or discipline, as specific fields of study are referred to in the academic community, has an inherent structure or framework. This structure or framework is a way in which the discipline is organized. It is important that the instructor be well-acquainted with this conceptual framework since part of the teaching process involves acquainting the student with the structure of the discipline. Detailed knowledge is important; however, the student needs a structural framework within which to relate knowledge elements. In a previous section, the instructional planning process was related to general systems theory in an effort to provide a framework to individuals with a technical orientation. This effort is an attempt to build a frame of reference for the relationships among the various elements involved in instructional design and planning.

Although instructors are infrequently involved in planning or revising of an entire degree program, they are frequently involved in the curriculum development process wherein decisions are made regarding the educational experiences that lead to the preparation of an individual to enter a given field. Even though the involvement at the macro level depends a great deal on the setting and the instructor's experience, instructors are directly involved in planning at the course and lesson level. Because of the instructor's direct and immediate needs in this area, this chapter focused on the essential elements involved in course and lesson planning. Course planning involves a substantial amount of decision making related to content, objectives, student learning activities and assignments, evaluation, as well as the environment in which teaching and learning occur. The instructor is well advised to go about the process of course planning in a systematic manner. Just as there is a structural framework in any field or discipline, there is a logical framework for course planning. The section of this chapter which described a course of study provided a structure or model for the instructor's use as decisions are made and plans formulated for carrying out instruction in a given course.

It is important that the instructor approach this process in a systematic and organized manner for at least two primary reasons. First of all, the systematic process of writing objectives, specifying and arranging content, describing learning activities and developing and/or collecting instructional materials provides for a structured approach to teaching that facilitates learning. It is easier for the learner to focus attention on the content to be learned if there is a discernable structure. Secondly, the process of writing things down helps to clarify them in the instructor's mind, and the results of the planning effort can be drawn upon and improved as the instructor teaches the course a second, third or fourth time.

Seldom does the instructor have the luxury of sufficient time to completely plan a course before it is taught the very first time. Nevertheless, as much of a course of study as possible should be developed prior to the initiation of the course. The instructor then adds to or more fully develops the course of study as the course is taught. In this context, a course of study is not just written, it is rewritten as it documents the results of the decision-making and planning process over time.

As indicated, one of the primary reasons for systematic and organized planning is to facilitate learning. This benefit from planning cannot be maximized unless key elements of the planning process are shared with students. Having a clear-cut direction facilitates learning. It should be obvious that the learner cannot have a clear-cut direction for learning if the instructor does not have a clear-cut direction for teaching. The old adage, "if you want someone to learn something, tell them what it is you want them to learn," is, indeed, a truism that is carried out effectively through a course syllabus. The course syllabus reveals the results of the instructor's planning and provides direction to the student as it gives an overview of the course content and organization, as well as the expectations revealed through objectives and the instructor's plan for evaluation.

Even though each learner develops a unique learning style, the effective instructor does not leave course organization up to each student. In fact, it is good strategy to provide an organizational plan for students to keep materials together for a given course which will facilitate the preparation of homework assignments, review for examinations and a collected body of materials for the course. Even though the well organized instructor could give each student a complete syllabus for the course, including assignment sheets for each unit and all handouts for the entire course on the first day of class, in most situations, this would not be the most effective procedure. Instead, the preferred strategy would be to distribute the first three or four pages of the syllabus on the first day of class and to point out to students that the pages have been prepunched for a looseleaf notebook and that subsequent handouts during the course will be prepunched to allow their insertion in a notebook. In this manner, the syllabus is cumulative throughout the course and allows the instructor to maintain control of assignments and handouts for appropriate emphasis at the time they are to be distributed and used. It is obvious that distribution of the entire syllabus, including handouts, on the first day of class would result in some students misplacing the handouts before they were to be utilized and some students not having the appropriate materials in class at the point in time when the instructor wished to refer to them.

The role of the instructor is to organize and deliver subject matter in a manner that facilitates the developmment of competencies by learners. The professional instructor has a responsibility to examine the subject matter in an analytical fashion in order that patterns or structures can be observed and communicated to learners. The instructor's task is to facilitate learning which requires the reduction of complexity and ambiguity. To bring about instructional clarity and efficiency of learning should be a major goal of all instructors.

Performance objectives provide direction for the educational process as well as standards by which competency development can be judged. An educational program should not be a "guessing game" in which instructional intent is somehow hidden from the learner. In an effective educational program, the learner should have knowledge of the instructor's expectation as well as the criteria by which performance will be judged. There is an old adage that the professional instructor should keep in mind, "If you want someone to learn something, tell him what you want him to learn." In football, the triple threat back is a valued asset. However, there is no value placed on the "triple threat instructor," i.e., the instructor who assigns one topic, talks about another and tests over a third.

At the micro level of planning, the instructor plans lessons which involve decisions regarding strategies and materials that will facilitate the learning of a given body of content. The results of this decision making process are written in a document which is referred to as a *lesson plan*. The wise instructor will develop and/or adopt a standardized format for the sake of efficiency. The results of planning are retained and reviewed as the course is taught again. This allows the instructor to revise, update, and improve the lesson plan rather than to waste time preparing a completely new plan each time the lesson is taught. Time is a precious commodity; therefore, the systematic use of time and the investment of the time that it takes to develop a format and to write down the results of planning and decision making will save time in the long run. All too frequently, instructors attempt to wing it and erroneously believe that they can remember all of the appropriate questions, activities, and sequencing, or even worse, believe that it will come to them during the lesson. There are numerous variables within each class period and the effective instructor must be flexible to adjust with changing conditions, e.g., students' questions, student confusion, or students' lack of prerequisite knowledge. However, the absence of a good plan from which to be flexible leads to a directionless class session.

Even though there is no universally adopted lesson plan format or format for student learning packages, the classic four-step method of teaching does provide a framework for developing materials for teaching and learning. An instructor will not go too far astray if attention is given to (1) the *preparation* of both self and the learner, (2) the *presentation* of the content to be learned, (3) opportunities for the learner to *apply* principles, concepts and skills that are being learned, and (4) *evaluation* activities that reveal both to the instructor and learner the extent to which objectives have been met. Regardless of the format employed, each instructor must develop a planning system that works. In reality, the nature of the system is not as important as the fact that one has a system. Having a system is the key to effective instructional planning.

REFERENCES ———————————————————— **2**

Ausubel, D., Novak, J., & Hanesian, H. (1978). Educational psychology: A cognitive view. New York: Holt, Rinehart & Winston, Inc.

Bloom, B.S. (Ed.) (1956). Taxonomy of educational objectives: Book 1, Cognitive domain. London: Longman Group, Ltd.

Bloom, B.S., Krathwohl, D.R. & Masia, B.B. (1964). Taxonomy of educational objectives: Book 2, Affective domain. Longman Group, Ltd.

Craik, F. (1979). Human memory. In M. Rosenzweig & L. Porter (Eds.), Annual Review of Psychology. Palo Alto, CA: Annual Reviews, Inc.

deBono, E. (1983). The direct teaching of thinking as a skill. Phi Delta Kappan, 64, 703-708.

Detterman, D., & Sternberg, R. (1982). How and how much can intelligence be increased? Norwood, NJ: Ablex.

Dweck, C. (1983). Theories of intelligence and achievement motivation. In S. Pareis, G. Olson, & H. Stevenson (Eds.), Learning and motivation in the classroom. Hillsdale, NJ: Erlbaum Associates.

Gagne, R. (1977). The conditions of learning. New York: Holt, Rinehart & Winston, Inc.

Good, T., & Brophy, J. (1986). Educational psychology: A realistic approach. New York: Longman, Inc.

Horton, D., & Mills, C. (1984). Human learning and memory. In M. Rosenzweig & L. Porter (Eds.), Annual Review of Psychology. Palo Alto, CA: Annual Reviews, Inc.

Loftus, G., & Loftus, E. (1976). Human memory: The processing of information. Hillsdale, NJ: Erlbaum Associates.

Long, H., McCrary, K., & Ackerman, S. (1980). Adult cognitive development: A new look at Piagetian theory. Journal of Research and Development in Education, 13, 11-20.

Maslow, A. (1970). Motivation and personality. New York: Harper & Row.

Mayer, R. (1979b). Twenty years of research on advance organizers: Assimilation theory is still the best predictor of results. Instructional Science, 8, 133-167.

Miller, P. (1978). Please hear what I am not saying. School Shop, 38 (2), 35.

Novak, J., & Gowin, D. (1984). Learning how to learn. New York: Cambridge University Press.

O'Neal, H., & Spielberger, C. (Eds.) (1979). Cognitive and affective learning strategies. New York: Academic Press.

Piaget, J. (1983). Piaget's theory. In P. Mussen (Ed.), Handbook of Child Psychology (4th ed.). New York: Wiley.

HUMAN LEARNING: FACILITATED OR IMPEDED

I t is possible for an electrician to wire a house or a technician to repair a radio without knowing much of the theory of electricity or electronics. Likewise, the cook may use the correct ingredients and procedures to produce a culinary delight without knowing the chemical composition of the ingredients or the scientific principles that caused the successful product. In the same way, an instructor may use good techniques of instruction without knowing much of the theory of learning. However, the electrician, the technician, the cook and the instructor will be more effective when confronted with new and changing situations if they have an understanding of the basic theory and principles related to the specific techniques of the job. This chapter deals with some of the factors and principles involved in the learning process on which effective instruction is based.

Individuals learn in many different ways—by reading, listening, watching, doing, thinking, and solving problems. The success of any of these learning processes depends on several elements of which intelligence, attention and interest are overriding forces. The intellectual abilities through which one acquires, processes, translates and applies information play a central role in the learning process. One's ability to reason, to see relationships and to solve problems can be facilitated through instruction; however, individuals do differ in their intellectual abilities and as a result they differ in their learning potential. Regardless of the student's learning potential, no instructional approach can be very successful if it fails to hold the students' interest and attention. It is much easier to learn when the learner is interested; it is most difficult when one lacks interest. The learner's attention will vary with the nature of the subject, the level and quality of the instruction, and with previous experiences of the learner both in and out of the classroom. Realizing that some students have longer attention spans than others and that some students learn more rapidly than others, variations in instructional strategies will be made by the effective instructor. It is important for the instructor to use techniques and learning activities that hold the attention and interest of the largest possible number of individuals.

Even though human learning has been the subject of a substantial amount of investigation, the exact nature of the process that occurs within the brain is unknown. However, there is a substantial body of knowledge that has been gained by observation and research that provide insight into the conditions that facilitate this mysterious process that transforms symbols, ideas, principles, and concepts into human behavior and performance. The effective instructor operates at a high level of problem solving; therefore, it is essential that he/she knows and understands much of the body of knowledge related to learning. This knowledge and understanding will enable the instructor to establish the conditions that are essential for learning to take place efficiently and effectively.

The instructor's knowledge of principles that influence the learning process is of little benefit without an understanding of key variables in the application of educational theories. Three sets of primary variables that influence learning are those related to the learner, the instructor, and the instructional process.

Variables that relate to the learner have the greatest influence since the individual learner is the central figure in the teaching-learning process. Each individual is made up of a myriad of physical, emotional, and intellectual characteristics as well as interests, attitudes, and experiences that influence the outcome (learning) resulting from a given educational experience.

The instructor introduces another set of variables to the teaching-learning equation. Just as no two individuals are alike, no two instructors are alike. Interaction between one instructor and a learner or a group of learners differs from the interaction of another instructor and other learners. While some principles of human interaction can be used by all instructors, the exact manner in which these principles are applied varies with each instructor.

For purposes of discussion, *the instructional process* is described separately *for learners and instructors*, but in reality these three sets of variables interact in the teaching-learning interface. The instructor's technical competence and manner of executing and evaluating instruction exert a substantial influence upon the learner's success.

LEARNING THEORY AND PRINCIPLES

In simplest terms, learning is said to occur as an individual develops new associations resulting from experience. The associations involve a mental process although in many cases there is a physical or "psychomotor" component. Although affected by many external factors, learning is primarily an internal event that occurs within the brain. The chemistry and neurology are not completely understood, but it is known that all of the associations (learning) are stored specifically and individually in brain cells. There is a substantial body of knowledge that has been developed through years of research and experimentation by early psychologists such as Ebbinghaus, Pavlov, E. L. Thorndike, Hull, Gagné (gon-yea), B. F. Skinner, and more recently Piaget (p-au-zhay), Bruner, and Ausubell. In addition, there has been a substantial amount of research related to the chemical and neurological structure of the brain itself which leads to the connections within the nervous system and the functions of the "left" and "right" hemispheres of the brain. There are literally volumes of literature available to the serious scholar who wishes to understand more about learning and the learning process. For the beginning instructor, it is important to understand the basic theory and principles related to learning and perhaps to understand that this is an imperfect science. However, there are a few general principles that need to be understood for the instructor to facilitate the teaching/learning process.

Learning Through Experience

Since learning is the process of developing associations through experience, it is a dynamic and active process. It is a process in which the learner is the central figure. The instructor cannot learn for the student. The instructor can help the learner develop new associations, but the instructor cannot learn for the student. Learning involves the acquisition of information and associating that information with previously learned information. Schools and educational programs are systematic efforts to facilitate learning and to bring about certain behavior changes. However, learning is not limited to school or other structured learning environments. Associations result from experience regardless of whether or not there was any overt effort to bring about the association. Learning can be incidental. In fact, the advertising industry is built on the premise that individuals learn and that they will behave on the basis of that learning. Nevertheless, it is important for instructors to recognize that learning is most likely to be thorough and certain when it occurs under conditions of direct attention and deliberate effort. In other words, the instructor directs the attention and effort of the learner. When an individual wants to learn something and is motivated to give careful attention to the task and to persist with any necessary repetition, the individual is more likely to learn efficiently.

Every individual has "learned to learn" over time, and information that comes to the learner will be decoded and then recoded in terms of their own individual style. This factor makes group instruction difficult since the instructor's style of organization and presentation may not be equally beneficial for all learners in the group. Individuals respond to a new stimulation in terms of its relevance to previously acquired knowledge. The individual's learning style, his/her previous knowledge base and a host of other variables will influence the "associations" that are made and thus the learning that takes place. Learning often involves proceeding through various levels of knowledge and understanding. One starts with brief and simple elements and builds gradually to more complex systems. Frequently, progress at higher levels is not possible until certain lower level or prerequisite skills are mastered. For example, a student who cannot subtract efficiently because of a lack of understanding of the principles involved will be continually frustrated by attempts to learn division.

Performance Indicators of Learning

Instructors must exercise some care in distinguishing between the process of learning and the evidence that learning has taken place through behavior or performance. Instructors may be too quick to judge learning by inadequate observation of the individual's level of performance or behavior. Behavior and performance are broadly used in this context to mean anything done by the learner to indicate to an observer (instructor) that learning has taken place. However, the absence of a "correct" behavior does not necessarily mean that learning has not taken place. For example, an individual may not be able to call the name of an individual at a given point in time even though he/she "knows" that individual quite well. Everyone experiences this inability to retrieve information that has been learned and stored in the long-term memory. An individual's performance or behavior at a given point in time may not be a clear indicator that the individual "knows" something. Many things are retained for only a few moments in our short-term memory before being lost altogether. Even those that are retained and mapped into the long-term memory may be difficult to recall in certain situations. Learning that has a substantial physical or motor component presents less problems related to retrieval than does learning involving primarily symbols and other abstractions.

Psychomotor Learning

The term *skill* most often refers to psychomotor learning in which associations are made that have a substantial physical or motor component. This type of mental/physical learning relates to gross motor skills which include one's general coordination and balance such as is involved in walking or running, as well as fine motor skills which are more specific and differentiated requiring a substantial amount of hand-eye coordination such as that required for writing, carving, drawing or making electrical connections. Psychomotor skills typically are developed gradually with practice. Refinement of skills requires practice. Most skills require a prescribed set of manipulations recognizing that there are always physical differences among individuals. There is typically a series of motions as well as a sequence of those motions that will allow an individual to gain a high degree of efficiency in performing a given task. One of the instructor's primary challenges is to determine and be able to relate the physical motions and the sequence of movements that will allow the learner to acquire the highest possible degree of skill in the shortest period of time.

Cognitive Learning

Cognitive learning refers to the development of associations that have minimal physical involvement outside the brain. It includes everything from the simplest associations between stimuli to the development of very complex insights. In fact, cognitive learning is often classified according to complexity. This leads to the levels of learning and "chaining" of associations that have substantial implications for the sequencing of instruction. In cognitive learning, the mental associations are not only simple associations between stimuli, e.g., smoke and fire, or between responses, e.g., inserting key in a lock and turning the key, but it can involve a very complex set of associations. Bits of information are not stored in isolation from one another but instead there is a very complex system of coding, sorting, filing and cross-indexing.

Even though the instructional process tends to focus upon the facilitation of new associations or insights in learning on behalf of the student, one must realize that new learning can result from the process of thinking. New associations or insight can come from thinking about past experiences as connections or "associations" are made between and among bits of information that are already stored in the brain. In this regard, thinking is somewhat similar to behavior or performance in that it leads to or results from learning rather than being learning itself. Nevertheless, thinking does involve the active use of knowledge and skills previously learned and does not occur in a vacuum. It must be recognized that individuals vary considerably in their ability to learn from both external and internal stimuli.

The Role of Memory in Learning

As previously noted, learning involves associations. Memory is a key factor in the learning process since the information that is received by the learner must, in some way, be organized or "mapped" into the memory. Learning theorists do not agree on the different processes that are involved in short-term versus long-term memory. However, it is generally agreed that everything (associations) that gets processed and stored in long-term memory must first be stored or "mapped" in the short-term memory. Even though some of the things (associations) that are stored briefly in short-term memory will not be retained. Forgetting is an interesting phenomenon that relates to one's inability to retrieve a previously learned association from the long-term memory. It is not a matter of the association being "gone," but rather it is not retrieved because of some strong interference from other associations which are similar. For example, there is a spelling rule that "i" comes before "e" except after the letter "c". There are exceptions in the English language and when the learner becomes aware of the exceptions, some confusion may result because of the previously learned strong association. In fact, this confusion may affect the spelling of words that do, in fact, follow the general rule. Therefore, interference from competing associations can cause one to "forget" or fail to retrieve something that remains stored in long-term memory.

Everyone experiences the process of reading a page of material and all of a sudden realize that the material being "read" was not being processed and then observing, "I don't remember a thing I read." This occurs because of distracting thoughts or other stimuli such as sounds, smells, pain, sights, that were sufficiently important to the reader that some of the words did not register even in the short-term memory. To the extent that this happens, the information will not be entered into long-term memory unless it is reread or perhaps encountered in another way. This happens because the brain has exercised a "gating" function in dealing with incoming stimuli. Even though the chemical and neurological process is not completely understood, it is known that all incoming stimuli are screened for relevance and that there are neuro mechanisms that "close the gate" on most stimuli and "open the gate" for stimuli that are of sufficient importance to enter the consciousness. These stimuli make connections (called synapses) in the midbrain that result in the stimulation of the higher brain or cortex. Only those stimuli that reach the cortex become part of the person's conscious awareness. The individual learner controls "importance or relevance" when one concentrates on material to be learned and as a result, other stimuli are "gated out."

One of the significant implications for teaching is that the attention and interest of the learner are central factors in getting information into conscious awareness and ultimately mapped into long-term memory. Material that is mapped into memory is selected systematically because it is perceived to be relevant for future reference. This systematic "filing" of information is somewhat analogous to the way that items in a warehouse are placed in specific locations so that similar items of precise size, color, etc. can be found quickly and easily. Somehow this information transferred into long-term memory is stored in ways that organize it on the basis of associational patterns. Each individual's associational patterns are unique although many patterns are common. This commonness can be observed in word association games wherein most individuals in a given culture will respond in the same manner when presented with one part of an association. For example, most U.S. citizens will respond with the word blue when given cues of red, white, and _____. The dissimilarities in associational patterns can be observed when other words are considered that do not have a single common or expected association as the words mountain, river, sky, dog. In a group of individuals it is instructive to note the extreme differences in the associations related to some of these terms which reveal the differences in the way associations are mapped.

The way in which memory works in the learning process has many important implications for the effective instructor. First of all, since information is not stored randomly but rather is mapped in an organized way, instruction is typically more effective if new information can be related to associations that already exist. Secondly, the learner is most likely to be motivated to learn something if they can see it as "relevant or important" to their future needs or their current interests. Motivation is important for short-term attention, but it is even more important to get the kind of active information processing that leads to long-term memory.

PROCESSES OF LEARNING

The processes by which individuals learn are numerous and varied. Because of the complex and individualized nature of learning, the effective instructor needs to be knowledgeable of the various processes involved in learning in order to select or develop instructional strategies that will facilitate learning for each individual in the class. Since most instruction takes place in group settings, the challenge facing an instructor who is serious about facilitating learning by individuals becomes painfully obvious.

Learning by Trial and Error

The baby's responses to discomfort are kicking and crying. If the discomfort is the result of being hungry, the kicking and crying stops when the child is fed. After a few weeks the child learns that a particular cry will bring food. Of course, the mother learns that cry, too. Later, the child and the mother learn that other activities, such as reaching for a cup, indicate the desire for food. The baby and the mother have learned to communicate by trial and error. The baby makes all kinds of movements and noises until the food comes. After a while the baby selects one kind of behavior to bring about the desired response from mother or father. In other words, the baby learns what to do to get results.

Adults as well as children learn many things by trial and error although the trials are seldom at random. Because of past experiences and their ability to reason or use knowledge gained previously, they don't have to make as many trials before acquiring the necessary results. Everyone uses trial and error to some extent, and the method is the only method that can be used at times. However, contrary to popular opinion, learning things "the hard way" is not necessarily the best way. In a humorous vein, it has been said that "good judgment comes from experience and that experience comes from using bad judgment."

From previously discussed principles of learning, it is obvious that trial and error learning is inefficient even though the experiences involved may cause strong associations to result. When correct information or the right answer is available, learning can proceed much more efficiently. When the learning process is purposeful and direct, learning is generally more effective than when one must wander through a process of several trials leading to limited or no success before the correct association is made.

Learning by Observation

Watching others can provide visual cues or mental pictures. This helps to eliminate some of the trials that a beginner might make. However, there are many important things that cannot be learned by observation alone. No amount of watching a pilot would permit one to develop the competence needed to become a pilot. Observing behavior would help one to mimic the physical movement, but the mental processes cannot be observed. Even more narrow motor skills that have little or no informational components such as tying a shoe or riding a bicycle cannot be learned by observation alone. One may get the general idea, but the skill cannot be acquired by observation. The acquisition of motor skills, such as using hand tools, walking, throwing a ball or typing require a change in the muscle and nervous systems. This is often referred to as psychomotor learning. This kind of learning comes only through doing and practicing over a period of time.

Such activities as operating a calculator, solving mathematical problems, running a metal working lathe, or even playing a card game is usually too complicated to be learned by observation alone. This method of learning, however, is a central feature of demonstrating or modeling which is one of the most efficient methods of teaching. The learner can observe the instructor or other models performing or exhibiting behaviors and in some cases can imitate these behaviors readily. In addition to physical skills, certain generalized attitudes or values can be taught through modeling as the learner gains insight by observation. Modeling, especially when combined with verbal instructions and mediation, can facilitate learning that might require long and frustrating trial and error under other circumstances.

Learning by Doing

Many instructors are too verbal as they use too many words in the process of telling. They have confused telling with teaching. Words are important, and no instructor can do without them, but words usually convey only part of the meaning. Some form of activity or participation is necessary for an individual to gain complete understanding. An individual from an urban area cannot have a very accurate concept of a farm until there is some direct involvement such as living or working on a farm. No amount of verbalization, television or films can take the place of real experience.

When physical skills must be acquired, there are obvious reasons for learning by doing. Physical skills such as driving a nail or hitting a ball are learned by executing correct movements and repeating these movements until they become a thoroughly established habit. This is the reason for following the instructor's demonstration with a direct "hands on" experience by the learner.

Although it is often neglected, the principle of learning by doing applies just as well for non-physical learning. Each major idea or concept in a lesson should be followed by carefully prepared student assignments and problems that make use of or apply the idea or concept presented by the instructor. Students must summarize, review, discuss and apply new material.

Frequently they should translate new ideas into their own words. Learning aids, including working models, performance tests and even achievement tests that require interpretation or application of facts are effective *learning by doing* processes.

Even while presenting material by lecture, it is possible to have the mental participation of learners as they relate new ideas to past experience or previously learned facts. The skilled instructor can apply this principle of learning by doing while lecturing by challenging the students through rhetorical questions and allowing time for them to:

1. Answer questions silently.

2. Critique ideas.

3. Disagree and try to defend their ideas.

4. See relationships of principles and specific applications.

In other words, the skillful instructor gets students to learn by doing through mental processing as well as through physical activity.

Transfer of Learning

In its simplest form transfer refers to the learning of something in one setting or situation that permits one to gain insight or solve a problem in a similar but different situation. Since learning involves associations, transfer involves the association of a new stimulus or response to a familiar one. This generalization of the "old" association is the process that occurs when a learner applies a previously learned mathematics formula to a set of variables in physics.

Transfer is not necessarily automatic, although persons of high intelligence can generally transfer quicker and more effectively than persons of low intelligence. Transfer can be facilitated by the teacher who continually causes students to think of alternatives, to look for new ways, to question and to apply knowledge. In other words, one must *teach for transfer* through generalized meanings and flexible habits.

A noted educator once said, "There is no single subject that has the key to rational thinking, any subject can make a contribution, but the way the subject is taught may make all the difference." Unfortunately some people think that one can train the mind like a muscle and that by mastering certain difficult subjects the mind can be strengthened and will, therefore, have greater intellectual or rational power and be more effective in learning another subject. This concept of learning is not generally accepted by psychologists, and careful experimentation has failed to support the theory. One does not learn to solve problems in human relations, for example, through the study of geometry, nor does a knowledge of human relations help in learning geometry. A respected historian whose work is of the highest level of scholarly endeavor may be unable to supervise others effectively, to lay out a good floor plan for a school building, or to understand a simple wiring diagram. This inadequacy is not because the historian does not have a good mind, but rather that he or she lacks certain competencies that are needed by a supervisor, an architect or an electrician.

Learning one specific task or subject may, however, help in learning some other specific task, if the two tasks or subjects are closely related or made up of the same elements and if the student recognizes these relationships. Knowledge of one language will help us learn another if the languages are related or similar. Because some English words come from Latin, a knowledge of Latin will help us to learn English. But it is just as true that a mastery of English helps us learn Latin. Mathematics will help us learn electronics because mathematical principles are a part of electronics. Simulators like electrical-mechanical trainers used for pilot training have great transfer value because they are designed to simulate the exact performance of the airplane. Great care is taken to keep such trainers in adjustment; however, since poorly designed or out-of-adjustment training devices may actually train the operator to do the wrong thing. The closer the learning environment resembles the actual occupational environment, the easier it will be for transfer to take place. Increasing use of these simulation techniques in instruction is being used at all levels of education.

Examples of transfer. If the student learns that $3 \times 8 = 24$, by transferring this knowledge he/she should know without further instruction that $8 \times 3 = 24$, and with minimum instruction that $30 \times 8 = 240$, and that $30 \times 80 = 2400$.

The geometry student knows that 5" is the length of the hypotenuse if the other sides of a triangle are 90 degrees to each other and one side measures 3" and the other 4". (The square of the hypotenuse equals the sum of the square of the other two sides.) If one understands the principle, and by using feet instead of inches, he/she should be able to lay out the 90 degree angles of a tennis court.

If such transfer does not take place, it could be because the instructor failed to illustrate the principle in a way that causes it to come to mind in new but related situations. The instructor may not have emphasized the generalizability of the principle or "taught for transfer."

Practice and drill are essential, but so is an understanding of the principles involved. A lot of unproductive student homework can be avoided when the principles are well taught and when examples are used to show how the principles can be applied.

The value of transfer. Teaching the principles of learning to potential instructors will not have much effect on their performance unless (1) the principles are applied in a variety of teaching situations, and (2) the relationship of these principles to specific teaching situations is evaluated and emphasized. It is not enough to know the specific steps of procedure. The principles and the why must be understood if one is to adjust to changing situations.

While most of the emphasis in transfer of learning relates to positive transfer in which previously learned material is generalized to new situations in ways that facilitate associations or learning, it should be realized that transfer may inhibit learning as well. This interference of something already learned with new learning is called "negative transfer." This often happens when two or more elements of learning are very similar and instead of being associated they become confused with one another. Negative transfer may also occur when an individual has learned to do something incorrectly and someone tries to teach them a correct procedure. The old learning gets in the way of the new procedures.

Teaching for transfer. Instructors can aid the positive transfer of learning if they:

1. Emphasize the underlying principles and ideas of the content being learned and make sure they are fully understood. Then the student will be more likely to apply principles to a new or different task or subject.

2. Help students to see the relationship of parts of the subject being taught to other parts of the course or to other subjects or courses.

3. Let students know when to expect transfer, the benefits to them, and how to facilitate the transfer.

4. Use projects, problems, discussion, and leading questions to give practice in transfer.

5. Give attention to the differing ways in which individual students learn and their approach to problems as well as to results.

Learning Curves and Plateaus

The phrase *learning curve* refers to a two-dimensional description of the gradual progress that is made as one learns a skill and practices over a period of time (see figure 3-1). Since changes are gradual over time, the points on the two-dimensional graph when linked together reveal a gradual curve. During the "trial and error" stage of learning, there is little progress since the practice or trials produce errors. However, with continued practice, instructor feedback and increased understanding as well as improved linkage between the neural and muscular systems, the learner begins to "catch on" and make more rapid progress. This progress continues until performance gradually levels off at a plateau after which increased learning may occur. However, at some point, the upper limit of an individual's ability in a given area will be reached. Therefore, it is difficult to know whether one is on a plateau with the potential of additional progress or whether one is at the point of "overlearning" beyond which further practice will not lead to improvement. If, instead of connecting the points on the graph into a smooth

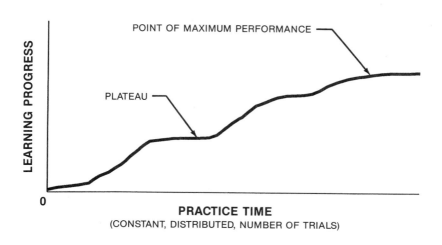

Figure 3-1. Learning curves reveal an irregular pattern of improvement by the learner over time.

line producing a curve, one were to draw horizontal and vertical connecting lines between the several points, the lines would form "steps". Therefore, the terms *learning curves* and *learning steps* are, in reality, only graphic representations of the progress that an individual makes in the process of learning or acquiring a skill.

If one uses the analogy of steps to describe progress in skill development, plateaus in the process of learning are like the landings in a long flight of stairs. They are particularly evident in the development of psychomotor skills which are complex combinations of physical coordination and mental processes. After mastering the steps of procedure in performing a skill, one may become discouraged because there may appear to be very little progress toward a higher level of skill. One cause may be that, although the individual may know how to perform the skill or task, they may not have practiced it sufficiently to make it a thoroughly established habit. Thought has to be given to each step of procedure as it is performed. At this point, the learner may feel that further progress is impossible and may feel like giving up. Golfers and other athletes experience plateaus in developing their game. Students should be informed of this characteristic of learning so that they will recognize it as natural and something experienced by everyone who strives for perfection.

One typically overcomes a learning plateau by continued practice assuming that the physical movements are correct; however, specialized instruction may be required to overcome the plateau if there is a flaw in the techniques of performance. As practice is continued and coupled with a strong effort to learn, and a thorough knowledge of the procedures involved in the task, the process will gradually become automatic, just as walking or talking is automatic to most human beings over three years of age. From this point on, progress is again possible in the same way that running is possible after walking has become automatic. However, other delays in progress are likely to occur as one strives to develop an additional level of skill.

Several plateaus may be encountered along the road toward a high degree of skill. The instructor should:

1. Recognize the existence of plateaus.

2. Inform students of the nature of the plateaus in learning.

3. Analyze student performance to detect any performance flaws that require remedial instruction.

4. Help to increase the learner's understanding of the task.

5. Emphasize the need for additional practice.

6. Recognize that emotions such as fear, hate and boredom may create plateaus in learning because the student's mind is not free to concentrate on the task being learned.

7. Provide encouragement and continued practice until the steps of procedure become so automatic that the student can concentrate on the next phase or level of achievement.

If plateaus are of long duration, it may mean that (a) improper habits have been formed, (b) the student is attempting to learn something beyond his/her potential ability, (c) the instructor has failed to give needed assistance and motivation, or (d) the individual's upper limit of ability on that task has been reached.

Repetition or practice. Cognitive learning as well as psychomotor learning is bolstered by frequent repetition of the same pattern of relationships. Even though learning does and can occur as a result of a single trial or event, most instructional strategy recognizes the value of repetition and practice. For example, only one trial may be required for a child to learn that a stove is "hot" even though no flame is observable. Obviously this is a dramatic event in which the strong sense of pain is associated with an event. Most classroom events are not this dramatic or sensory and as a result, most learning takes more than a single trial. As the learning task becomes increasingly complex (more and more associations are to be made) then repetition or practice becomes increasingly important. Little or no practice may be needed for very simple or isolated behavior like verbalizing the names of objects or pronouncing words. However, practice becomes important as one seeks to learn to apply general or abstract principles; when one uses mathematical or statistical principles to solve problems or when one seeks to develop skill such as playing a musical instrument, soldering an electrical connection, or learning to type.

All too frequently in school settings there is insufficient time for the needed repetition and practice. As a result, the learner may not develop the level of skill necessary for efficient application. Usually, distributed practice involving frequent but small doses of repetition is better than long periods of repetitive practice, particularly if the learner begins to tire or lose interest. This is why review sessions, frequent quizzes, drill and other strategies involving application are so important in the teaching/learning process. Frequently, instructors must decide whether to teach a subject by breaking it into small parts and teaching each part well before going to the next or to teach the whole subject, to some extent, before drilling on the parts (this is often referred to as the *whole versus part* method). Learning a five-minute speech should probably be learned in one setting. A longer speech might be learned in segments over a period of several practice sessions before "putting it all together." A basketball coach would probably allow some team play almost from the start but most of the practice sessions would be devoted to drill on the elements of the game such as shooting, passing and dribbling.

Complex tasks involving many separately identified skills as well as information obviously cannot be practiced as a whole from the beginning. In these situations, logical divisions must be made and learned separately.

The principle of repetition also applies to oral instruction. Emphasis on key points to be learned and repeating them in different ways has a positive influence on learning. An important element of effective instruction involves the emphasizing of key elements in a lesson so that they get the learner's attention. The following are techniques that may be used by the instructor:

1. Repeating the statement several times during the period.

2. Writing the word, term or phrase on the chalkboard, overhead projection transparency or on a chart or poster.

3. Preceding the material with such words as "remember this," "make note of this," "now this is an important part," etc.

4. Pausing before and after a statement that has particular importance.

5. Reinforce the information or idea with a visual device (diagram, photograph or illustration).

6. Vary the speech pattern (speaking more slowly or loudly or softly).

7. Use dramatic physical gestures.

It should be kept in mind that the overuse of a given technique may decrease its effectiveness. The instructor's personality, style as well as the nature of the subject may dictate which form of emphasis is most appropriate.

Feedback and reinforcement. An instructor makes an indirect assessment of learning by observing the student's behavior or performance. Likewise the learner judges progress by evaluating his/her behavior or performance.

The learner's own personal appraisal as well as the instructor's judgment of progress can serve as important feedback regarding the teaching/learning process. In reality, practice does not involve the precise repetition of the exact same behavior over and over. Instead, there are variations in behavior with each trial which may yield different results. These different results provide feedback to learners about the relationship between specific behaviors and the results. By using this feedback, learners gradually become more skillful. As a result, performance increases with practice until a plateau is reached or until the skill is mastered, or until the individual reaches his/her maximum performance level.

All behavior produces some type of outcome, and as a result, individuals receive feedback which may be either positive or negative reinforcement. Thus, reinforcement guides behavioral change and provides motivation for continued action. Reinforced behaviors tend to be repeated and behaviors that are not reinforced tend to be extinguished or discouraged. Generally speaking, feedback or reinforcement is effective when it is immediate. Self-instruction materials make use of this principle by presenting learning tasks that can be completed successfully. These correct responses provide immediate feedback and reinforcement in the form of success. Incorrect responses are not reinforced since the immediate feedback spells failure.

TYPES AND CONDITIONS OF LEARNING

As indicated in the initial section of the chapter, learning results when associations occur within the brain. Learning is primarily an internal process within the brain although there may be related motor or physical manifestations. These associations may be very simple and involve only two or three elements, e.g., the relief of discomfort associated with a bright light or the relief of discomfort of cold ears by wearing ear muffs to a very complex set of associations in which a number of previous associations are retrieved from long term memory and brought to bear upon a unique problem requiring a novel solution not previously experienced. It is, however, necessary for learning to be distinguished from changes that occur from the natural processes of human growth and development. The fact that a child six years of age can jump twice as high as he/she could at age four is more the result of growth than learning.

Educational psychologists have typically referred to this range of learning complexity as types or levels of learning. Although there are many explanations and descriptions of these levels or types of learning, one of the most comprehensive is provided by Dr. Robert Gagné (gon-yea) in the publication, *Conditions of Learning.* At the risk of oversimplification, the levels of learning as classified by Gagne' are summarized under eight categories from signal learning to problem solving.

Learning as a System

As indicated previously, learning is not synonomous with behavior or performance. However, an individual's behavior or performance may be the only way that the instructor has to judge the extent to which learning has taken place. As a way of thinking about the eight levels or types of learning one might find it useful to consider the stimulus (S) to learning as an input and the response (R) resulting from learning as the output. A stimulus can be anything brought into the learner through the sensory mechanism, e.g., sight, touch, hearing. A response is typically an observable behavior that permits the instructor to judge the extent to which the individual has changed or learned. In its simplest form, a system consists of input — processor — output. (See figure 3-2.) Utilizing a systems analogy, learning (associations) occurs in the "processor." The association and the mapping that occurs cannot be observed directly. As a result, the instructor must infer learning from the observation of behavior or performance. The

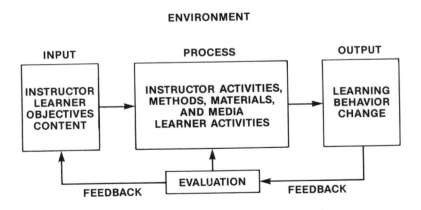

Figure 3-2. Application of general systems theory to instruction reveals the interrelationships among elements of the teaching-learning process.

educational psychologist will diagram the process as S-R or some variation of this symbolism.

For the instructor to apply or take into account the "simple to complex" levels of learning categorized by Gagné, it is important to focus attention on the conditions, both internal and external, that facilitate learning. External conditions are those that can be controlled, at least to some extent, by the instructor. The instructor, can control certain conditions by using the concepts presented earlier in this chapter, e.g., repetition or practice, feedback and reinforcement, teaching for transfer, learning by doing and others. To return to the "systems theory" analogy of input — processor — output, the instructor's influence on the external conditions has a direct controlling effect of the stimuli or input. These conditions indirectly affect learning and the resulting "output" through which the nature and extent of learning are judged.

Levels of Learning

The eight levels or types of learning identified by Gagné are signal, stimulus-response, chaining, verbal association, discrimination, concept, principle or rule, and problem solving. Regardless of the level or

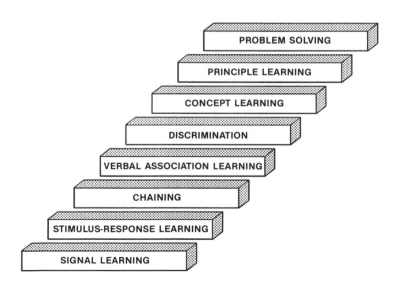

Figure 3-3. Gagné classified the levels of learning into eight categories.

complexity of the learning event, the conditions under which it takes place will determine, in large measure, the extent to which the mental or mental/ motor associations are mapped into memory and/or coded into the central nervous system. Therefore, it is important for the instructor to (1) specify the content structure, (2) identify prerequisite capabilities, (3) plan instruction carefully, and (4) assess the results or changes in behavior following a learning event. The fundamental question related to learning is, "What capability exists following the learning event that did not exist before?"

Signal Learning. This type of learning is familiar to everyone. It takes advantage of involuntary responses, e.g., eye blinking, tearing, nerve reflex, saliva. Perhaps the most frequently cited example relates to Pavlov's experimentation with canine learning. When feeding was accompanied by a given sound such as a bell, it was found that the dogs would begin to salivate when they heard the sound even though no food was present. The signal or stimuli produces an involuntary response. Another example would be an increased heart rate and the tingly feeling associated with fear of heights, water or the dark. Military commands are designed to evoke alertness.

Stimulus-Response Learning. This type of learning is more important to the typical instructional process in that it involves a voluntary response to a signal or stimulus. Typically, the responses are motor responses such as moving one or more parts of the body or even speaking. In fact, the stimulus itself is generally motor related. For example, the parent may teach a child to say "daddy" or "mama" by presenting the stimulus (the word itself) immediately followed by reinforcement (praise, hugging, a pat on the head) for any sound that is close. Learning to type or "keyboard" involves stimulus—response since one learns to press keys when the letters or numbers are presented visually. Learning to write a message (response) from Morse Code signals that are heard (stimuli).

Chaining. Another relatively simple and frequently occuring type or level of learning involves the connecting of two or more previously learned stimulus—response patterns. The English language is replete with chains of verbal sequences as revealed in studies of word association. Examples such as "table and chair," "horse and buggy," or "lock and key" imply two different objects about which one has learned and then chained the two together. In this type of learning, it is obvious that two separate learning events or association patterns (links) are prerequisite to the chaining. For chaining to occur efficiently, the two links should occur close together in time. This timeliness or close sequencing is referred to as contiguity.

Verbal Association. Even though Gagne' lists this type of learning separately, it is actually a form of chaining. Adults with considerable verbal facility are in command of a sizable vocabulary. Therefore, when they encounter a new word that depicts a piece of equipment or process, the chaining process occurs with ease. However, individuals with limited vocabularies may not know the prerequisite "root" word, the prefix or suffix that would greatly enhance the verbal association. Previous knowledge of the words spontaneous and combustion greatly facilitate the meaning of "spontaneous combustion." When there can be visual stimuli such as a picture along with sound, verbal association between and among words will be facilitated.

Discrimination. The previously described types or levels of learning were relatively simple in that a relatively small number of discrete stimulus—response associations were involved. Learning to classify and make multiple discriminations is a complex task involving a host of variables and associations among those variables. This requires differentiation among stimuli that are similar and responses (names) that are assigned to each group of stimuli. A good example is the learning that occurs whereby many adolescent boys can identify new car models. Each year brings about change in body style, grill, chrome features, insignia, and the combination of materials and color. A young man with sufficient interest will soon be able to discriminate among this year's models by name as well as among those learned previously. Each model comprises a complex set of stimuli that evokes a response (model name). When a number of these S-R connections are brought together multiple discrimination is involved.

It is important for the instructor to recognize the phenomenon of interference that is involved as the learning task becomes more complex (an increase in the number of associations with previous S-Rs). In reality, the new chain or set of associations interferes with the retention of a previous learned set of associations. This interference is the basis of forgetting or being unable to recall something previously stored in one's memory. Discrimination is the type of learning involved as the instructor learns to call each student by name or to select a cabinet door key from a set of keys.

Concept Learning. These higher levels of learning distinguish clearly humans from other species. Abstract representations such as up and down, near and far, left and right, larger and smaller, outside and inside, between, above, beneath and many others are formed through an internal neural process. For example, when an individual learns the concept of cubic, he/she cannot be fooled because of its color, its size or the material of which it is made. Likewise, when the concept of middle is grasped the learner can identify anything (animal, vegetable or mineral) in terms of its position in the middle.

Principle Learning. Formal education is highly dependent upon the learning of rules or generalized principles upon which future action is dependent. These rules or principles involve the linking or chaining of two or more concepts, e.g., round objects roll; gasses expand when heated; fire burns things. This form of learning involves more than the memorization of these "principles" or "double barrel" concepts since it requires the idea inherent in the principle. In fact, one can "know" the idea of the principle without saying the words. From a practical standpoint, the instructor must be certain that the learning observed is really a conceptual chain of understanding as opposed to a verbal chain. In the evaluation process, the student should be required to apply a rule or principle instead of just identifying or writing the rule.

Problem Solving. When an individual applies principles or rules to make decisions that allow him/her to deal with or control circumstances, problem solving is involved. This process of thinking in which previously learned rules or principles are applied to a situation that is novel or unique to the individual is referred to as problem solving. Because of the relatively lengthy chain that may be involved in each of several principles or rules to be applied in a given problem situation, it is important that the learner be lead to define the "goal" or the problem to be solved. Once the goal or problem is clearly in focus, the relevant principles must be recalled or located. The next step is the critical dimension through which the human mind combines or interrelates the principles through the thinking process. Sometimes through a "flash of insight" the solution is revealed and a new *higher order* rule emerges for the individual's use.

INDIVIDUAL DIFFERENCES

It is obvious that no two individuals are alike, but from an instructional standpoint, it is important to recognize which differences among individuals cause them to learn differently. Individuals differ in their physical characteristics: height, weight, length of legs, color of skin, eyes and hair, and size of head. However, most physical characteristics have little or no effect on learning. More importantly, the instructor must be sensitive to the many other less obvious differences which have a tremendous impact on learning such as mental ability, interests, keenness of senses, emotional stability, experience background, and knowledge level. As a result of basic aptitudes, training, and experiences, learners differ widely in what they have learned and the level of competence they can reach in a given period of time. Certain learners respond best to written materials while others respond better to materials presented orally. Genetic differences lead to differences in learner capacity and potential. Likewise, individuals develop differently because of their environment and their response to a variety of instructional strategies.

The fact that individuals differ in a variety of ways provides a significant challenge to an instructor. The professional instructor consistently observes, listens to, and tries to understand each student. In our casual thinking about learning and teaching, one tends to visualize an instructor and a group of students, the one teaching, the other learning. However, the instructor must understand and teach each individual in the group. The group does not learn anything, only individuals within the group learn. The instructor must decide which individuals need guidance, encouragement, extra instruction, more practice, or more challenging assignments. Decisions must be made regarding each individual's level of achievement and ways must be found to assist learners achieve their maximum potential. Individuals differ in emotional maturity, in the ability to understand complex concepts, in physical coordination, in learning rate or speed and many other ways that may influence performance in a learning situation. The instructor must know each member of the group as a unique person and this knowledge will help to determine the approach to use. This is one reason why large classes in our public schools are not very successful and why mass media such as radio and TV can only supplement, or be a part of the educational process rather than take over the instructional process.

Aptitude, Ability and Achievement

The capacity of an individual to learn is one of the most obvious individual differences that is of primary importance to the instructor. To put it simply, one cannot learn something that is beyond one's capacities regardless of the time or instructional method used. Even though the educational processes tend to cause a given group of students to be more alike, there are still substantial differences in capacity of individuals within a given group of students. In addition to differences in learner capacity, Piaget and others contend that certain kinds of learning is possible only after certain prior development has taken place. Instructors must recognize that students may not be able to comprehend or gain from a given learning experience unless they have certain prerequisite information. Even though the material to be learned is within the learner's capacity and the learner may be able to understand it later, it is quite possible that circumstances at the moment will not allow learning to occur. Learners clearly differ in their general patterns of strengths and weaknesses. Some are strong in verbal abilities but weak in quantitative or spatial abilities while others have the opposite pattern of strength and weakness.

Aptitude refers to the individual's potential to achieve in a given area. A student may have great aptitude for music, but not able to play any instrument because of lack of training. Aptitude, then, is the potential or "built-in" characteristics that can be developed through training and experience. Aptitude may be thought of as clay in the ground. It can take the form of mud in the street, bricks for a building, or in the hands of the artist, into a great piece of sculpture. The aptitude is the same. The result is dependent on the way it is used.

Aptitude tests, of which there are many types, attempt to measure or predict what the student can do after appropriate education experiences. Aptitude refers to latent or potential ability. The specific aptitude that has the greatest impact on most cognitive learning in the school setting is *intelligence*.

Ability refers to the individual's actual level of performance as contrasted to aptitude or potential. It refers to what a student can do after education or experience.

Ability means demonstrated performances over a period of time. The skilled carpenter with a sore hand may not perform well today but has the ability to perform and may do very well a few days later. The sick student may fail an examination, but he/she may still have the ability to pass the examination because of adequate knowledge of the content.

Achievement refers to the present. When a student gets a high mark on a test, this is evidence of achievement as measured by the teacher's standards. A good aptitude test given, perhaps years before the course, would have predicted that the student could do this. When an aptitude test predicts success but achievement does not result during the educational process, it may be concluded that the student's interest in the subject, the instructor's methods , or other factors have affected learning.

If the student gets good grades in mathematics but not in English, this may mean a difference in aptitude for the two subjects. However, it may mean that one teacher is doing a better job than the other. It may mean simply that one teacher has different standards than the other. Or it may mean that the student, for some reason, works harder in mathematics than in English. These factors and many more must be considered in understanding the progress of a given student. It is sad that so much emphasis is placed on school grades by some parents who have little understanding of the basis for such grades.

Intelligence and Learning

Intelligence is hard to define, but basically it refers to a general aptitude based on many specific aptitudes. It is measured by aptitude for such factors as solving problems, speed in learning, understanding of relationships, and dealing with abstract ideas.

Controversy continues regarding the relative amount of one's intelligence that is predetermined by genetic structure and the impact that environmental infulences have on intellectual development and especially upon measured intelligence. The most common position that is currently taken in the scientific community is that each individual's unique genetic pattern sets upper and lower limits on the possibilities for development. However, it is important for instructors to realize that very few individuals maximize their aptitudes. Therefore, the instructor's responsibility is a never ending quest to help individuals achieve at higher and higher levels as they seek to maximize their aptitude. It is important for instructors to understand that although IQ tests may yield a single score, they do not measure a single aptitude. There are a large number of correlated but nevertheless different factors involved in intellectual functioning. There is not a single aptitude that can be designated as *intelligence*. For this reason, IQ scores are often described as "what the test measures." There is no simple and direct relationship between an IQ score and the size or functional efficiency of a particular area of the brain. As of this time, there is no common agreement about the number of human abilities that exist or how these abilities are related. Nevertheless, most of those who study this phenomenon accept the general developmental ideas of Piaget concerning the emergence of specific abilities as opportunities are provided for individuals to engage in specific developmental tasks.

Intelligence always refers to aptitude rather than achievement. An individual an be very intelligent yet accomplish very little in an educational setting. The term I.Q. (Intelligence Quotient) refers to a means of relating general aptitude to age. It is determined by standard intelligence tests given under controlled conditions. If we want to know how one person compares with others of the same age, as measured by intelligence tests, their scores can be compared with the average of hundreds of others of the same age. A person may have a score on a test that is equal to the average of others who are the same age or it may be higher or lower. If the individual is twelve years old and his/her score on the test is the same as the average of thousands of other twelve year olds from a given population for which the test was constructed, the individual is reported as having an I.Q. of 100.

Traditionally, the I.Q. was a ratio of mental age (MA) and chronological age (CA). For instance, if a 10 year old had a mental age of the average 12 year old, the mental age (12) was divided by the age in years (10) and multiplied by 100, giving an I.Q. of 120. A mental age of 8 and a chronological age of 10 would result in an I.Q. of 80.

However, the 1972 Stanford-Binet standardization testing program revealed that the average mental age in the U.S. has shifted upward and as a result a child five years of age must have a mental age of 5 years and 6 months to be classified as average. As a result, I.Q. is now derived at each age level rather than calculated as a direct ratio of chronological age and mental age.

The growth of mental ability, like physical growth, is more rapid during the early years of life, and then gradually levels off. For practical purposes, we can assume that full mental maturity is reached by most people by age 20 to 25. The mental growth rate of the very intelligent person is faster and continues to a higher level than that of the person of average or below average intelligence.

If the intelligence test were well constructed, and if the person being tested were from the same cultural background assumed by the test development team, and if the test were taken under ideal conditions when the individual is free from emotional or physical discomfort, a true measure of intelligence can be expected. Under the above conditions, the same test or similar forms of the test could be administered to an individual at different times during life, and the I.Q. would remain relatively stable although the M.A. and C.A. would both increase. Even though the Intelligence Quotient is fairly stable and constant for individuals, the mental growth rate may fluctuate in individuals.

Factors such as intensity of interest, attitudes resulting from home conditions, as well as physical and emotional health may affect scores on a specific intelligence test. These same factors, affect success in learning.

The distribution of Intelligence Quotients as found by intelligence tests known as the Stanford-Binet Scale is shown in figure 3-4.

It is estimated that General Grant had an I.Q. of about 110. Lincoln, 125, and Jefferson, 145. Of course, they didn't take an I.Q. test so the estimate is based on what they said or wrote at various times during their lives.

INTELLIGENCE TESTS

NAME	AUTHOR(S)	DEVELOPED OR REVISED	FORM
Stanford-Binet Intelligence Scale	Binet	1908	Individual
First Revision	Terman	1916	Individual
Second Revision	Terman	1937	Individual
Third Revision	Terman & Merrill	1960	Individual
Wechsler Intelligence Scale for Children (WISC)	Wechsler	1949	Individual
Wechsler Adult Intelligence Scale (WAIS)	Wechsler	1955	Individual
Lorge-Thorndike Intelligence Test	Lorge & Thorndike	1957	Group
Davis-Eells Test of General Intelligence or Problem Solving	Davis & Eells	1953	Group
California Test of Mental Maturity	Sullivan, Clark, & Tiegs	1963	Group

Figure 3-4. Intelligence tests are designed to be administered in individual and group settings.

As instructors, we must bear in mind that achievement is based on much more than I.Q. What a person does with the gift of intelligence depends on opportunity, personality, general health, ambition and other factors. Many people have done very well on difficult tasks in spite of handicaps of all kinds. The individual with a measured intelligence of average or below, under the right conditions of education, environment and with appropriate personal characteristics, can make contributions that are clearly above average and frequently superior to those who may be more intelligent. Instructors must not limit an individual's performance level by low expectation any more than they should frustrate a learner by demanding a higher level of performance than aptitude will permit. This is a fine level of distinction that the superior experienced instructor can make much more easily than the novice. It is an instructional skill worth cultivating as it permits individuals to maximize their potential as human beings.

Physical Characteristics and Learning

As previously noted, physical characteristics, such as shape of head, distance between eyes, angle of chin, give little or no indication of intelligence, ability, or personality. An instructor's feelings and attitudes toward physical characteristics, however, may cause distortions in observation. Too frequently, an individual over generalizes from one or two examples which cause misjudgment. One may perceive differences that are not really there. An instructor who thinks a high forehead indicates high intelligence is more likely to think that students who have high foreheads achieve better.

The professional instructor does not put all people of the same physical characteristics, sex, age, or race into one classification. For example, some older persons are "set in their ways" while other older people are liberal-minded and flexible. Members of a given racial group may be either good or bad, but the professional instructor must not prejudge others of the same group. The instructor must realize that very little, if anything, can be really known about a person's ability, personality, honesty, etc., by appearance and even less from a photograph.

While physical characteristics, such as shape of head and brow, size and shape of nose and color of skin, in and of themselves do not determine the individual's aptitude for learning, they may have an influence upon the learner's self-concept which does impact learning. Any characteristic from freckles and red hair to small stature may cause feelings of insecurity and embarrassment which may prevent students, especially young or timid students, from feeling that they are accepted by their fellow students or by their instructor. Unfortunate social experiences caused by the reactions of others to the student's physical characteristics or home background often lead to learning and behavior difficulties.

The effective instructor is alert to these possibilities and should promptly take whatever action is necessary to help the individual fit into the group in a normal way. Sensitivity to the feelings of students is part of the instructor's role, but even more important is the strategy used to help individuals overcome their "hang ups" so that they can achieve their full potential.

Sex and Learning. In addition to the obvious physical differences between males and females, for which most of us are grateful, there are other differences. Adult males usually test higher on mechanical aptitude, but it is recognized that most of this test difference is due to early experience with mechanical things. Little girls traditionally have not been encouraged to play with mechanical toys but rather with dolls. Probably, most differences in the averages between men and women, except in physical strength and related characteristics, are due to environment and educational experiences. The evidence is overwhelming that many women perform well in jobs traditionally reserved for men when they are given an equal opportunity for educational experiences whereby they may gain the necessary competencies.

Age and Learning. It is easy to exaggerate the importance of age. Often a difference in performance is attributed to age when other differences actually caused the performance differential. As a result, older persons may not always get the same chance to show their abilities. Compulsory retirement, regardless of the individual's level of competence, is being challenged by many competent psychologists and administrators.

In the ability to learn new mental skills, most individuals reach a peak by age 25. From then on, during the person's working life, there is usually no significant decrease in the capacity to learn. Of course, some older people do not wish to learn anything new or are out of the habit of learning because of their life style or circumstances. These factors do influence the rate or speed of learning. It must be recognized that some physiological factors related to aging such as visual or hearing impairment can adversely affect learning.

Scientists, business leaders and writers often reach their peak performance between age 50 and 60. It should be recognized, however, that younger persons might do as well if they were in the same favorable position to demonstrate their ability.

In skills of a physical nature, age is more significant. The average age of maximum performance in sports varies with the sport. For football it is between 20 and 30, but for less physically demanding sports like golf the maximum is between 20 and 45.

Needs, Desires, and Interests

Needs, desires, and interests are significant instructional factors because they affect an individual's motivation to learn. A frequently cited way of classifying and describing human needs and desires is the structural hierarchy developed by Abraham Maslow who theorized that experienced needs are the primary influences on an individual's behavior. According to Maslow's Hierarchy of Needs, an individual's behavior is determined to a large extent by a real or perceived need. In other words, individuals behave in certain ways in order to satisfy some need they perceive. According to Maslow's theory, an individual's unsatisfied needs become the prime source of motivation.

People's goals are a motivating force that can be channeled to help them learn more effectively. To gain insight into goal-related behavior, Maslow developed a hierarchical structure in which all human needs are categorized into five levels. These five levels of need relate to the natural process whereby individuals develop from an immature, primitive state to a more mature, civilized state. Individuals progress through these five levels of need as they would climb a ladder. They must experience security on the first rung in order to experience a need to step up to the next higher rung on the ladder. People's inability to fulfill a lower order need may cause them to maintain immature behavior patterns even though any one level of need may never be completely satisfied. There must be at least partial fulfillment of a given level of need before an individual can become aware of the next level of need and have the freedom and confidence to pursue it. Maslow's Hierarchy of Needs recognizes the five levels of need as (1) basic, (2) safety, (3) belongingness, (4) ego-status, and (5) self-actualization. See Figure 3-5.

The first level of the hierarchy represents basic needs of a physiological and survival nature. Needs at this level include shelter, clothing, sex, and food. In a culture where basic needs can be met by most people, there is little tension created concerning their fulfillment. Some individuals redefine this basic level upward to include such needs as physical comfort, a pleasant working environment, or money to provide for creature comforts.

The second level of the hierarchy relates to the individual's well being or *safety* needs. As the individual at least partially fulfills basic needs, other desires will be created that relate to security, environmental orderliness, and the avoidance of risk. These needs are often satisfied through an adequate salary, insurance policies, fire and police departments, alarm systems, and door locks.

Figure 3-5. Human needs are classified in Maslow's Hierarchy of Needs. Needs at the lowest level must be met before an individual is motivated to pursue needs at higher levels.

The third level of the hierarchy relates to *belongingness*. This is the need for belonging, acceptance, and appreciation by others. When one's needs for protection or safety have been met, there is less preoccupation with self and a need to form interpersonal relationships. This level of needs is met traditionally through the family, friends and group membership.

The fourth level of the hierarchy relates to the *ego-status*. This is the need to gain special status within the group as an individual begins to feel secure about relationships with others. This need-related tension is associated with ambition. These ego-status needs motivate the person to seek out opportunities to display competency that will secure social and professional rewards. Ego-status fulfillment is not within the individual's control because it depends on the appropriate response of others to the individual's efforts to perform in a superior way. However, if the person has gained satisfaction on level four, it is easier to move up to level five—self actualization.

The fifth level of the hierarchy relates to *self-actualization* or an individual's personal growth. The individual may fulfill this need through internal motivation to become more creative, demand higher achievement, establish personal success criteria, and become more self-directed.

In formulating instructional strategies and dealing with individual learners, effective instructors are sensitive to the needs, desires, and interests of students. Students' needs for physical comfort and security must be met. Also, provisions must be made to accommodate students desires within the context of the class setting.

Need for Physical Comfort. The temperature level of the classroom or laboratory is significant. Students are easily distracted when they are either too warm or too cold. Substantial research evidence indicates that a higher level of achievement can be expected when students and instructors are comfortable. When feasible, the student should be seated for lectures, discussion sessions, and demonstrations.

Need for Security. Clean, well-lighted classrooms and laboratories as well as safe working conditions help meet student needs for security and provide a positive learning environment. Learning is not easily facilitated in an environment where a student is afraid or anxious. The instructor must provide a setting where students feel that they will not be injured or subjected to physical or emotional abuse.

Students need to feel that with reasonable effort there is a good possibility for success. A threatening environment in which failure is highly possible leads to insecurity. The instructor must be approachable so that a student's anxiety level can be minimized.

Need for Acceptance. Students should be treated as individuals. Encourage friendships and acceptance in the group. Showing respect for students, without becoming their pal, wins students' respect. The effective instructor is rewarded by the achievements of students and their respect through the years.

Instructors should learn the names of students as soon as possible. Knowing a student's name has numerous positive values. Initially it sends a message of individual worth to the student. Subsequently it reinforces that sense of worth. Recognizing individual differences in students and responding to those differences encourages learning. Students realize when an instructor has a genuine interest in them and will work hard to maintain that interest.

Need for Recognition and Approval. The effective instructor finds ways to provide recognition for achievement. Students must understand class standards and have opportunities to measure themselves against those standards. It is a sure sign of a poor learning environment when a student says, "I don't have any idea how I am doing in this course." Students must know when they have done a good job. Grades are not the only way in which this recognition can be accomplished. Sometimes a few words or a pat on the back from the instructor meets a substantial need.

The instructor must be discreet in providing words of praise through private conversation or a note on the student's paper. An instructor's good intention may work to the disadvantage of students if those who are praised for good work become the scapegoats for poor achievement of others in the class. While it is appropriate to post examples of good student work, it is better to omit students' names. Likewise, when posting examination results, the students' identity should be masked. This practice saves embarrassment for both low and high achievers. Calling students by name and providing recognition for something well done pay dividends in terms of student motivation and higher levels of productivity.

Need for Self-Respect. Students' attitudes and feelings have great impact on the effectiveness of learning. All students desire to be respected. As indicated in Maslow's Hierarchy of Needs, the ego-status level represents a substantial set of needs. Society provides many examples of people who have sought recognition in both positive and negative ways in order to gain self-respect.

Need for Success. It has often been said in educational circles that "success begets success and failure begets failure." The need for success is important in terms of Maslow's Hierarchy of Needs. First individuals need to have others recognize their success. Then, at the level of self actualization, the most important need is for individuals to consider themselves successful according to their own internally defined criteria.

In an educational setting, success is typically defined as the achievement of certain standards or objectives preestablished by the instructor. Students should understand the basis on which they are being judged so that they have a reasonable chance of being successful.

Projects, problems, and other learning activities should be consistent with the objectives of the course. The evaluation process should also be consistent with the objectives of the course and should be well known. All assignments should be prepared carefully so that success is possible with reasonable effort. Assigned problems and tasks should increase in difficulty as the course progresses so that students are challenged to do their best, continually working from one level of success to another. In some types of instruction, provision can be made for assigning tasks of varying complexity so that each student can achieve to a maximum level irrespective of the achievement level of others.

Time requirements can be varied so that slower or less able students can achieve success even though it may take longer. However, when occupational competency is required, all persons who are to be certified by the instructor as occupationally competent must reach some established standards, and time may be a variable that cannot be compromised.

Whenever possible, challenging experiences should be provided for the more able students in class so that they may exceed the standards and move on to higher levels of self-actualization if their ability permits.

Learner Frustration

When one wishes to do something and cannot for one reason or another, a feeling of annoyance and tension results. This condition is often referred to as frustration. Frustration resulting from the complexities of a fast-paced technological society is frequent and unavoidable. It can come from simple things like rain when a picnic is planned, a car that won't start, a telephone busy signal, or at the other extreme, from unsatisfactory progress in one's occupation.

Frustration occurs whenever there is conflict between an individual's desires and his/her level of achievement at a given point in time. The greater the number of variables that must be accommodated in one's daily life, the more difficult it is to be "in control." When a person is frustrated, strong emotions affect behavior in ways that, to the casual observer, make very little sense. The person, whose behavior is difficult to understand, may be frustrated. Regardless of the cause, frustration may interfere with the individual's attention to the learning task. While it should be acknowledged that some degree of tension may be desirable in a learning situation as it can cause an individual to pay attention and work harder at the task, too much tension leads to frustration and interferes with the learning process.

It is important for instructors to have a working knowledge of the causes and reactions to frustration in order to understand better their own behavior as well as that of supervisors, students, and others with whom they work. Some of the common sources of frustration are:

Impersonal Frustration. A busy intersection, a stalled engine, a flat tire, are all examples of impersonal things that cause frustration. It is not unusual for anyone faced with such situations to feel tension and perhaps to become angry. Nevertheless, this tension and level of frustration must be controlled and kept in perspective. "Controlled" does not mean that the frustration or anger should not be revealed, but rather that the tension or frustration should not cause the individual to allow a condition to influence their life out of proportion to the importance of that particular occurence or event.

Frustration with People. Although other people may help us obtain our goals in life, they may also stand in our way. Every person is a complex combination of needs, characteristics, values, abilities, desires, opinions and attitudes. It is inevitable that people get in each others' way. Good human relationships satisfy many needs and desires; however, even the most perfect relationships are likely to be frustrating at times. The parent loves the child, but sometimes the one frustrates the other because each wants something different at any given point in time. For example, the boy wants to build a treehouse; his mother wants a neat yard.

Most adults learn to let someone else have their way at least temporarily and to at least partially hide their feelings. Frustrations in adults, therefore, may be less obvious than in children. There are fewer fistfights among adults, but frustration shows up in other ways.

Frustration with Rules and Regulations. Whenever there is an organization, there must be rules and regulations. Most of these are recognized as necessary and beneficial to the well being of the organization in the long run. At the same time, these regulations seriously interfere with one's freedom since they restrict an individual's actions from time to time. The people enforcing the regulation, whether they be instructors, policemen, supervisors, or members of a committee become the target of frustration even though the source may be a rule or regulation.

Frustration from Limitations. Individuals become frustrated when they cannot remember something as quickly as they want, when they cannot get someone to see their point of view, when they cannot drive a nail without bending it or when they cannot back into a parking place.

Sometimes a choice must be made between two equally appealing goals. The skilled technician may have to choose between staying at the bench where there is satisfaction from doing high quality work or moving to a supervisory position, which means more money and responsibility. Regardless of the choice made, there is likely to be frustration at first and from time to time thereafter. It is not uncommon to hear a supervisor express a wish to be back in the production area where life is remembered as being simpler with fewer frustrations. Instructors who become school administrators frequently long for the "good old days" when they were classroom teachers.

Another type of frustration occurs when the achievement of a highly desired goal is in conflict with the individual's code of conduct or personal conscience. A common example is the ruthless "go getter", highly motivated toward financial, social or similar goals whose desires in those areas are in conflict with the desire to be well-liked and have positive social relationships.

Reactions to Frustration. As pointed out in the preceding sections, there are many situations that lead to frustration. However, regardless of the specific situation with which one is confronted, frustration results from some type of barrier to the achievement of a goal. For a time, the individual may look for some way of getting around the barrier. For example, different ways to start the car, or to make money without hurting anyone else may be attempted. If these alternate routes to goal achievement are not successful, there is a tendency for the individual to become somewhat emotional, which may give some temporary relief, but the resulting behavior may seem very strange to others who do not realize the source of frustration. One of the most common forms of emotional reaction is referred to as *aggression* in which one becomes angry and attacks someone or something in an emotional rage. Behavior such as kicking a door, hitting a wall, or swearing at a car are examples of aggression. A more complicated form of aggression is seen in a parent who returns home from work and takes out his or her frustration on other members of the family. It should be understood that the parent may not understand or admit the cause of the frustration. There is simply a feeling of need to kick the dog, argue with the spouse, or yell at the child. A job-related frustration has triggered an emotional response. Another form of aggression is seen when individuals blame their problems on a convenient scapegoat such as their supervisor, the president of the company, a relative, or a fellow worker.

Another reaction to frustration is regressive behavior. Regression may take the form of childlike or unquestioning dependence on another person or group to solve a frustrating problem. Likewise, a strong and continuous desire to return to the "good old days," or crying in the face of frustration are also examples of regression. These latter examples may not always be undesirable in that they may relieve frustration and permit resumption of normal activity. While it is quite normal for anyone to exhibit an occasional aggressive or regressive behavior in the face of frustration, repeated behavior of this type is not helpful or healthy.

When there is repetition of certain negative behavior in the face of frustration long after it should be apparent that the behavior is not solving the problem, the individual is referred to as exhibiting fixation. For example, one may observe a driver continue to turn the car starter after it should be clear that something else must be done to get the car started. Likewise, the person who dwells on questions of world affairs, economics, the meaning of life or other complex problems to which there are no real answers but who, nevertheless, continues to insist on simple answers may, in time, develop a pattern of beliefs and attitudes which are very fixed. Such individuals do not meet new problems with an open mind. Any information contrary to preconceived beliefs is rejected. New ideas and points of view that are in conflict with preconceived answers are painful. An individual with such a *fixation* may blindly follow and fight for some group or movement that happens to fit a given pattern of thinking. Milder forms of fixation are observed in individuals who have very narrow conversation patterns such as their children, their work, football, etc.

Another reaction to frustration may be apathy and negativism. Some individuals, when faced with many frustrations and perhaps even the frustration of poor health, simply give up and quit trying. They may take on a negative and sour attitude toward almost everything. They expect nothing good to happen and make no effort to cause positive events to occur in their lives.

Such an individual who has faced many frustrations with little success may try to escape either physically or emotionally. Some may keep moving to another geographic location, another job, another friend, or in the case of a soldier, going "away without leave" (AWOL) may be seen as the answer. Others may escape emotionally by daydreaming, by going to the movies, or the nearest bar, by taking up a hobby or by just "going fishing." A certain amount of escape of this type is normal. It may bring about some change of pace and provide helpful relaxation. Such psychological escape is harmful only when carried to extremes, for example, when one breaks with reality and does not separate reality from fantasy. Milder forms of this behavior occur when one has an inflated view of their own importance. However, if you start wearing a three-cornered cap, walk around with your right hand inside your waistcoat and insist that everyone address you as Napoleon, you need help now! .

Learning to Live with Frustrations. Individuals differ in their ability to adjust to frustration. Some seem to have more ability than others to cope with frustrating situations. The ability to withstand or cope with frustration comes partly from early experiences with frustrations that were not too severe or too frequent. Parents, by necessity, frustrate their children because the child's demands cannot and should not always be met. This is a normal developmental process in which a human being learns that the needs for self cannot always be achieved. Sometimes the needs of others must come before the needs of self. Individuals need these developmental experiences as a normal part of living. On the other side, however, the child who is consistently frustrated in all or most of his/her desires may develop habits of mental escape that will be harmful when reality must be faced and dealt with in a positive and constructive way.

Individuals can learn to tolerate frustration and cope effectively when they understand the nature of frustration and attempt to make reasonable adjustments. Instructors must keep in mind that individuals learn and act as they do because of their own drives, frustrations and attitudes. The existence of frustration in instructional situations may be recognized by certain symptoms such as poor achievement, discipline problems, damaged school equipment, the spreading of gossip and rumor, exaggerated complaints, absenteeism and accidents in shops and laboratories. The effective instructor must remember that behavior is always a result of something. People are not born lazy, mean, aggressive, stubborn or fearful. The instructor must look for the causes rather than just trying to deal with the behavioral symptoms. For example, the student may not know exactly what the instructor expects. The effective instructor who does a good job of planning knows what he/she wants and communicates clearly this direction to students. Frustration can be caused by the absence of needed instructional materials and supplies. As the instructor looks for cause rather than symptoms, he/she must be willing to remain open to new and more objective information in judging the student's motivations, attitudes and behaviors. If a student is resorting to daydreaming, why? What is the reason for a student's sarcasm?

Remember that most of us at times become frustrated, if only to a relatively mild degree. No one is completely free of frustration. Remember that a degree of tension is necessary if one strives to achieve at a higher level. Recognize but don't try to treat extreme cases of reaction to frustration. If you think you recognize a case of extreme frustration, seek assistance from the school's counselor, psychologist, or other professional sources to whom the students should be referred.

To some extent, an instructor can reduce frustration by helping to reduce or eliminate the feelings shown in figure 3-5, which are commonly found in the instructional setting. An instructor may be able to help some students face reality and live with situations that are beyond their power to change. They should be helped to see that there are times when the attitude of "if you can't lick them, join them" is the best approach. There is no sense in beating one's head against a stone wall forever. An individual can work hard and take pride in achievement and still accept the fact that many things cannot be changed. The instructor must not advocate or encourage cheap compromise or "copping out" when the going gets rough. But at the same time, reason and reality may dictate acceptance of a new course of action if long range and more important goals are to be achieved.

Performance Differences

If everyone in the group receives the same instructions, differences in performance should be expected and the larger the group the greater the range of differences to be expected. Even in simple types of work one person may produce several times the amount of the another. Instructors must contend with built-in differences. Educational programs will not erase these differences among individuals. In fact, if individuals who have different aptitudes and different levels of achievement receive the same instruction, the differences among them with regard to achievement is likely to become greater. The person with the greatest aptitude for a given task is likely to perform the task better at any stage of training and typically can gain more from the training received. Instruction will improve the performance of each student, but it usually has the greatest effect on students who have consistently demonstrated good achievement. For many reasons, success tends to beget success. What should you do about individual differences in a class? Here are three important suggestions:

Name _____ _____ _____ Date _____
                Last   First   Initial

Address _____ Phone _____

Age _____

Do You Have Any Health Problems? _____

With Whom Do You Live? _____

Work Experience (Start with Present Job)	Starting Date and Approximate Months on Each Job
_____	_____
_____	_____
_____	_____

Military Experience

_____	_____
_____	_____

Education

School	Length of Time	Did you Graduate? Degree or Diploma
_____	_____	_____
_____	_____	_____
_____	_____	_____
_____	_____	_____

Hobbies and Special Interests

_____

_____

Do Not Fill in Space Below This Line.
- -

Notes on Interview _____

_____

_____

Figure 3-6. Instructors should use a form to gather basic information about a student.

Encourage Individual Abilities. Don't try to force everyone into the same mold. Make use of the students' best abilities so that they can develop at their own rate of speed. The instructor will find that it is not possible or desirable to keep all students on exactly the same problem or assignment. Students should develop to the full extent of their abilities, and it would be foolish to hold the fast learner back to the pace of the slow learner.

Know the learner. In order to facilitate student learning, the instructor needs to gather a few facts about each student. A simple form, Figure 3-6, will help to compile these facts in an orderly manner. In designing your form avoid asking for unnecessary information. An interview should be held with each student after the form has been completed to help you get better acquainted and to assist you in interpreting the facts. Because of the number of students involved, you may have to extend this process; however, getting to know individual students helps you and them.

Provide both group and individual instruction. The characteristics of typical classroom instruction are well known to anyone who has attended school. The chief advantage of group instruction over individual instruction is the saving of time which can result when the students are at the same level of accomplishment and need the same instruction. There is also a tendency for instructors to make more thorough preparation and to put on a better demonstration for a class than for an individual. This is one of the advantages claimed for instruction by mass media such as television or films.

The chief disadvantage of group instruction is that individuals who make up a group rarely need exactly the same instruction at the same time. The more advanced students are held back to the rate of progress made by the group as a whole. When demonstrations are given to a group, considerable time may lapse before some of the students have an opportunity to apply the information or procedures, and much of it may be forgotten.

The best plan in most instructional situations is found in a compromise. Instruction to the group should be given when the material is basic and needed by the entire group. Individual instruction should follow and be continued throughout the program by means of written instruction sheets, short on-the-spot demonstrations, and coaching of individuals.

There are some real advantages in group instruction which result from the interaction of individuals to the group as a whole and to other individuals within the group. Because of the interplay of ideas and the resulting motivation, group instruction is most effective in some situations.

Relationship of Instruction to Learning

In addition to the individual learner and the instructor, the teaching/ learning equation includes another set of important variables which are involved in the process of instruction. These variables encompass the setting in which teaching and learning takes place. This body of knowledge relates to instruction and evaluation, and the instructor's personal qualities and professional competence in guiding the learning process.

Learning Environment. The setting in which the teaching/learning process occurs can have a substantial influence on the outcome of the process. Some types of learning require a substantial amount of physical performance, and in these cases a laboratory with appropriate equipment is essential. Other types of learning require simulation and the "real world" authenticity of the environment is essential. Regardless of the nature of the learning environment, it is a well known fact that the physical comfort of learners is a primary factor in effective learning. Human beings are too easily distracted by such factors as glare, movement, poor circulation, lack of visibility, or an environment that is too hot or too cold.

Organization for Instruction. The manner in which an instructional program is organized has a substantial influence on learning. Whether the instructional program is a course, a unit within a course, a lesson, a workshop or a seminar, instructional effectiveness begins with organization. Advanced planning and "anticipatory thinking" are essential components to the effective organization of instruction.

Clear Directions for Learning. The first step in providing clear direction for learning is for the instructor to have a carefully conceptualized instructional plan. The instructional plan must include specified objectives and a prepared outline of the content to be covered. It is only when the instructor has a clearly thought out instructional plan that clear directions can be prepared for the learner. However, the instructor has only done a partial job by developing an instructional plan for the course. An essential next step is to design a strategy for communicating the instructional plan to the students. Students need to know the objectives they are to achieve and understand the instructor's conceptual framework for the content being presented. As indicated previously no two individuals can be expected to have the same map of associations. However, it is much easier for learners to make meaningful associations (learn) if they are aware of the structural framework from which the instructor is proceeding. Unfortunately, some instructors have a mistaken view that the objectives and the conceptual framework of the discipline must be "discovered" by the learner. This attitude makes the instructional process a game in which the learner often becomes a frustrated loser. There is much wisdom in the old adage, "if you want someone to learn something, tell them what it is you want them to learn."

Meaningful Learning Activities. After the instructor has developed objectives for the educational program and clearly identified the content to be learned,appropriate learning activities must be designed or selected to aid the learner in the process of achieving the specified objectives. Designing or selecting appropriate learning activities requires the instructor to understand the principles of learning as well as the content to be mastered. For example, if psychomotor skills are to be developed, the instructor must have the physical movements demonstrated and provide opportunity for the student to learn by doing. In addition, there must be opportunities for systematic practice and repetition. Provision must be made for positive reinforcement. The learner must perceive a need for engaging in learning activities in order to be motivated to give the activity the attention and time that it requires. The selection and preparation of instructional activities and the process of involving the learner in these activities become the focus for Chapter 4.

Consistent Evaluation. For instruction to have the most positive influence on learning, there must be consistency within the organizational framework. After the objectives have been specified clearly and articulated and after meaningful learning activities have been provided to help the learners achieve the specified objectives, the evaluation plan must be developed in a manner which is consistent with the objectives, the content and the learning activities. It is not only important for there to be an evaluation plan that is consistent with other elements of the educational program, but it is equally important for the learner to perceive and understand the relationships among the various components of the educational program. Evaluation should not be viewed as a "guessing game" between the instructor and the students. There should be no surprises when tests or other evaluative activities are conducted. Students should know what is expected of them even though they may not know the answers to questions that are asked or they may not be able to perform the task that they were expected to learn. It is no compliment to be referred to as a "triple threat" instructor. Loosely translated, this means the instructor assigns one thing to be learned, talks in class about another, and tests over something that was neither assigned or discussed in class.

There is an inherent structural framework for the course, unit and lesson that must be understood and organized by the instructor. The nature of this framework and instructor's organization must be revealed, at least in part, to the learner in appropriate ways so that learning is not a series of isolated and unrelated events.

Knowledge of Results

When one takes target practice, it is only natural to want to know if the bullseye was hit. If missed, the individual typically wants to know how far and in what direction the bullseye was missed. Knowing how well one is doing helps to improve performance. This is true whether the subject is target practice, chemistry, or English composition. Knowledge of results (KOR) or one's progress toward a goal or level of skill can provide motivation to improve. The instructor should evaluate students' work at frequent intervals and let them know how well they are doing in comparison to a known standard. The instructor plays an important role in helping students establish appropriate standards and in evaluating their achievement in terms of those standards.

Competition among individuals and groups may provide motivation to greater effort; however, intense rivalry and the "win at all costs" attitude may be counterproductive. Ruthless competition between students in an instructional program can be counterproductive when emphasis is shifted from learning to winning.

Repetition and Drill

Repetition and guided practice are essential in skill development. Practicing a selection on the piano, drilling on multiplication combinations and swinging at many golf balls provides essential repetition to make certain neuro-muscular (mental and muscle) connections correctly so that they can be repeated without conscious thought. When this occurs, one is considered to have developed a skill which is defined properly as a thoroughly established habit of doing something in the most efficient and effective manner.

Since drill takes instructional time, it is often necessary to provide this kind of repetition in a laboratory setting or outside the regular class period. Large group instruction does not provide a good setting for individuals to get the kind of supervised practice that is essential for skill development. For drill or practice to be effective, there must be a clear understanding of the process rather than mere imitation. There is much evidence, experimental and otherwise, to support the assumption that distributed practice in learning is more effective than long periods of continuous practice. For example, in learning free hand lettering as a part of a drafting course, it is more effective to schedule five, 15 minute periods per week than to have one concentrated practice session of 75 minutes. Factors such as boredom and fatigue are critical to decisions regarding length of practice sessions. The periods of practice should not, however, be too brief nor necessarily of equal length.

The principle of distributed practice is most important in the development of physical skills. However, the principle is still valid in a general way for all types of learning. Nevertheless, there are times when one reasonably long period of concentrated study is more effective than several shorter periods. A two-hour period of concentrated effort in the drafting room as a sequence of design elements is being applied to a practical drafting assignment may be better than several shorter periods. Adults can generally profit from longer periods of study than can children because of their longer span of attention.

The experienced instructor learns to judge the effectiveness of various lengths of concentrated study and practice for each level of student and each type of subject matter. When the number of errors in a student's performance begins to increase, it may be time to stop the practice until the student is more rested or until more time can be given to thinking through the task to get the steps of procedure and the principles more clearly in mind.

Continued practice after something is understood and can be remembered readily or performed with a high degree of accuracy results in a high level of competence. Some refer to this as *overlearning*. This is a point where additional practice or attention to the task does not really improve performance. Subject matter that can be remembered without hesitation after a considerable period of time may be overlearned. Many facts and principles that are used for further learning need to be learned beyond the point of mere understanding. They need to be overlearned. Skills such as writing, spelling, and speaking need to be mastered to the point where they can be put to use easily without much thought.

The Instructor's Personal Influence

The instructor's personal characteristics and behavior as well as professional competence has a substantial influence on learning. As previously indicated, an individual's physical characteristics, although very evident, do not have much influence on one's ability to learn. Likewise, these characteristics have little impact on the instructor's effectiveness. There are, however, a number of other personal factors such as attitude, intellectual ability, creativity and interpersonal skills that do have a substantial impact upon student learning.

Attitude of Instructor. The unconscious influence of the instructor's attitude on students is difficult to estimate, but there is much evidence to indicate that it is substantial. The genuine enthusiasm displayed by the instructor is a major factor in motivation because it tends to be contagious. A positive attitude by the instructor engenders a pleasant atmosphere in the classroom and contributes to student interest and motivation. Enthusiasm can be shown in many ways. Some instructors are, by nature, more expressive than others. Instructors must use their own personality to reveal their interests in the subject matter and in their students.

The key to a positive attitude and enthusiasm is the instructor. If instructors are interested in their jobs and the importance of their work, and well-prepared, their interest and enthusiasm will show. Students will tend to respond in the same way. The instructor who looks continuously for a better way of presenting material and of adding new and interesting material will bring the instruction alive. Being well-prepared for each class period demonstrates the instructor's interest in both the subject and the class. Enthusiasm and pride in the job of instructing leads to improved performance. These characteristics are transmitted to students and reflected in their attitudes. Likewise, instructors who do not like their jobs or the organizations in which they work, too frequently project a negative attitude in their classrooms. The development of positive attitudes on the part of students is frequently an objective of instruction. Most educators agree that "attitudes are more often caught than taught." While this cliche may be an overgeneralization, it does point out the significant impact of modeling on learning in the affective domain.

By the time an individual becomes an adult and chooses to become an instructor, most of the personality traits that have a substantial impact on one's interpersonal skills have been substantially developed. By being aware of the importance of certain instructor behaviors upon student motivation and interests in learning, the instructor can begin to maximize instructional effectiveness. Research has not revealed one dominant personality type that ensures instructional effectiveness, although there are certain instructor traits that enhance positive relationships with students and certain traits that foster negative relationships. This section highlights some personality traits and behaviors that should be encouraged or avoided if instructors are to maximize their effectiveness in the instructional role.

Identification with the Learner. One common difficulty with the technical specialist who becomes an instructor is the lack of appreciation or understanding of the student as a novice. The specialist with a high level of competence has long passed the beginner's level and often has forgotten the difficulties faced by a beginner. The specialist, as an instructor, is often unable to appreciate the students' feelings. The specialist who takes on the instructor's role frequently talks as though the class is comprised of other specialists. Too often the subject is the specialist's only concern and the classroom may become a stage from which to impress the audience.

The effective instructor, however, knows the students' entering capabilities, knows the language they understand best, and knows how to pace the instruction. To the professional instructor, the student and subject matter are both important. It can be assumed that most adults who have voluntarily entered an educational or training program want to learn. Yet many come with only a vague notion of the nature of the instructional program and the expectations of them as learners. Some come because of the expectation of others. Others think that going to school will result in a better career or a changed lifestyle which will bring about increased prestige and status. Few will recognize that it takes self-discipline and time on the learning task to succeed. At the college level, the payoff in terms of employment, job advancement and the benefits that these bring are often too far removed to provide day-to-day motivation for learning.

It has been said that an education is the only thing students will pay for and not try to get their money's worth. In other words, the student may want the diploma or degree but may care little for the learning experiences that are part of the educational process. No instructor will be successful in the long run who is unable to set the stage or stimulate students to want to learn. Most courses of instruction can, at best, provide only a start toward the goal of subject matter mastery. Students should be motivated in such a way that they continue to learn and develop their abilities long after they complete a given course. Students who are driven by external motivation to get high grades or by the constant threat of failure or punishment often lack the motivation and self-discipline that will carry over to life outside of the course. Too frequently, a student learns the subject matter in a course, but in the process, also learns to dislike the subject. If this is the result of the educational process, what has been gained? Would it not have been better to have had another type of instruction through which one enjoyed the subject matter and wanted to continue the relationship beyond the course. In the type of technically oriented society of which we are a part, every occupation requires continued growth and development through learning experiences.

Instructor Behavior. Although much of one's effectiveness in the interpersonal relations area is determined by personality traits that are so much a natural part of the person that very little change can be expected without a substantial commitment over a sustained period of time. There are a number of behaviors that can be cultivated which will allow a more positive reception by students.

An instructor's behavior, the spoken word and the way the words are spoken, as well as the things a person does and the manner in which they are done conveys certain messages to the student. Because of the leadership role of the instructor and the impact of the instructor's behavior on a learner, the instructor may have to control his/her behavior at times. Instructors may not be able to have the luxury of "letting it all hang out," which loosely translated means being completely honest and saying what they think or acting the way they feel. Obviously, the instructor does not gain the respect of students by being dishonest, but there may be times when it is better to control one's feelings than to be "brutally honest." There are many factors which must be weighed at a given point in time, and the instructor will have to make an on-the-spot decision regarding the appropriateness of a specific behavior at a specific point in time under a set of conditions that only the instructor can assess adequately.

In most classroom situations, the instructor's attitudes or feelings may be subject to misinterpretation by students. Often instructors will express themselves or assume a physical posture out of habit that inadvertently sends the wrong message to students. Too often, it may be a message that the instructor does not intend to send, but the reception by the student is based on his or her past experience with other people and may not be the message being sent by the instructor at all. For example, the instructor's facial expression when "thinking hard" or concentrating may convey a frown of disapproval to a student who asks a question. The instructor who stands with crossed arms may strike a "defensive" posture as perceived by students. The instructor who seeks to be definite or very clear about a given standard of performance may be viewed as being "hard nosed" and inflexible. In Chapter One, attention was given to several important behaviors as instructors were urged to be considerate, cooperative, complimentary, friendly and involved with their students. The complexity of the teaching/learning interface requires many decisions to be made quickly and, all too frequently, without the benefit of all the facts that one would like to have in order to make the best possible decisions.

Motivation. One seldom does anything except as a result of a felt or perceived need that provides the motivation for action. Sometimes the motivation is obvious. There have been examples of individuals who have lifted a tremendous amount of weight to free a person who was in danger of being crushed. That kind of need provided motivation. It is not always easy to discover the type of motivation to which a person will respond. The individual who says, "I don't know why I did it," may be telling the truth. The motivation to "do it" was there, but the need that supplied the motive may not be clearly understood. Sometimes the motivation is known to an individual but purposely concealed from others. The person may have needed attention but certainly would not want to acknowledge that as the motivating factor.

Of course, the thoughtful instructor attempts to provide the student with reasons for studying the content at hand and the importance of learning the content. All too frequently, however, the instructor has a difficult time relating the subject to immediate needs of students. In some courses, this may be more difficult than others. Unfortunately, if an instructor has no better reason than "because I said so" or "because it will help you in the next course," this obviously will not provide much motivation. Effective instructors continually seek out relevance for their subject area in order to provide motivation for learning.

Some instructors think of motivation as sort of a pep talk at the beginning of a lesson. However, real motivation cannot be a separate and distinct step in teaching. Everything that happens in the instructional process has an impact on the student's level of interest and motivation. In reality, the methods and techniques described in the following chapters of this book are beneficial only to the extent that they have a positive effect on the student's desire to learn. For instruction to be effective or meaningful to the learner, it must be initiated at the learner's level. If the learner does not know or understand the material, it is the instructor's responsibility to see to it that the student gains the prerequisite level of knowledge before going on to new content. This may require supplementary assignments for individual students. It may mean securing help from individualized instructional materials in the library or learning center. It may mean that the student will need to take a prerequisite course. When this situation occurs, some action must be taken. Students faced with continual failure cannot be motivated to extend their best efforts to learn.

Reward and Punishment. Both reward and punishment are useful tools for the instructor. Reward or positive reinforcement is, by far, the most useful. When learners are rewarded for doing something correctly, they are being provided with positive reinforcement. When one focuses on things that are wrong and on the mistakes that are made, negative reinforcement is being provided. Negative reinforcement tends to make a learner concentrate on errors rather than on the correct procedure. Even dog trainers know that it is better to pet the dog for holding up the right foot for the handshake than to punish the dog for holding up the left foot. Obviously, errors must be corrected, but this should be done in a helpful and positive manner that is mixed with the recognition of good performance. An encouraging smile or a positive comment from a respected person is a reward for most students.

While reward or approval from the instructor is a common form of positive reinforcement, the intrinsic reward that comes from the individual's competence, demonstrated through performance, is the highest level of reinforcement. The instructor should encourage and help students to develop the ability to judge and take pride in a job well done. In this way, the greater skill or accomplishment becomes its own reward.

Some instructors find it much easier to criticize than to praise. This is somewhat a matter of an individual's personality or orientation. Students seldom do perfect work, but the instructor should see the good elements of even a mediocre performance rather than to emphasize the errors that must be corrected. Even though honest praise can be given in almost every situation, praise loses its effect when it is given too frequently and when not deserved. The effective instructor knows the students and understands the type of recognition that works best for them. Often a friendly remark over the student's shoulder is all that is needed. It is safer to praise when the student and instructor can talk privately since peers may resent the appearance of a "teacher's pet." Nevertheless, praise may be given publicly if the achievement is truly outstanding and when it is recognized as such by everyone.

Grades, properly used, can provide useful motivation. However, there is often too much emphasis on grades in some programs since a letter or numerical grade is, at best, only a partial indicator of competence. To be effective, grades must not become the major source of motivation for learning. Also, grades, if they are to motivate and not discourage, must be determined by careful judgment of a number of factors or criteria. The instructor has a responsibility to grade in a manner that stimulates rather than discourages students.

Reprimand. Attempts to coerce or compel students into good habits of thought and action nearly always fail. The instructor who applies more force than support is more likely to arouse resistance than compliance. However, when the student is compelled from within and when the instructor is able to spark a desire or interest within the student through a fair, firm and friendly relationship, the results in terms of student achievement are often outstanding.

Too frequently, reprimands are carried out in a way that provoke resentment and a strong desire on the part of the student to retaliate or "even the score" with the instructor. Obviously, such experiences do not pay dividends for anyone. When it is necessary to reprimand, only those methods which will help the student to progress to a higher level of achievement should be used. If possible, the reprimand should be provided in such a way that it will stimulate a feeling of respect for the instructor and an increased desire to participate in the learning process. In most instances, the reprimand should be a private affair between the student and the instructor. Seldom will a public reprimand accomplish any positive ends. The old adage, "praise in public but criticize in private" is a good rule of thumb. When a reprimand is necessary, the effective instructor will:

1. remain calm,

2. know and use the facts,

3. consider the feelings of the student,

4. discuss the matter with the student alone,

5. include some encouragement and praise for work well done,

6. suggest a constructive course of action,

7. criticize the mistake or behavior, not the individual, and

8. end the conversation on a positive note by acknowledging past achievement and the student's positive attributes.

CONCLUSION

As the instructor gains insight into the ways by which individuals learn, he/she will become increasingly effective as a facilitator of learning. When one understands that learning takes place through experience and that the role of the teacher must be more than that of a dispenser of information the concept of the instructor as a *director* or facilitator of learning takes on real meaning. It is important for instructors to realize that the body of knowledge related to the principles and theory of learning is incomplete and that, at best, it can only provide guidance and direction. The discipline of educational psychology is not an absolute science based on universal laws that lead to the consistency and predictability of a science like chemistry or physics.

Nevertheless, the summarization of the principles, processes and levels of learning described in this chapter, when understood and applied by the instructor can result in more effective instructional strategies that do, in fact, facilitate learning. The effective instructor understands that a learning event must be organized with direct learner involvement. This will enable the learner to gain a depth of understanding that maps the associations into long-term memory. Likewise, an understanding of the various levels of learning through which an individual progresses, as well as the part which repetition, reinforcement, contiguity, and prerequisites play in establishing appropriate conditions, will enable the instructor to function effectively in a setting which places a premium upon effective decision making.

This chapter has been designed to encourage the instructor to be sensitive to the myriad of variables involved in the teaching/learning process that influence the extent to which students learn. The most significant set of variables relate to the individual learner. The learner's aptitude and abilities when combined with interests and needs have a primary influence on the extent to which an individual will achieve.

The learner is influenced not only by his/her assets and liabilities but also by the nature of the instructional leader. The instructor's attitude and behavior influence the learner's level of interest and desire to learn. Just as learners are different, instructors are also different. Many of the variables resulting in physical differences among individuals have little or no impact on learning, but it is important for instructors to realize that the variables related to their own personality and behavior do have positive and negative influences on learning.

The instructional program directed by the instructor and experienced by the learner is another major factor that impacts directly on the level of learning that occurs. The instructor has a primary responsibility for the environment in which learning is to take place as well as the organization of the instructional program. Learning can be facilitated through the organizational structure of the course, unit or lesson. It is of utmost importance that the purpose for learning and the content to be learned are communicated to the learner. Learning is facilitated when students have a clear understanding of the what as well as the why of the learning task. Learners desire feedback and knowledge of the results of their efforts. This implies relatively frequent appraisal as well as prompt grading and return of tests, papers and reports. When the development of skills is desired, students must realize that correct procedures are essential and that a high level of skill will not be possible without a substantial amount of repetition and practice.

The process of teaching involves the instructor in a substantial amount of decision-making. Successful instructional decisions result from (1) knowledge and understanding of the subject matter to be taught, (2) the principles of learning and instruction, (3) an understanding of the learner's interests, abilities and limitations, and (4) a careful consideration of timing and appropriateness under a given set of circumstances.

In this chapter, the author has attempted to introduce the body of knowledge related to learning and the factors that facilitate or impede the learning process. The student is encouraged to supplement this information by selecting readings from the list of references found at the end of the chapter.

REFERENCES ——————————————————————— 3

Ausubel, D., Novak, J., & Hanesian, H. (1978). Educational psychology: A cognitive view. New York: Holt, Rinehart & Winston, Inc.

Craik, F. (1979). Human memory. In M. Rosenzweig & L. Porter (Eds.), Annual Review of Psychology. Palo Alto, CA: Annual Reviews, Inc.

deBono, E. (1983). The direct teaching of thinking as a skill. Phi Delta Kappan, 64, 703-708.

Detterman, D., & Sternberg, R. (1982). How and how much can intelligence be increased? Norwood, NJ: Ablex.

Dweck, C. (1983). Theories of intelligence and achievement motivation. In S. Pareis, G. Olson, & H. Stevenson (Eds.), Learning and motivation in the classroom. Hilldale, NJ: Erlbaum Associates.

Gagné, R. (1977). The conditions of learning. New York: Holt, Rinehart & Winston, Inc.

Good, T., & Brophy, J. (1986). Educational psychology: A realistic approach. New York: Longman, Inc.

Horton, D., & Mills, C. (1984). Human learning and memory. In M. Rosenzweig & L. Porter (Eds.), Annual Review of Psychology. Palo Alto, CA: Annual Reviews, Inc.

Loftus, G., & Loftus, E. (1976). Human memory: The processing of information. Hillsdale, NJ: Erlbaum Associates.

Long, H., McCrary, K., & Ackerman, S. (1980). Adult cognitive development: A new look at Piagetian theory. Journal of Research and Development in Education, 13, 11-20.

Maslow, A. (1970). Motivation and personality. New York: Harper & Row.

Mayer, R. (1979b). Twenty years of research on advance organizers: Assimilation theory is still the best predictor of results. Instructional Science, 8, 133-167.

Miller, P. (1978). Please hear what I am not saying. School Shop, 38 (2), 35.

Novak, J., & Gowin, D. (1984). Learning how to learn. New York: Cambridge University Press.

O'Neil, H., & Spielberger, C. (Eds.) (1979). Cognitive and affective learning strategies. New York: Academic Press.

Piaget, J. (1983). Piaget's theory. In P. Mussen (Ed.), Handbook of Child Psychology (4th ed.). New York: Wiley.

4

DELIVERING INSTRUCTION

As indicated previously, teaching requires numerous decisions involving a host of variables related to (1) the competencies to be acquired, (2) the students themselves, (3) the instructor, and (4) the instructional process. As the instructor plans the lesson, decisions must be made to select the most appropriate methods and techniques whereby students will encounter the subject matter and gain the expected competencies.

Effective instruction requires a competent instructor who can design effective instructional procedures and activities and who can choose and execute appropriate methodology at the right time and under the appropriate conditions. Delivering instruction is a complex matter that requires a high degree of decision making skill and judgment on the part of the instructor. For this process to be effective, the instructor must be well informed regarding the various methods of instruction and the conditions under which they can be expected to be used most effectively.

In this chapter, primary attention is focused upon the process by which the instructor presents information orally as well as through demonstrations and follows up on those modes of presentation with questions to identify points that need to be clarified, amplified, or explained differently. In addition, basic techniques involved in group discussion and other means of participation are described.

THE LECTURE METHOD

The "lecture" is perhaps the most frequently cited as well as the most maligned method of instruction. The bad "press" of the lecture is the result of abuse by instructors who talk too long with very little audience involvement. Nevertheless, when properly used with the right content for appropriate lengths of time and integrated with other instructional strategies, oral presentations can contribute to effective teaching and learning.

A traditional but inappropriate form of the lecture method is one in which the "lecturer" mounts the podium, transmits his/her notes orally to students who write down as much as they can of the oral presentation in their notebooks for 45 minutes, asks "are there any questions," and then quickly steps down from the podium and walks briskly to the office. Professional instructors know that there is much more to teaching than "telling." Effective instruction always provides for two-way communication between instructor and student. Therefore, the traditional form of the lecture method is seldom employed. The length of oral presentations vary considerably with the age and verbal ability of the students as well as the subject matter. Nevertheless, direct teacher talk without some type of involvement of students should seldom exceed 10-15 minutes, even for adults. The lecture is typically supplemented with written handouts, projection transparencies, chalkboard illustration, student questions, student activities in the form of writing, sketching, instructor questions or other means of interacting with the subject matter, which contribute to instructional effectiveness. In other words, the lesson for a given class period may involve the lecture method in which oral presentation is a significant component. However, as previously indicated, a good lesson has several components and the effective instructor seldom relies solely on a single instructional method.

Even though teaching methods are presented separately in this chapter, it should be emphasized that a variety of methods are used by effective instructors and that a single method would seldom be used exclusively during a given class session. Questioning is used extensively by effective instructors in combination with the lecture as well as the demonstration. For this reason, the strategies for utilizing oral questioning in concert with the oral presentation and demonstrations are presented together in this chapter.

Planning the Presentation

The lecture method has often been criticized because it (1) involves too much teacher talk, (2) forces the learner into a passive role, (3) wastes students' time by presenting information that they have already or could gain through reading, and other means. However, it should be noted that most of these criticisms are caused by overuse or inappropriate use of the lecture method and these problems are not inherent in the method itself. Nevertheless, the effectiveness of the lecture method will depend largely on the care and skill with which the instructor prepares and delivers the lecture.

Planning for an oral presentation or lecture is not an isolated activity as it must be viewed in the context of planning a lesson. A review of the components as well as the format for a lesson plan in Chapter 2 will reveal that the "presentation" is a key element in the lesson; however, there are several other components that must be considered in the instructor's planning. For example, the objectives for the class session must be identified clearly in order that the substance of any presentation relates directly to the student's mastery of the lesson objectives. Likewise, appropriate resources must be identified that will enhance learning, and there must be an opportunity for participation by students to reinforce or supplement an instructor's presentation.

Most lesson plan formats refer to an "introduction" or "set induction" as a separate component of the lesson plan. This is done for the purpose of highlighting or underscoring the importance of the lesson. Often times, however, this will immediately precede the instructor's presentation. In this regard, it is, in reality, a part of the oral presentation. Effective teachers use "set induction" to put students in a receptive frame of mind that will facilitate learning as the instructor seeks to (1) focus attention on the objective(s) for the day, (2) create an organizational framework for the information which is to be presented, and (3) stimulate interest in the topic which will gain and hold the attention of students. The fact that it is separated on the lesson plan format should not be a point of confusion.

Prepare an Outline. Within the context of the lesson plan, the presentation or "lecture" must be prepared in a manner that will contribute both to instructional efficiency and effectiveness. In full consideration of the objective(s) to be achieved and the set induction to be established, the effective instructor prepares a topical outline of the oral presentation to be made. The preparation of a topical outline permits the instructor to consider all elements of the topic to be presented so that the complete structural framework can be conceptualized. This organizational framework is important as it establishes major and minor points as well as a chain of reasoning within the topic that provides for the logical linking of associations by the learner. Without a carefully developed outline, the instructor will have difficulty in giving proper attention to the scope, sequence and timing of the presentation.

The amount of detail included in an outline is dependent on many factors and is a variable that can only be determined by the instructor. The nature of the subject itself, the student's level of development and the instructor's knowledge of the topic are important variables in this regard. It would be somewhat logical to assume that an experienced instructor might require a less detailed outline than a beginning instructor. Unfortunately, teaching experience is not a primary determiner of outline detail. One of the greatest failings of experienced instructors is their tendency to "jump around" or "wander," which interferes with instructional clarity and makes it difficult for the learner to perceive the structural framework of the content.

Preparation for Presentation. After the content of the presentation or lecture has been outlined, the instructor needs to complete the preparation of the lesson plan which provides the context for the presentation and provides for other activities that will increase instructional effectiveness and learning on the part of students. While it is not necessary to prepare a complete manuscript for a lecture or presentation, and it certainly would not be necessary or desirable to try to memorize an entire oral presentation, it is desirable to have a rather thoroughly developed introduction which provides the set induction for the lesson. This sets the stage for the entire class period, and its influence should not be underestimated or taken lightly.

As indicated in the lesson plan, appropriate questions that might be asked during or following a presentation need to be formulated. In the lesson plan format, these are indicated as "interaction items." Appropriately worded questions are critical. Therefore, it is important that the instructor preplan the questions and have them written out in advance in the lesson plan. In order to insert them at the appropriate point in or following the presentation, the number of the question or interaction item can be placed in the outline without rewriting the question. Interaction items may be questions; however, they could be "alternatives to questions" such as the following suggested by Charles Schmittou of Clemson University:

(a) Use declarative statements. These statements may reflect the teacher's thinking or they may summarize or rephrase student remarks. It might begin with "So you think that" or "I think you are saying that."

(b) Make declarative restatements. These usually reflect students' thinking. They may summarize or rephrase student remarks. The statement might begin with "So you think that" or "I believe from what you say that."

(c) Pose indirect questions. "I wonder why you think . . ."

(d) Use imperatives. "Show me the reason for that" or "Tell us more about that."

(e) Use student questions. Teacher invites students to pose questions to fellow students.

(f) Provide deliberate silence. When a student finishes speaking, the teacher maintains deliberate silence (3 seconds or longer). It has been found that when the teacher waits, the student will often resume speaking or another student will speak up.

These techniques do not replace, but merely supplement the skill that a teacher might develop in questioning. Research has revealed that the more the teacher asks questions, the less the student participates. Questioning as such, does not always stimulate student participation.

After the detailed introduction has been prepared and questions have been formulated, the instructor will prepare overhead projection transparencies or other audio-visual aids. If handouts will be needed by students prior to, during, or following the presentation they must be prepared in advance. Any other appropriate application activities or assignments will need to be prepared. Handouts might include diagrams, illustrations, definitions of key terms, or a topical outline for the purpose of facilitating student note taking. In addition, notes should be made to remind the instructor of relevant examples, antecdotes, or analogies that will facilitate student understanding. These notations may be placed in the margin since they are intended as "memory joggers" and, as a result, would require only a few words to stimulate the instructor's memory.

Making the Presentation

It is obvious that much of the "success" of an oral presentation is built into the planning process. However, careful planning, in and of itself, cannot insure a successful presentation. Environmental factors such as the temperature and humidity as well as the events of the previous hour or even sudden shifts in the weather can have a profound effect upon the learner's attention to the learning task. Nevertheless, the instructor must make every effort to capitalize on the results of planning by maximizing student interest and involvement and minimizing student distractions and apathy.

Getting Attention of the Audience. Too frequently, instructors become so interested and involved in their subject matter that they assume students will be equally interested because of the nature of the subject matter itself.

Even though some students will be inherently interested in the subject matter, the instructor should give considerable attention to "selling" the lesson to the students since a disinterested and unmotivated student will not be an effective learner. The planning for the introduction should have been substantial and the instructor needs to work at the task of getting and maintaining student attention. An effective way to begin a presentation is to pose a provocative question, present a dramatic quotation, tell an interesting and related story, mention a puzzling or paradoxical set of facts from the content of the lesson or use some other means of arousing student interest and curiosity.

The instructor's enthusiasm about the subject is catching. The more interest that is shown in the subject, the greater will be the student's level of interest. The instructor's level of knowledge impacts directly upon the instructor's level of interest. The more someone knows about a subject, the more potential applications can be perceived and the more interest and enthusiasm can be generated. Without knowledge and experience and the resulting interest, it is difficult for the instructor to be enthusiastic. There is no substitute for first-hand experience about the subject matter out of which real life examples and illustrations can be drawn. This gives life and vitality to a presentation. One cannot expect students to be interested in something that does not seem to be of interest to the instructor.

In addition to knowledge of and interest in the subject matter, the instructor can gain the attention of students by knowing more about the students and their interests. When the instructor shows an interest in the students by learning their names and treating them as individuals of worth, there is a reciprocal level of interest and attention generated toward the instructor.

Even though the focus is upon the introduction and getting the attention of learners, it is important that a high level of student attention be maintained throughout the entire lesson. In order to accomplish this, the presentation must be varied by moving from one type of student activity to another and by limiting the amount of teacher talk at any one time. A variety of stimuli must be utilized throughout the class period. Stimulus variation, in its simplest form, represents movements, sounds or visual impressions that change or vary during the time period. Some of this stimulus variation refers to those teacher actions which are sometimes planned and are sometimes spontaneous that can develop and sustain student attention.

Physical Behavior. Although there is no substitute for appropriately selected and well structured content, the success of a lecture depends in large measure on the lecturer's communication skills. The instructor's method of delivery significantly affects the learner's attention, which in turn, affects the extent to which learning takes place. By the time an individual becomes an adult, their pattern of speech, manner in which they carry themselves, their posture, their nonverbal communication through gestures and facial expression have become a habit. Some elements of that physical behavior contribute to instructional effectiveness and some elements interfere with instructional effectiveness. The purpose of this section is to highlight the types of behavior that contribute to a positive instructional setting in order that instructors become aware of behaviors to cultivate as well as those to avoid.

No two individuals are exactly the same, and as a result, behavior patterns of one effective instructor are not exactly the same as those of another instructor who may be equally effective. Nevertheless, research and observation have allowed the identification of positive and negative behavior patterns of which instructors should be aware.

Movement. The effective instructor cannot be "lectern bound" or seated motionless at a desk or table. The plain truth of the matter is that motion gets attention even though too much motion may be distracting. Body movements should be natural—neither too rigid, rapid or jerky. The research literature in the field refers to the instructor's physical movements for the expressed purpose of maintaining attention and improving communications as "kinesic variation". The physical shifting from one part of the room to another focuses student attention directly on the instructor during the presentation. The movement does need to appear natural rather than mechanical and some care needs to be given to assure that the movement is not distracting. Moving freely from left to right and then from right to left or stepping back and forward, sitting on a stool or leaning against a lectern, represent changes in the instructor's physical position that help to maintain student attention.

Attending. The instructor exhibits an *attending* behavior when communicating with the student in a manner that reveals interest, concern and respect for the student. It is not easy to make everyone in a group feel that they are receiving the instructor's personal attention. However, the instructor's eye contact with each individual in the group several times during the course of a presentation will be very helpful in this regard. The instructor who looks out the window, looks down at the floor, or looks above the heads of students does not exhibit attending behavior. Knowing the students' names and addressing students by name is also important. Showing interest in individual students, even the way that the instructor responds to a student's question, can affect the way the student feels about the instructor and the amount of attention and respect that will be given in return. For example, the instructor that responds in a manner that causes a student to feel foolish or of little worth contributes to a negative learning environment. By smiling and stepping toward the student who has asked a question and by tactfully dealing with the response in a manner that does not "put down" the student or make light of a response that may be incorrect helps to provide the learner with positive attention.

Focusing. The type of behavior used by a teacher to intentionally control the "direction" of student attention is referred to as *focusing.* This type of controlled attention is gained either through specific physical gestures or by verbal statements or a combination. Gestures, facial expressions and pointing can be used appropriately and can provide additional animation. This type of directed movement can increase comprehension if it supplements oral communication effectively and is not overly dramatic or otherwise distracting. Gestures are used to reinforce ideas and to help in conveying meaning. A shrug of the shoulders, a glance at the ceiling, or crossing one's arms may convey more meaning than dozens of words. The timing of gestures is as important as the gestures themselves. It is important that key points are emphasized with gestures rather than to use gestures continually and, therefore, not be able to direct the students' attention to a key point that is made. Gestures such as using the hands expressively, motioning with the arms, pointing at something, clapping the hands, raising the eyebrows, smiling, or frowning, can be used to direct the learner's attention to a particular thought, word, concept, or thing. Verbal focusing may be accomplished through expressions such as "listen carefully," "this is important," "you can drive a stake down by this," "listen closely to this," and "watch what happens when we do this."

Pacing and Pausing. *Pacing* refers to the rapidity with which things are done. The pace of the class session is affected by the rate of the instructor's speech pattern, physical movements, and the shift from one activity to another. The instructor's personality and habit patterns tend to influence the pace of class activity. Unfortunately, the natural pace of the instructor may not be the appropriate pace for the content being delivered or the learning style of the students. An overly slow pace may induce boredom and cause students to loose interest while an overly rapid pace may leave students frustrated and confused. Thus relatively familiar, easy or low level content may be taught best with brisk pacing while relatively unfamiliar, difficult or complex content requires slower pacing. Remember that the student is supposed to apply mentally as the instructor presents orally. If the learner does not have sufficient time to process the information that is being presented before having to give attention to a new idea or concept, the desired associations (learning) will not be made.

The concept of *pausing* is related to that of pacing. Too frequently, students are "covered up" with a barrage of words. Recent research has focused on the effect that pauses have upon the process of communication. A moment of silence is not only necessary for the learner to "process" information, but it can also be used as a device for getting attention. Although speech and theater people have long used the "dramatic pause," educational researchers have only recently begun investigating such matters as the frequency, duration, and uses of planned silence or pausing. Unfortunately, too many instructors overlook the value of pauses within the oral presentation. The insecure instructor may be afraid of silence as there is a compulsion to fill the silence with the sound of one's own voice.

As a stimulus variation technique, pausing can enhance instruction in several ways:

1. It can create expectation or suspense.

2. It can provide a model of listening behavior or thinking.

3. It can be used to emphasize an important point.

4. It can provide an opportunity for the student to process information and mentally apply that information.

5. It can capture attention by contrasting silence with sound.

6. It can be a cue or signal that the teacher is moving to another point or idea.

7. It can be used to show disapproval of undesired student behavior.

Mannerisms. As previously indicated, stimulus variation is important to maintain attention of the learner. Behavior that is meaningless and even repetitive can be distractive. Instructors frequently develop patterns of movement or speech referred to as *mannerisms* that are distracting and interfere with learning. These types of movements and expressions are typically repeated without regard to the meaning they might convey. Such mannerisms as rattling coins in one's pocket, repeating the expression "you know" or the excessive use of any other word or phrase, leaning over the lectern, tossing a piece of chalk in the air repeatedly or pacing back and forth in a rythmic or routine manner are examples of distracting mannerisms. These behaviors are often so much of a habit pattern that the instructor may be unaware of their use and the extent to which they have an adverse impact on learners. Instructors may use a video and audio recorder to help in the analysis of their behavior and speech patterns. Students will provide feedback in this regard on course evaluations if they are assured that their identity will not be revealed as they often hesitate to be critical of their instructor if there is a chance that the instructor could use such a "candid observation" against them.

Clarity of Presentation. The extent to which a presentation is easily understood and free from confusion or ambiguity determines its *clarity*. In other words, the presentation judged to have clarity is clear, logical and orderly. In recent years, educational researchers have been giving an increased amount of attention to instructional or teaching clarity. As a result, there is a better understanding of the dimensions of instructional clarity as well as the consistent and positive effect that it has on student achievement. The two major dimensions that are involved relate to the structure of the oral presentation, i.e., the logical process of linking ideas, concepts, principles, etc., while the other dimension deals more with the words, sounds and expressions used by the instructor in conveying the content of a presentation. In the first dimension, clarity has a great deal to do with the instructor's knowledge and ability to plan the presentation while the second dimension involves primarily the manner in which the content of the presentation is delivered.

Of particular significance are the observations of Land and Smith, who have focused on the teacher's use of vagueness, mazes, structure and content. *Vagueness* refers to the use of words or phrases which are ambiguous, involve approximation or show a lack of assurance (e.g., X is a theory or a model or a paradigm). *Mazes* refer to slips of the tongue, stammering, or garbled speech. In addition, they may become word pathways (blind alleys) through which students must wander in their search for meaning. Mazes sometimes involve pauses filled with sounds like (uh, ah, um), false starts and phrases that do not make any semantic sense. *Structure* in their research refers to the frequency with which the instructor repeats concepts from one sentence to the next, reviews previous work, prepares students for the next learning task by describing the work to be done and how it will be done, and allowing time for students to think about, respond to and synthesize what they are learning. *Content* within the dimension of instructional clarity involves visual and verbal examples, creative redundancy, review of difficult concepts on the chalkboard or overhead projector and/or showing examples of work to be done as homework.

Thinking and Speaking. Before an instructor can express an idea clearly, the idea must first be thoroughly understood by the instructor. Furthermore, thought must be given to the idea during the preparation stage, as well as during the presentation. The faulty choice of words which makes for weak expression is indicative of inadequate preparation. Some rules to remember are:

1. Use terms which are common to the vocabularies of students. Consider the educational level of the group. It is better to oversimplify instruction than to run the risk of talking over the heads of students.

2. Do not try to impress students by using words with which they are not familiar. The purpose of the presentation is to express ideas, not to display one's vocabulary.

3. Use technical terms when they are essential, but define each new term the first time it is used. Remember, many words have several meanings.

4. Do not allow the presentation to become alphabet soup. Acronyms are words composed of the first letters of each word in a formal title or phrase. These are an important part of the communication process, but they must be taught just like new words. The same is true for abbreviations such as VCR, CRT, etc.

5. Use short sentences for emphasis.

6. Eliminate unnecessary words and phrases.

7. Be specific. Whether the primary objective is to have students acquire a general understanding or to learn detailed facts, make statements exact and precise in meaning.

All ideas expressed must bear a positive relationship to the main idea of the lesson. Maintaining this continuity is largely a matter of planning. In the actual presentation, the instructor can maintain continuity by making careful transitions from one point or sentence to the next. This may be done by using such terms as, however, nevertheless, consequently, furthermore, therefore, then, accordingly, in addition, and finally. Do not overwork one word.

In order to make a transition from one phase of a lesson to another, the instructor may introduce the new phase with a statement or two explaining the nature of the next concept to be taught and also its relationship to the whole lesson. Lead the students from the summarizing or concluding statements of the phase just completed to the new content to be taught. Use a variety of expressions for introducing the new materials. Avoid the monotonous repetition of such introductory remarks as, "Next we take up the," "Now we go into the."

Remember no verbal description of an object or process can make it possible for the student to reproduce the object or process exactly because words don't include all details. Other means of communicating including pictures, blueprints, tables and charts are usually required.

Voice. Every student in the class should be able to hear without difficulty every word said by the instructor. Here are some suggestions which may be useful to remember:

1. Relax.

2. Vary the volume with the size of the class and with the conditions under which instruction must be given. Be particularly attentive to this when giving instruction in the open air or in a room which has poor acoustics.

3. Watch the reactions of students. The instructor can usually tell if students are having difficulty in hearing. If there is any possibility that the volume is not satisfactory, ask students at the back of the class if they can hear. In an unusual speaking situation, such as a classroom with a large fan or blower, a good idea is to arrange ahead of time with a person in the back row to signal when more volume is needed.

4. For most people there is a range of tones which can be made without straining the voice. Whether you normally speak in a high or low pitch is not particularly important. However, students find it monotonous to listen to the same pitch. Therefore, the skillful speaker may change the volume from low, but audible and confidential, to loud and firm to compensate for a small range of voice pitch. Practice with a tape recorder may prove helpful.

5. Strive for variety.

Articulation. The clarity of spoken words is more important than the production of sounds and syllables. Therefore, the instructor should strive for good articulation in oral presentation. Above all, speak at a rate and with pronunciation that will enable students to distinguish the words being used. It is suggested that one should:

1. Practice pronouncing each word distinctly and clearly. It may be necessary to speak more forcefully and deliberately when instructing a large group than when carrying on a conversation.

2. Be particularly careful in pronouncing words which may not be common to the vocabulary of students. It will be necessary to spell out some words or write them on the board or overhead projector.

3. Not slur or run words together.

4. Not speak too rapidly.

5. Face the group when speaking. Instructors often forget that their voice does not project well when facing the chalkboard.

Rate of Speaking. An average of approximately 100 to 150 words per minute is considered satisfactory for oral instruction. (Franklin D. Roosevelt spoke about 110 words per minute). Even though many instructors can speak clearly at a rate faster than 150 words per minute, students ordinarily have insufficient time to think about and understand the ideas expressed if the rate of speaking is increased much above that point. Here are some suggestions to try:

1. Present simple materials at a fairly rapid rate.

2. Speak more slowly when presenting difficult material.

3. Pause frequently. Give students a chance to comprehend remarks and to make any necessary notes.

4. If the available time for a particular lesson is decreased, do not merely talk faster in an effort to cover the same material as before. Re-plan the lesson to fit the shortened time.

Correct English. Some otherwise competent instructors fail to realize the far-reaching significance of bad habits of English usage. No one is perfect and most students will not condemn an otherwise skilled instructor who occasionally makes an error in language usage. However, the habitual use of grossly bad English is a handicap few instructors can afford. Improper usage also undermines the importance of effective communication skills that should be part of every educational program.

Suggestions: Ask a friend to help in the identification of the errors and practice the correct wording. Use the tape recorder. Listen carefully to those who have a reputation for speaking well. Consider signing up for instruction in speech or communication. Review a good reference on oral communication.

Concluding the Presentation

Rather than simply coming to a halt, lectures should have a planned conclusion designed to accomplish certain objectives. This process is often referred to as achieving *closure*. Closure refers to actions or statements by the instructor that are designed to bring a lesson presentation to an appropriate conclusion. Typically, the conclusion will involve a review of the main points that the instructor wishes students to remember. Closure seeks to help students bring things together and to help them gain greater meaning from the presentation. Following this review and emphasis on the structuring elements that tie the major points of the presentation together, the instructor would ordinarily shift from lecture to some other mode of instructional interaction such as questioning, applying or evaluating.

The instructor who uses closure effectively understands the importance of reinforcing the fact that students have reached an important point at the conclusion of the presentation and that they have now arrived at that point. As viewed within the context of the psychology of learning, it is important to recognize that closure helps to imbed the newly learned material into the learner's network of relationships which facilitates storage into the long-term memory and provides a number of different possibilities as cues for the retrieval process. Another way to think about closure is to consider it as the compliment of set induction. As you recall, "set induction" is the initiating activity for the lesson while closure is the culminating activity. Research on the psychology of learning indicates that learning increases when instructors make a conscious effort to help students organize the information presented to them and perceive relationships based on that information. In summary, closure is the teacher's way of (1) drawing attention to the end of a lesson or lesson segment, (2) providing assistance to the student in seeing relationships within the conceptual framework of the content to be learned, and (3) consolidating and reinforcing the major points to be learned.

THE DEMONSTRATION METHOD

The demonstration is an instructional method in which an instructor shows and explains. Demonstrating may be used to enrich or increase the learner's understanding of principles or concepts in science, the use of a formula in mathematics or an arrangement in music.

For example, a demonstration of the principle of "leverage" would be an effective strategy. With a simple table top model, the instructor could demonstrate the factors of force, fulcrum and resistance which would enhance the explanations of the scientific principles involved. This method is often used to show and explain the procedures involved in carrying out a series of steps necessary to accomplish a task. If the lesson objectives call for the student to perform a series of physical movements or to develop a skill, the demonstration method is an appropriate strategy. For the purpose of skill development the demonstration is characterized by the process of showing the student the step-by-step process necessary to accomplish the task.

Even though *showing* is the principal component of the demonstration method, the method also involves *telling, questioning, testing* and *application*. If the student is to be able to perform the task that is being demonstrated, each of these elements or components of the demonstration method is important to the process of skill development on the part of the learner.

In the development of a skill, the learner must not only know the steps to be followed but also understand the purpose of each step as well as the interrelationship among the steps that determine the sequence. After the learner knows the steps and has seen the steps performed in sequence by the instructor, the learner must be guided through an initial performance correctly and successfully. The application and practice stages are also critical dimensions of the demonstration method when skill development is the desired outcome.

While there are a number of instructional strategies and methods that are utilized in the process of helping students achieve cognitive objectives, the demonstration method is the primary means by which students receive instruction related to psychomotor objectives.

It is important for the instructor to realize that there is more to the demonstration method than showing. The effective demonstration involves telling, showing, questioning and application. When skill development is the desired outcome, *practice* must be included as a major component of the method.

Appropriateness

One of the real challenges to the effective instructor involves the selection of the most appropriate methodology to employ with a given element of content for a given group of students under certain conditions. This essential decision making is part of the job of the instructor. It would not be possible to determine in advance that an instructor should teach all of a certain subject by any particular method since the objectives of each lesson as well as the content to be taught within the lesson must be taken into account to determine the appropriate method or methods to be used. If students need specific information in order to solve a particular problem in physics, a chalkboard demonstration of the problem-solving procedure may be necessary to follow a short lecture in which the specific information was provided. However, if the instructor merely intends to introduce new developments in a subject area for the purpose of providing a lesson overview to advanced students, a brief lecture rather than a demonstration may be more appropriate.

Textbooks on the teaching of technical subjects emphasize the demonstration as a teaching method. The demonstration is generally effective in teaching science, mathematics and mechanics as well as the subject areas within veterinary medicine, agriculture, engineering, business and office education, physical education, art, home economics, health, design, technical and industrial education.

As valuable as the instructor demonstration is, it may be necessary to supplement this method with models or films, particularly if the equipment is small or if the movements are quite intricate. Because of the involvement of the sense of sight as well as the tactical sensory mechanisms involved in the showing and application phases of the demonstration method, it does provide an effective means for student learning. As a result, it should be used as much as feasible. Many simple skills such as shooting the free throw in basketball or driving a nail in carpentry demand the demonstration methodology. In general, the demonstration is most effective for teaching:

1. scientific principles and theories,

2. movement or relationship of parts,

3. the proper utilization of tools and equipment, and

4. manipulative operations or motor skills.

Effective instructors can utilize the demonstration when teaching (1) a principle, (2) steps of procedure, or (3) ideas and relationships with the use of instructional aids and devices.

Timing. The best results are secured from the demonstration, as is true with most methods, when it is given at a point in time when students feel a need to learn the content. Obviously, it is easier to have a demonstration ready for a scheduled point in time. It is much more difficult, and under some conditions impractical, to have all of the students in a class "ready" for a demonstration at that time. In order to accommodate the principle of *timing*, the following alternatives are suggested:

1. The demonstration may be given to the entire class whenever a few of the advanced students need to perform the operation or task. Later, individual or small group demonstrations can be given as needed. This scheme may seem wasteful of teacher time; however, it provides for individual instruction which should be anticipated. Any "lag time" that exists prior to the *application* step of the demonstration method creates a problem. Nevertheless, if written instruction sheets related to the operation are available, they can be used successfully for review by the individual student prior to performing the operation or procedure which was previously demonstrated.

2. The students may be divided into groups based on the instructor's judgment of the anticipated needs for a demonstration. In this way, the demonstration can be given to each group at a point in time when the individuals are nearly ready for the instruction. This scheme is also useful in situations where a number of different student activities are going on simultaneously or where a limited amount of equipment is available.

As a general rule, the knowledge content related to the task to be demonstrated should be taught prior to the *showing* phase of the demonstration. Caution must be exercised by the instructor to avoid too much "teacher talk" in the demonstration setting as students are interested in seeing the instructor perform the steps in the process. When a substantial body of information is necessary for students to maximize the benefit of a demonstration, this information should be taught prior to getting students in the demonstration setting.

Skill Development. The demonstration is the major teaching method in those situations where the objectives require the development of a high degree of motor skill. The instructor should keep the following key points in mind when planning demonstration lessons to facilitate skill development:

1. The learner must know the steps of procedure to be followed and the physical motions necessary to perform.

2. The learner should understand the purpose of each step and the relationship among steps that determine the sequence.

3. The learner should be guided through an initial performance correctly and successfully.

4. The learner must practice the physical-mental steps until the process becomes automatic.

It is important to remember that skill is *doing something in the most efficient and effective manner.* Therefore, it is important that the instructor analyze carefully the steps involved in the process in order that the student can learn the proper movements that will lead both to efficient and effective performance. When skill development is an objective of instruction, a substantial amount of practice under supervision is necessary. Practice without supervision may be wasteful when the proper movements are not being made and as a result the practice may lead to the development of bad habits.

After the formal demonstration is completed, the instructor has only begun to teach. Effective instruction often occurs best through supervision and individual coaching as the student begins to apply and practice.

There has always been some disagreement between those who would advocate "accuracy" in the skill development process and others who would emphasize "speed." Probably the best answer to this argument is to recognize that some skills can be learned best by practice with emphasis on accuracy and the gradual development of speed. Other skills can be learned best by performance at the required speed with the graduate development of accuracy. When learning to throw, one must concentrate on the proper arm and leg movements and use proper speed from the start. Accuracy comes with practice. However, when batting skills are being learned, the ball should not be thrown so hard that the batter cannot make contact. The speed must be adapted to the batter's hand-eye coordination and then gradually increased. In typing, the emphasis is placed upon proper hand position and stroking techniques so that speed and accuracy are developed simultaneously in recognition that neither one without the other will be effective. In learning such basic mental skills as spelling and arithmetic, the emphasis is upon accuracy first and the development of speed with practice.

Planning the Demonstration

Careful planning is essential to effective instruction. Some instructors, however, make the mistake of preparing less for a demonstration than for other instructional methods. This is especially true of individuals who possess a high degree of skill in the process to be demonstrated.

The instructor must identify the steps of procedures and the physical movements involved in the operation or task to be demonstrated. It is essential that these steps be written down. This forces the instructor to think through the process from beginning to end, and the written steps also provide the basis for an instruction sheet that might well be provided to the students either during or following the demonstration.

The skillful individual may perform many of the steps in such an efficient and automatic manner that the identification of detailed steps of procedure may be difficult. However, it is essential that the instructor recognize that the learner must have every step and movement identified if he/she is to be able to learn and as a result be able to perform each of the steps in proper sequence. There may be times when the task or operation to be performed may need to be taught through two separate demonstration processes or combined with another performance element. This is a decision that the instructor will need to make depending upon such factors as the background of the learner, the content, the time available and the learner's level of readiness. A general rule of thumb is that a demonstration should not exceed 15 to 20 minutes. However, as with all other generalizations, the instructor must take a number of variables into account during the planning process when determining the appropriate length of the demonstration.

Tools, Materials and Equipment. It is essential that the tools, materials and equipment needed for the demonstration be identified and assembled in advance of the demonstration. Too frequently, instructors find it necessary to send a student for a tool or a piece of equipment during the process of a demonstration. This occurs because the instructor did not invest the time to rehearse the demonstration and lay out the necessary items in advance. Such distracting interruptions diminish the effectiveness of a demonstration. A list of items needed should be a part of the written lesson plan in which the demonstration method is involved.

Tools and equipment should be arranged so that they do not draw attention away from the process or the concept to be learned. Familiar tools and equipment present no problem in this regard; however, a particularly interesting instructional aid or unusual item of equipment should, if possible, be brought into sight only at the time it is needed.

Occasionally, a special arrangement or "set up" may be made to surprise the student; and by this means, cause an important element of the lesson to be highlighted. For example, an instructor might emphasize the light weight of balsa wood by having a large hammer made of the wood and stained to look real.

At the right moment in the demonstration, a student may be asked to hand the hammer to the instructor. The result might bring a touch of humor to the demonstration and contribute to its effectiveness.

Performance Standards. The instructor, in preparation for the demonstration, should actually go through the physical performance, work the problem, or manipulate the equipment effectively and skillfully to insure that there are no awkward gaps or mistakes. While it is desirable that students recognize that the instructor has a high degree of skill in the subject, the demonstration should not be used as a "showcase" for the instructor's speed of performance. After the demonstration has been presented carefully and slowly, it may be desirable to repeat the performance steps another time at the normal speed in order to set high standards of performance toward which students should strive. Nevertheless, it should be emphasized that the basic *showing* process must be careful and deliberate in order that students understand each step and the physical motions involved. Skillful performance by the instructor has its place since it does help to give the students an idea of the standards of speed and accuracy required of them within the work setting. In this case, it is not one way or the other, but rather, it is the appropriate timing that is important in the instructional process.

Conducting a Demonstration

Even though planning and preparation for a demonstration are vitally important, the demonstration must be conducted effectively. Too frequently, an instructor will show several methods of conducting a given procedure during a single demonstration. Even though there may be several acceptable procedures, it is important to limit a demonstration to one procedure in order that this might be taught and understood before other variables are introduced. Few things are more confusing to the student than changing from one procedure to another during a demonstration. Obviously, these decisions should be made in the planning process.

The Physical Setting. Since a critical component of the demonstration method is *showing*, the demonstration must be seen; however, arranging students so that all can see and hear is a frequently neglected aspect of instruction. The seating or standing arrangement will vary with the type of demonstration to be given. Chairs arranged in a semicircle may meet many requirements; however, in other cases where it is important that all students see materials or equipment from one perspective, bleacher type seating or standing may be necessary.

When demonstrating around stationary machines or equipment, it is necessary to prevent students in the front from obscuring the view of others. Some instructors have found it helpful to use masking tape or chalk to make a line behind which observers should stand. In some cases, it may be well to arrange the first row of viewers in chairs and the second row can stand so all can see the demonstration. Cooperation of the class members can usually be obtained by a short explanation of the need for all to see.

It is important for the instructor to be sensitive to the arrangement of the students since the demonstration method depends upon the sense of sight to transmit movement and relationships. The physical setting in which the demonstration is conducted is of such importance that it warrants special attention during the planning process as well as attention during the actual conduct of the demonstration.

In addition to arranging the group so that all can see the demonstration, it is important that other distractions be kept to a minimum, e.g., movement by other groups, noise from other classes. Comfort factors such as temperature and light must also be considered since these factors do impact student learning.

Telling and Showing and Questioning. The central focus of the demonstration is on the process of telling and showing each of the steps involved in the performance being demonstrated. It is important that the "telling" portion of the demonstration be kept to a minimum and carried out in an efficient manner. In addition to the steps required to conduct the procedure, operation, or task, it is important to include small elements of informational content that make the steps meaningful and/or contribute to the students' understanding.

Demonstrations are often too long, and the student is given too much information before having a chance to perform the steps of procedure. Demonstrations should seldom exceed 15-20 minutes even for the more mature learner. Inexperienced instructors, unless they have made a careful analysis of the steps of procedure to be learned, are likely to underestimate the difficulty which students will encounter in remembering the complete process.

The most skillful way to perform an operation or task is typically also the safest. Therefore, safety is a part of the demonstration lesson. When teaching the steps of procedure, it is logical to emphasize the key points of safety as they relate to each step of procedure being performed. This helps the student to remember the safety precautions at the right time. Rules about safety and long discussions about safety that are separated from the skills to which they apply are often a waste of time. Obviously, certain safety instructions may well be the subject of special demonstrations, lectures or discussions. Generally speaking, safe work habits can best be taught as the individual learns the steps in performing a task or operation.

Basic theory and elements of technical information which take a considerable amount of time to teach and learn should be the subject of separate lessons. However, there are smaller elements of informational content that can be included in the demonstration because they apply naturally and contribute to understanding and learning. The instructor must, however, screen the material carefully to make certain that the information and concepts taught during the demonstration are essential and closely related to the steps being demonstrated. To stop in the middle of a demonstration and give a five to ten minute lecture is generally not economical in terms of student or instructor time. The important point to remember is that information and theory given with the demonstration must be kept to a minimum and must apply directly to the steps of procedure being demonstrated.

Just as it is important in any type of group instruction, the instructor should be sensitive to maintaining good eye contact with the students. Since demonstrating a procedure, an operation, or task requires attention to tools, materials and equipment, the instructor must be especially sensitive to the need to stop periodically and look at the students. This is necessary to judge the students' reactions, provide an opportunity to ask or respond to questions, to repeat parts of the demonstration, or whatever else is necessary to assure understanding. The periodic pause or hesitation also keeps the instructor from pacing the demonstration too rapidly for the student.

After each part or major step of the demonstration, the instructor should provide for questions. Students may not ask questions for many reasons including the fact that they may not know how to ask what they judge to be intelligent questions. Students often hesitate to ask questions because they are afraid of feeling foolish in front of their peers. In these cases, a stimulating question from the instructor will suggest questions to the student. Also, experienced instructors can anticipate the questions that students should be asking because they realize the points in the lesson that are typically difficult to understand. The instructor must ask questions to make sure that the demonstration has been understood and to emphasize key points of procedure. The effective instructor does not assume that no questions means "everything is understood." Use good questioning techniques and allow an appropriate interval for a student response. Always ask questions on key points and safety procedures during a demonstration. Assumptions regarding student understanding from an initial experiences is seldom warranted.

Instructional Aids. When using the actual equipment, tools or materials, it may not be necessary to use visual aids with a demonstration. However, many demonstrations are made more effective with the combination of the actual equipment and special instructional aids. Such aids might be used to show the relationship of small or hidden parts of the equipment, to enlarge very small parts so that they can be seen, or to emphasize graphically the effect of an incorrect procedure. A very common example is the use of a large facsimile of a slide rule even though the instructor and all members of the class have individual slide rules.

When demonstrating how to read a micrometer, a large scale demonstration micrometer is often used. It consists of a specially constructed micrometer built so large that it can be easily read from several feet away. The overhead projector may also be used to project a large image on a screen. In demonstrating the operating principles of an engine, the piston strokes, the valve operation, and the timing and firing cycle may be done easily and clearly by the use of a simple wooden model with moving parts.

Sometimes it is expensive and wasteful to demonstrate with real materials. For example, the clothing instructor will frequently demonstrate cutting and fitting with paper instead of cloth. Likewise, architectual drafting instructors often use cardboard for demonstrating layout and construction.

Assistants. Depending on the type of equipment being demonstrated and the nature of the subject matter, it may be wise to consider the use of assistants during the demonstration. Another instructor or advanced student may be brought into the demonstration to help. Variety may be added to a demonstration by having an individual who is particularly skillful to present that part of the lesson. This helps to create the desirable atmosphere of instructors and students working together.

The use of assistants may help to make demonstrations effective when the instructor, for physical or other reasons, is unable or does not wish to perform the demonstration personally. In this situation, the instructor is free to observe with the students and point out key factors as they occur while the assistant demonstrates. One of the most common examples of this procedure is seen in athletics where the head coach may no longer have the coordination and stamina to demonstrate but can analyze and highlight the techniques as they are being demonstrated.

Following up a Demonstration

After a demonstration has been carefully planned and conducted, the application process must occur if the time and effort involved in planning and conducting the demonstration are to be maximized. The "follow up" or application step which normally occurs after each demonstration provides learners with an opportunity to "test" their understanding and ability to perform. This step provides for *learning by doing* as the student attempts to apply procedures that have been demonstrated. The application step may be for the purpose of helping the student to understand the content more clearly or for the purpose of enabling the student to begin to develop a degree of skill. Without the application step, a demonstration, even though skillfully presented, can fail to have a significant impact on student learning.

Normally, the first part of the follow up consists of assigning work to the students, letting them start, and then through supervision and coaching correct any errors or provide supplemental instruction on an individual basis. This instructional step should be carried out carefully and thoroughly. No student should be allowed to practice incorrect methods which lead to bad habits. Likewise, it is psychologically sound to have the student succeed from the beginning.

When giving individual instruction at the student's bench or desk, care should be taken not to take the work away from the student. Occasionally an instructor will stop at the student's workplace and quickly run through the process without making sure that the student has understood or can perform the procedure. It is a better strategy to direct the student's attention to an error while leaving the tools and equipment in the student's hands. The student then can apply the new or altered information and experience the personal satisfaction of doing the task him/herself.

Even though it is important for the student to feel a measure of success by correct performance early in the learning process, it must be recognized that consistent performance at a high level requires the correct procedure and a substantial amount of practice. When the objective to be achieved is a high level of skill, the student must be willing to repeat the performance numerous times to make the mental-muscle association essential to efficient and effective performance.

ORAL QUESTIONING STRATEGIES

Ever since Socrates, teaching and questioning have been viewed as interrelated activities. Questioning strategies are an integral part of both the lecture and the demonstration. For one to be an effective instructor, one must be an effective questioner. Unfortunately, the instructor who believes that telling is teaching and that the primary role of the instructor is dispensing information too often overlooks the learning outcomes that result from questioning. All too frequently, questioning is viewed as an evaluation technique rather than part of the instructional strategy. Effective teachers ask many questions and for a variety of reasons such as (1) to check the student's understanding of key points, (2) to check for mastery of basic concepts, (3) to encourage critical thinking, and (4) to stimulate interaction among students as well as between instructor and student. The first step in effective questioning is to recognize that questions have distinctive characteristics, serve various functions and provide opportunities to develop higher level thinking skills by applying, analyzing, synthesizing or evaluating the content being learned. As instructors learn about the different kinds of questions and the different functions they serve, they can draw upon this understanding to utilize all types of questions effectively.

Educational research in the area of questioning indicates clearly that most questions asked by teachers demand nothing more than the recall of facts (isolated bits of information). This "echo" approach places undue emphasis on rote memorization of facts. One way to avoid asking questions leading to the mere repetition of facts is to start each question with a word or phrase that calls for thought on the part of the students. Such words as *why, how, summarize, justify, trace, describe,* or *define* tend to encourage thoughtful answers and meaningful interaction. Through the process of questioning, the instructor is interested in stimulating the learner to make use of information, to put together facts which may not have been understood thoroughly or assimilated, and to draw logical conclusions which become evident when the pertinent facts are interrelated.

The questioning technique is effective if it is carried out at the appropriate time, causes the student to learn by thinking and doing, and changes the student's role from passive listening or watching to thinking and applying while listening and watching. Skillful questioning like any other teaching technique can be learned or improved through study, practice and feedback. Instructors can improve their questioning techniques by learning to formulate more thought provoking questions and encourage critical thinking by students. Instructors can also learn to avoid practices which interfere with students' responses.

Types of Questions

In a very generic sense, questions are typically categorized into two main groups: (1) factual or recall and (2) application or problem. However, a more meaningful classification system for questioning would be to relate questioning to Bloom's Taxonomy of Educational Objectives and differentiate questions by cognitive level. As indicated in Chapter 2, Bloom classified educational objectives in the cognitive domain into the following six levels: (1) knowledge, (2) comprehension, (3) application, (4) analysis, (5) synthesis, and (6) evaluation.

Knowledge. At the knowledge level, the instructor's questions require the student to recognize or recall information. To answer a question on the knowledge level, the student must simply remember facts, observations and definitions that have been learned previously. Even though there is substantial criticism among educators of factual or knowledge level questions, this level of question does have its place in the instructional spectrum. The criticism is actually at the overuse or abuse of this level of question rather than the type of question per se. It is important for instructors to realize that the learner functions first at the knowledge or memory level. Students cannot be expected to think at higher levels if they lack prerequisite information. Such memorization of information is also required in order to perform a variety of tasks. The meaning of words, correct spelling, multiplication facts, the combination for a lock and rules of the road are examples of important information that must be committed to memory.

Even though the knowledge category is very important and knowledge questions are appropriate, this type of question does have its drawbacks. The primary drawback is that instructors tend to overuse this type of question and do not demand that their students exhibit behavior beyond this level. Questions at this level may lead the learner and the instructor to assume a deeper understanding than actually exists. Parroting someone else's thoughts does not, itself, demonstrate understanding.

Comprehension. Questions at the comprehension level require students to interpret and translate information that is presented on charts, graphs, and tables as well as specific facts. It is important to realize that the student must have certain factual information in order to gain the understanding necessary to organize and arrange the material mentally. For questions of this type, the student must demonstrate a level of understanding by rephrasing, describing or making comparisons.

Application. A question at the application level would require a student to apply previously learned information to solve a specific problem. At this level, it is not sufficient for the student to be able to relate information previously memorized or even to paraphrase and interpret something that has not been memorized previously. Instead, students must be able to utilize the information to answer a question or solve a problem. For example, a student who has learned the definitions of latitude and longitude may be asked to locate a given point on a map by applying knowledge of latitude and longitude.

Analysis. Questions at this level of cognition require students to think carefully and critically about information that they have acquired as they look for hidden meaning or inferences of the facts. As information is analyzed, one must think carefully and critically to reach sound conclusions or draw a generalization based on available information. Analysis type questions ask students to (1) identify motives, reasons and/or causes of specific occurrences or events, (2) reach certain conclusions, draw inferences or generalizations based on given information, or (3) identify evidence needed to support or refute conclusions, inferences, or generalizations. In many instances there are no absolute answers to analysis questions as several answers may be plausible. Furthermore, because it takes time to think and analyze, these questions cannot be answered quickly or without careful thought. Therefore, there are limitations to the use of this type of question in oral form.

Synthesis. Synthesis questions like those involving analysis and evaluation require higher order thinking processes. Synthesis questions require students to make predictions, to use their creativity in developing original approaches or to solve problems that do not have single answers but rather a variety of creative solutions. Instructors can use synthesis questions to help develop and reinforce the creative abilities of students. Obviously, this type of question demands a substantial amount of information and a thorough understanding of a number of factors as students consider possible responses.

Evaluation. The evaluation question may not have a single correct answer as it requires a student to judge the merit of an idea, to assess the plausibility of a solution or to offer an opinion on an issue. These actions on the part of a student require that they possess substantial information, but they must also be able to establish criteria by which a judgment might be made. Both objective and subjective criteria may be used as an evaluation is made. The important thing to remember about evaluation questions is that some type of standard must be used. If the student is not supplied with a standard set of criteria, then the instructor must be prepared for multiple answers because that is the natural outcome if different sets of standards are applied.

Characteristics of Good Questions

In order to formulate appropriate questions and use them effectively, it should be obvious that instructors cannot rely totally on the words and phrases that come to their mind at a given moment during a class presentation. Some questions, of course, will be spontaneous in response to a given set of circumstances. However, as indicated in the lesson plan format in Chapter 2, interaction items need to be developed in advance and keyed to specific sections of the presentation. When asking the questions during the class period, it should not be necessary to read them. The instructor should be able to state questions with reasonable accuracy from memory after a glance at the lesson plan. As indicated, these carefully prepared questions should not be the only ones raised by the instructor. They should, however, provide a skeletal framework around which impromptu questions may be asked as the situation dictates.

Clearly Stated. Questions should be stated in simple, straightforward language. The instructor should be efficient with words so that the question is as brief as possible yet sufficiently complete to assure understanding. The first word should be the key action word, e.g., explain, define, compare. A list of sample terms that relate to the several cognitive levels are found in Chapter 2. In addition to the action terms suggested in Bloom's Taxonomy, direct questioning words such as why, when, who, what, where, and how allow the instructor to communicate clearly the direction of the question and the response mode desired from the student. Questions ordinarily should be phrased in language adapted to the level of the class. If students do not understand the question, they cannot respond along the lines expected by the instructor.

Common Vocabulary. Questions should be designed to assess knowledge and understanding of the subject being taught. If the instructor's vocabulary is beyond the common usage of the students, they may not be able to respond even though they know the content. The words used within the question itself may be confusing. In a teaching/ learning environment, the purpose is to provide reinforcement, identify concepts that need to be retaught, and provide opportunities for students to gain greater understanding through verbal descriptions.

Thought Provoking. Questions should challenge the student to go beyond the knowledge level whenever possible. Questions should be phrased to reach beyond the simple "yes—no" response. If the answer to the question is so easy that the answer is obvious to most students, then it is probably not necessary to be asked. Questions which are thought provoking arouse the curiosity and interest of students and help them clarify their ideas as well as to analyze and synthesize facts in addition to merely listing them. This aspect of questioning is especially important to the adult student.

Value of Questioning

For maximum effectiveness, the instructor should prepare questions carefully and use them to:

1. Stimulate interest in the lesson.

2. Establish communication between the instructor and students.

3. Focus the students' attention on the major points or principles to be remembered.

4. Stimulate mental "learning-by-doing" by causing students to apply facts and principles as they analyze problems.

5. Help students develop a feeling of confidence and success which leads to greater motivation, further study and experimentation.

6. Develop the ability to organize ideas and speak effectively.

7. Stimulate students to think for themselves rather than follow the pattern of the text or the thinking process of the instructor.

8. Build cooperation in the class through group activity and responsibility.

9. Provide for a democratic approach to learning.

10. Evaluate the effectiveness of instruction and provide valuable clues to better methods.

Using Questions Effectively

In full recognition of the potential which questioning has for making a positive impact on student learning at the several levels of cognition, it is important that the instructor develop the techniques that will enable questioning strategies to be utilized effectively.

To whom is the question asked? Students should understand that questioning is a part of the teaching process and that questions are asked for a variety of purposes such as clarification, verification, implication and evaluation. It will be helpful to the process if certain ground rules are established. For example, the instructor needs to get everyone's attention before posing a question. When students are not listening as a question is asked, this provides an undesirable learning environment. Pausing to secure the attention of the class before asking a question and refusing to repeat it for those who were not "tuned in" can save time and lead to more effective listening habits.

It should be understood that the instructor wants the whole class to hear the question and that each individual should be prepared to respond. However, it is poor practice to allow the entire class to answer in a chorus type response. This method of response decreases individual thought, gives the lazy student a chance to do nothing and results in a noisy class. Perhaps an even more serious defect is that it gives the instructor no opportunity to evaluate an individual student's level of knowledge or understanding. Even though it is important to specify that a given individual will be asked to respond, it is equally as important to be sure that every student hears the question and is a potential respondent.

With regard to calling on specific individuals, some system should be employed to insure that everyone is called upon with reasonable frequency. A number of systems which may appear feasible at first have serious drawbacks; for example, if members of the class are called on according to a seating arrangement or in alphabetical order, it is quite easy for an individual to estimate when the instructor will call on him/her. Thus, the lazy student will not think very hard about questions when asked to students on the other side of the room. An equally inappropriate strategy is to call a given individual's name before posing the question. This practice encourages the listening of only one student—the one whose name is called. Posing the question and then waiting a few seconds before calling on a particular student is a much better strategy. Some instructors have used cards with the names of class members on each card. Shuffling these cards results in alerting everyone, but it does not assure equal distribution of question to all individuals or within the several areas of the classroom. A more practical approach is to call on individuals in a somewhat random fashion but record the number of questions that individuals have been required to answer.

Do you provide enough time for a response? Just as pacing is important to oral presentation, it is essential to effective questioning. To the extent that questions are intended to stimulate students to think about the content and formulate responses rather than merely retrieve information from memory, it is important to give time for these processes to occur. This is especially true for complex or involved questions where students may need several seconds merely to process the question before they can even begin to formulate a response. The basic idea is that pacing and wait-time should be appropriate to the question being asked and ultimately to the objective that the question is designed to accomplish.

All too frequently, the instructor feels uncomfortable with a wait time that extends beyond one second. Classroom interaction is too frequently characterized by an incredibly rapid rate of interaction as instructors fire one question after another without giving students sufficient time to think, to formulate their answers, and to respond. When instructors can master the skill of increasing their wait time from one second to as much as three to five seconds, particularly for questions at the higher levels of cognition, they will find some very positive changes in both the quantity and quality of student response. Both instructors and students need to realize that it is "okay" to have a few seconds of silence. Too often, the instructor feels compelled to fill the silence with the sound of his/her voice. Research evidence reveals that teachers tended to wait less than one second before calling on someone to respond. Furthermore, even after calling on a student, instructors tended to wait less than a second for the student to give an answer before they supplied it themselves, called on someone else, or attempted to help by rephrasing the question or giving clues. This behavior on the part of instructors suggests that they are actually underestimating the value of their question by failing to give the question adequate time to have the desired effect on the student.

Does the question match the individual? Some effort should be made to match the questions to the individuals being asked to respond. Following the practice of calling on students after the question has been asked demands that the instructor learn the names of students quickly, and even more importantly, become knowledgeable of the variation in ability that exists within the class. In recognition of the individual differences, it is appropriate at times to give the most difficult questions to the most advanced students. Obviously, it is undesirable to indicate the questions that you consider to be the most difficult; however, recognition of these individual differences and making some effort to take them into consideration is important.

Student answers should be evaluated carefully so that the individual as well as members of the class can be made aware of the extent to which an answer may be correct or partially correct. Since individuals may not attach the same meaning to a given statement, the instructor may need to rephrase the answer in order to clarify meaning. In most instances, however, the exact wording of the student's response should not be repeated in parrot-like fashion by the instructor. The student responding should be encouraged to speak clearly and loudly enough for all to hear; the classroom should be quiet enough for the response to be heard. Students need to learn to listen to their peers. In fact, sometimes the wording chosen by a student will have greater impact on other students than the phrasing that the instructor might utilize.

What is the instructor's reaction to the student's response? In addition to being certain that student responses are heard and repeated or clarified when necessary, the instructor needs to provide appropriate reinforcement. The most frequent types of reinforcement utilized by teachers are verbal reinforcers consisting of a one word or brief phrase response such as "good," "that's right," "excellent," "okay," or "nice job." An even more powerful reward to the student results from building on the student's response to reinforce or elaborate upon a point. A similar strategy can be employed even with the student who does not give a complete or completely accurate response. The instructor can separate out the correct part of the response and then ask another student to provide additional information. For example, "Jane, that idea is quite good, but we need to take that idea a bit further," "John, how would you suggest that the answer Jane provided could be applied to a case where the ph value is known?" It is important to provide verbal reinforcement to even partially correct responses in order to increase the student's desire to participate. Responses such as, "That's not right," "Where did you get that idea?" or "You should know better than that" are negative reinforcers that discourage student participation. There is no good place in teaching for sarcasm or the "put down" of students. With some students, these can result in undesirable consequences as they feel compelled to "save face" within their peer group.

Even as powerful as verbal reinforcement is, nonverbal reinforcement may be even more powerful. Nonverbal reinforcement refers to physical messages sent by teachers through cues such as eye contact, facial expression and body positioning. A teacher's smile or frown communicates something to students. The way the instructor is standing may imply defensiveness or disapproval. The nonverbal cues may imply that the teacher is interested, disinterested, pleased or displeased with the student's response. In various subtle ways, nonverbal reinforcement encourages student participation or inhibits participation. Unfortunately, many instructors are insensitive to the way that they provide either positive or negative reinforcement to students; and as a result, the power of this kind of behavior is lost or misdirected. For example, a teacher who relies totally on one or two favorite types of reinforcement and uses these reinforcers repeatedly may find the eventual result to be completely ineffective. The teacher who continually says "okay" after each student's response is, in reality, not reinforcing but simply verbalizing a comment that has lost its reward power.

Are questions developed sequentially to lead to higher levels of understanding? While an increased wait-time and reinforcement are two strategies that instructors can utilize to increase student participation, it is sometimes desirable to enhance the quality of student thinking through the questioning process. The strategy employed here is to lead the student from one level of thinking to another by a careful series of probing questions. Probing questions follow up on a student's response and attempt to stimulate students to think through their answers and expand on their initial responses. This type of questioning may be used to prompt student thinking on any level, but it is probably most effective at the higher level of analysis, synthesis, and evaluation. The instructor may note that a student is groping for an answer to a question when it is known that the student has already learned the information necessary for correct response. In this case, the instructor may ask additional questions using key terms or phrases which provide cues to the response chain. These questions are sometimes referred to as leading questions. The following question/answer dialogue is used as an example.

Instructor: In using a T-square and drawing board, we only use one edge of the board. Why is this important?

Student: We use the T-square for horizontal lines, but we use a triangle on the T-square to draw vertical lines.

Instructor:　In other words, we have no need to use more than one edge of the board. Suppose we wanted to draw a series of long vertical lines. Would it not be easier to use the top edge of the board to guide the T-square?

Student:　Yes.

Instructor:　Do we know that the left edge and the top edge are exactly at 90° to each other?

Student:　They seem to be but I'm not sure. I'm not sure either whether the head of the T-square and its blade are exactly at 90° to each other.

Instructor:　If we use only one edge of the board, is it important that the T-square head and blade be at exactly 90° to each other?

Student:　No, because the triangle will assure us that vertical lines will be at 90° with the horizontal lines.

Instructor:　What would be the result if we draw lines from the left edge and also from the top edge of a board that is not exactly square?

Student:　Vertical lines and horizontal lines would not be at exactly 90° angles to each other.

Instructor:　And that's the reason for not using both the left edge and the top edge for accurate drawings.

In addition to reacting to student responses to instructor questions, instructors must also react to student initiated comments and questions. Relevant student questions indicate a need for clarification or a desire to know more about the subject. Relevant student comments suggest that students are thinking actively about the subject matter and relating it to their past experience and knowledge base. These questions and comments present unique opportunities or "teachable moments" that demand attention. Even though the instructor's response to such questions or comments may have to be kept brief or delayed until after class since a complete or more adequate response would take too long or move the discussion too far from the lesson's focus, instructors should indicate that they welcome such questions and comments, and when possible, should respond positively.

DISCUSSION AND OTHER GROUP PARTICIPATION METHODS

Even though the lecture method and the demonstration method, when applied properly in a classroom setting, provide for some student interaction with the instructor, these methods place the instructor in the primary role of presenter. The instructor is the central focus of attention as the principal actor. Whereas, the discussion method, as well as modifications of this method, require the instructor to assume a different role. When the discussion and other group participation methods are employed, the instructor becomes a leader of a group that shares ideas, information and opinions in order to (1) clarify issues, (2) relate new input to prior knowledge, or (3) attempt to resolve some question or problem that may have no single "correct" solution.

When utilizing this participatory or "learner-centered" approach, the instructor acts as a leader who structures the activity by establishing its focus, setting boundaries and facilitating interaction. In this role, the instructor is less dominant and less judgmental. In groups that contain mature learners or adults, the instructor may be removed completely from the discussion to serve only as a resource person in the process. Learner-centered participatory methods should not imply that learners are free to talk about anything they wish. This type of methodology takes considerable planning on the part of the instructor so that the groups have clearly defined objectives, know the process to be utilized, and understand the expectations of the process. When the group process is used, there is a shift of authority and responsibility. Involvement in setting goals and directing their own learning activities provide unusual growth opportunities for many individuals. This methodology also provides a change of pace and an opportunity for learner participation and application after the foundation has been provided through lecture, demonstration, reading, etc. The discussion or "group" process is not the most efficient means of providing new information; however, it is quite valuable when seeking to achieve objectives that relate to *application, analysis, synthesis,* and *evaluation.*

The term "discussion method" is used generically to encompass learner-centered group procedures which provide for a substantial amount of learner participation and interaction. However, there are specialized group procedures that utilize discussion methodology such as "role playing," "brainstorming," "the nominal group process," and "quality circles," which will be described in some detail within this chapter.

The Instructor's Role in Group Participation

It is important to remember that the discussion methodology is not the most efficient or effective for the acquisition of factual information or to secure precise information of a procedural nature that leads to skill development. However, it is an excellent methodology for the sharing of prior knowledge or experience which can lead to a new or enhanced perspective by the participant. The instructor must identify the point or points in the lesson where discussion or some other type of group participation would be appropriate. Decisions also have to be made regarding the number and size of discussion groups or whether the entire class can function effectively as a single discussion group.

If ideas are being collected, the instructor can assist by recording the ideas on the chalkboard, a chart pad or on an overhead projection transparency. However, they should not be evaluated at this point since the important thing is to generate ideas through free and open participation. The instructor must not place a value on student input as either *good* or *bad*, *right* or *wrong*. When someone else is leading the discussion, the instructor may wish to withdraw from the discussion and re-enter only to make a connection between ideas, to point out similarities or contrasts, to request clarification or elaboration, to invite students to respond to one another and to summarize the progress at various points in time. The fact that the leader does less talking than with some other types of instruction does not suggest less preparation. Just the opposite is usually the case. Preparation in depth is necessary if the instructor is to set the stage, and develop the problem to be discussed.

The role of the instructor or leader in group participation is to get every one involved in an effective and constructive manner. The leader must guide the discussion when necessary without being too obvious and bring the session to a close with an adequate summary and a feeling of accomplishment on the part of the participants. Above all, the instructor must be sensitive to individual responses as well as the feelings and attitudes of all participants. A few suggestions are as follows:

1. Set the stage. Explain the method to be used and the nature of the problem to be discussed. Use questions to get participants involved from the start. Make sure that everyone understands that the objective is to learn by experience and that no one will be criticized as they experiment with ideas and human relations behavior.

2. Assign the problem and discuss it sufficiently to be sure that it is thoroughly understood.

3. Start the discussion and keep it going. Be prepared to ask a question or suggest another facet of the problem whenever necessary to avoid any situation that tends to cut off free and open discussion. It is important to keep individuals out of too much conflict or controversy which may cause them to withdraw from any further participation. This can often be accomplished by giving credit where needed, by tactfully clarifying meaning, by suggesting a review of what has been said, or by asking a question to draw individuals back into the discussion.

4. Listen and think. Do not become emotionally involved in the problem or do too much talking. The leader's job is to draw out the thoughts and feelings of individuals in the group. Try to salvage something out of anything that is said.

5. Summarize the discussion and clear up any misconceptions of fact that may have occurred. This may be done on the chalkboard or by verbal comments and discussion.

The instructor's role changes substantially as the learner-centered or participation methodology is used. The instructor is no longer viewed as the central source of authority. A different source of group authority emerges through the structure outlined by the instructor, the specific content focus as well as the group's sense of cohesiveness and competence. The effectiveness of the group process often depends upon the willingness of the instructor to lead the group without being the "expert" unless called upon as a resource for information not otherwise immediately available.

Physical Arrangements. As part of the planning process, instructors must decide upon the physical arrangements necessary for effective discussion or other group participation methods. For example, the seating arrangement needs to be different for this methodology than either of the more traditional lecture or demonstration methods. With large groups, this demands that several discussion groups exist and function simultaneously. For this type of methodology, it is necessary that each member of the group be able to see the other members of the group including the leader. Several geometric seating arrangements that will permit "line of sight" among the participants as well as between participants and leader indicate the several patterns of group interaction appropriate for the variations in methodology being employed (see Figure 4-1).

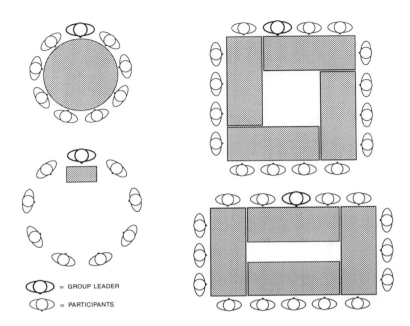

Figure 4-1. Seating arrangements should allow eye contact among discussion group members and their group leader.

Directed Discussion

Directed discussion is different from the lecture in that the instructor causes the students to provide most of the information. In a directed discussion, the instructor acts as a leader and directs or redirects ideas and information produced by members of the class. The term "directed" is used to emphasize the planned and purposeful nature of this method used by a skillful instructor in an educational setting. Through the directed discussion method, the instructor draws upon the experience of the group, while in the lecture the instructor directly relates ideas and information to students. Directed discussion can be used effectively only when students have some knowledge of the subject being discussed. This is a key point, information can not be drawn from a vacuum. If the learners lack a base of prerequisite information and/or an experience background upon which to draw, discussion may not be the most appropriate method.

Primary advantages of discussion methodology are that it stimulates the students to think and tends to produce an informal situation in which learning may be facilitated. Since gaining the respect of the group is a strong desire of each member, the discussion method is far more effective in the development of attitudes. In addition, this methodology facilitates the active participation of students and permits the instructor to give some individual attention to each student. Personal contact between instructor and students is an essential part of any effective approach to teaching and learning.

The discussion method enables the instructor to identify misunderstandings and confusion on the part of one or more students. The instructor, therefore, is in a position to judge when a fuller explanation and review are necessary. Through discussion, the instructor can discover which students are developing positive attitudes and making satisfactory progress in the subject and which ones need more attention or additional instruction. The directed discussion gives the instructor a chance to evaluate teaching success.

The directed discussion usually requires greater resourcefulness than the lecture because the instructor must allow maximum freedom, yet reach a predetermined goal. During discussion, constant attention must be given to each individual's comments as the instructor gains insight into the level of knowledge and understanding of each student. Instructors must imagine themselves in the position of the learner and try to visualize the problems from the student's point of view. Patience must be exercised with those who fail to grasp ideas which seem obvious to the instructor who must at all times act with fairness and understanding.

The directed discussion consists of an orderly exchange of ideas with a goal in mind. It is not a "bull session." An effective discussion helps to:

1. Arouse interest because the students take part and are challenged to think.

2. Bring out points of view from individuals that are helpful to the group as a whole in understanding the issue, problem or content.

3. Give the instructor valuable feedback regarding the progress and ability of individuals in the group.

4. Locate misconceptions and give the instructor an opportunity to correct them and to strengthen teaching effectiveness.

5. Get students and instructor better acquainted.

The discussion method is frequently quite effective as an introduction to a lesson. The instructor may start a lesson by asking questions to focus attention on the new content and its importance. Discussion may serve as a quick review with a gradual shift to the need for more information. Since everyone learns new things in the light of past experience, this is a sound technique.

A discussion provides a good means of application. When new content has been presented in a lesson, the instructor should provide ways for the student to apply this material as soon as possible. One way to do this is to start a discussion which causes the student to think through and use facts and principles presented in an earlier part of the lesson. This requires thoughtful preparation on the part of the instructor, but it pays dividends in terms of student progress.

Since students may acquire knowledge and skills in several different lessons, without seeing the relationship of these to each other, some means must always be provided to integrate or tie the knowledge and skills in the proper relationship. Do not forget about *transfer of learning*. A carefully planned discussion, with leading and challenging questions by the instructor, provides students with an opportunity to grasp the full meaning and to gain deeper insight into concepts and principles presented previously.

Advantages and Limitations

As is true with any educational methodology, the directed discussion method has certain advantages and limitations that need to be understood by the instructor in order that this methodology might be used at the right time and under appropriate conditions. As mentioned previously, discussion is dependent on participation of members of a group. However, participation among individuals within the group must be purposeful and directed toward the achievement of certain desired ends. Directed discussion is judged to be an effective methodology where some of the higher order cognitive outcomes are desired such as "analysis," "synthesis", "application", and "evaluation." The methodology is also quite effective as a means of "team building." It is important for individuals to get to know each other better and to feel more comfortable in expressing their opinions and sharing information. Directed discussion helps to achieve these ends. In addition, this methodology can be helpful in the attainment of certain attitudinal changes whereby individuals gain respect for the ideas of others and learn to disagree without becoming disagreeable. This kind of interchange among individuals provides a better condition for attitudinal change than does the more teacher directed methods. Objectives such as "gaining competence in expressing oneself orally" or "learning to listen more effectively" are also outcomes that can be gained from the use of the discussion method.

In many applications of discussion methodology, the instructor serves as the group discussion leader. However, in large classes or in groups of mature learners, several small groups can be created with each group having its own discussion leader and recorder. In these instances, the instructor serves as a resource person and coordinator of the group activity. For this technique to work effectively, there must be a considerable amount of pre-planning so that the groups can stay on target and go about the discussion in a systematic manner in order to achieve the objectives specified for the activity.

In addition to some of the "process" advantages typically cited for discussion methodology such as increased interest through learner involvement, it is important to realize that discussion promotes cognitive development as it helps to stimulate and clarify thinking. As students attempt to explain a concept or explore an apparent discrepancy between theory and practice, greater insight into the relationship and structure of the content will be gained. Secondly, learners gain an increased appreciation of the complexity of the subject matter being studied as they listen to different viewpoints expressed by participants. A good discussion inevitably exposes the ambiguities as well as the complexities of a topic. A third cognitive benefit of discussion is that learners increase their identification with the subject matter under consideration, and as a result, they become more interested and have an increased commitment to learning.

Directed discussion is certainly not without its limitations. The instructor must recognize that discussion methodology is time consuming. It is not an efficient means for transmitting and acquiring new information. After the instructor realizes the conditions under which discussion methodology can be used most effectively, most other limitations relate to the inadequate or ineffective planning and conducting of discussions. In other words, if the instructor (1) uses discussion methodology under appropriate conditions (e.g., objectives to be achieved, maturity of learners, assurance of prerequisite information), (2) does an adequate job of planning for the discussion process, and (3) follows through on the procedures described in the following section, discussion methodology can contribute substantially to the teaching/learning process.

Planning a Discussion

1. Decide on the outcome expected from the discussion. Is the purpose to find out the level of the student's knowledge and understanding, or to reinforce ideas and concepts through group interaction? Keep the objective clearly in mind throughout the advance planning and during the discussion process.

2. Plan the introduction carefully as in all types of lessons.

3. List the main headings of content to be covered.

4. Under each heading, write challenging questions that focus attention on the content to be discussed.

5. Estimate the time for each step in the lesson and write this in the margin of the plan. Since a discussion may tend to get off the track, it is necessary for the instructor to set a time limit for each segment of the discussion and to stay on schedule in order to achieve the objective of the lesson.

6. List the main parts to be covered in the summary of the discussion. Since many ideas will be presented by the participants in a good discussion, the instructor must plan the summary to emphasize, organize, and tie together the essential points.

Concepts Underlying Effective Discussion Leading

While some purists of discussion methodology might argue that "directing" discussion places serious limitations on possible alternatives that might come from the group for which the instructor's background or knowledge would not anticipate, directing discussion is judged appropriate because of the need to stay within the framework of time and purpose. Through research and experience, a number of ideas have been identified that increase the effectiveness of the discussion process. Several of these ideas or concepts will be helpful to the instructor who seeks to be an effective discussion leader or who helps class members become effective discussion leaders. First, the group members need to agree on a set of rules for group discussion. For example, the group members must be willing to accept an idea or opinion from anyone in the group. The idea or opinion needs to be recorded so that it will have an opportunity to be explored in depth at a later point in time. There must be a willingness to listen to each member of the group. A one-way or even two-way dialogue is not sufficient for group discussion. After several basic rules have been agreed upon, the leader should be sensitive to the principles of group dynamics whereby some individuals will have to be forcefully drawn into discussion and others will need to be prevented from dominating the process. This, of course, has to be done tactfully so that the process continues smoothly. Careful consideration of the following eight ideas will permit the instructor to lead the discussion with a reasonable degree of effectiveness.

1. It is easier to create favorable attitudes toward an idea or project than to change negative attitudes.

2. Individuals are more inclined to accept new ideas from persons whom they respect.

3. Policies, procedures and practices are more acceptable when one is involved in their development.

4. Ideas are more likely to be accepted when they offer immediate and personal rewards. Individuals respond favorably to praise. Ideas which add to one's prestige are more readily accepted.

5. A new method is less likely to be accepted if a number of procedures or skills must be mastered before the method can be put to use.

6. People resent being manipulated by selling techniques. Resentment of obvious selling techniques is likely to be strong among well-educated persons.

7. Even though the leader must have a target (objective), the leader must be flexible and not appear to be closed-minded or autocratic.

8. The individuals will participate more freely if there is a climate of openness so that any comment is valued and recorded. If individuals are embarrassed or ridiculed, they will cease to participate.

Teaching Through Discussion

As indicated previously, the discussion method provides opportunities for individuals to share experiences and ideas related to a given topic or problem. The discussion method may be used in a variety of ways within a given lesson. However, if the instructor or leader is not skillful in leading a discussion, the inherent value within the methodology cannot be maximized. Discussion is frequently used at the beginning of a lesson to stimulate interest and gain attention. Student involvement in discussion helps to stimulate interest in the subject. During the course of a lesson, discussion can be used to take advantage of the experiences of group members, to help them gain greater insight and understanding or to achieve objectives that require analysis, synthesis, application or evaluation. At the end of a lesson, discussion techniques can be utilized to summarize or review key points.

Initiating the discussion. The physical setting affects the manner in which individuals interact. Participants respond more favorably when they can look at each other. Whenever possible, instructors should arrange the group in a circle, square or small rectangle. To create the feeling of equality and openness, everyone, including the leader, should be seated. Allow about ten minutes to provide an introduction to the topic, establish ground rules and define the task. Facial expressions and other "body language" are part of the communication process. There are several ways to start a discussion. The method one uses will depend on the type of content and the background of the students. One of the most practical ways is to announce the topic and indicate that each person is to express his/her ideas on the subject. Then ask a challenging question and call on an individual to respond. The questions should not have a yes-no or factual response. Since the lead question should be challenging, instructors usually get only a partial answer. At this point, they may draw others in by allowing them to express their opinions and add to the response.

Guiding the discussion. As the discussion progresses, it may move on a tangent or the students may focus attention on unimportant details of the topic. The instructor must then summarize what has been said and ask a leading question to bring the group back on the topic. If there is a tendency to spend too much time on one part of the lesson, the instructor may summarize the discussion thus far, add a few facts to cover the initial content more adequately, and then ask another question to bring in the next part of the subject. In this way, the discussion can be kept moving in the proper direction and on the planned time schedule.

The chalkboard and a large chart pad are excellent aids to the discussion method. By recording significant points as they are made, the discussion can be guided, the students can see the progress being made, and the proper relationship between facts and ideas can be established.

One of the most challenging tasks of the discussion leader is dealing with individuals on each end of the communication continuum—loud, talkative, or disruptive as well as quite, inhibited and passive individuals. The leader must deal firmly and frankly with those individuals who talk too much, and as a result, prevent others from participating. The leader should be polite and courteous with such phrases as "Don, all of us appreciate your comments. Now let's hear what others have to say.", "Joann, why don't we give Jane, Sue and some of the others a chance to add something?" For a discussion to be successful, no one should be allowed to dominate.

The strategy for bringing the quite, shy, reserved individual into the discussion process is quite different. In this case, the leader must be subtle and cautious. While the leader should be encouraging and provide every opportunity for participation, some individuals may not wish to talk, and they do have a right to remain silent. Some of the techniques that can be used to bring individuals into the discussion are:

1. Establish eye contact with the quiet or reserved individual.

2. Involve the quiet person with an easy question or ask a "low-risk" opinion question such as "Pat, what do you think of Ken's idea?", "Andy, would you agree or disagree with that?", "Karen, what is your personal opinion about _____?"

3. It is not good practice to single out an individual as the "quiet one" or in any other way focus the groups' attention on the individual. Instead, try to involve everyone in the discussion, including the individual who seems reluctant.

4. When you get the slightest bit of participation, give the individual a quick compliment such as "thank you," "good," "interesting point," which are all non-elaborate.

Closing the discussion. During the discussion, the individuals in the group will have interpreted the comments in their own way and in the light of their own past experience. It is, therefore, necessary that the instructor sum up the ideas discussed and emphasize the key points and their relationship. Do not fail to summarize. If students see that progress has been made, believe that they have taken part in the discussion, and have contributed to it, they will tend to be cooperative and helpful in the next lesson.

Group Participation Methods

Direct involvement or participation is generally recognized as essential to effective learning and is often referred to as "learning by doing." Participation can be provided in several ways: through discussion and questions, through the application step in a formal lesson, or through techniques which involve individuals as members of groups. When the objectives are to develop human relations abilities, group participation methods are the most promising.

Lifelong learning must become a reality for individuals who are to continue to grow and develop and make a contribution. Some fields change more rapidly than others, but in the type of society in which we live, change is inevitable and each individual must continue to grow and develop in order to keep abreast of change as well as be a part of the change process. As individuals move from a structured school setting, they must be willing and able to assume an increasing amount of responsibility for their own learning and development. It is helpful for learners to have experiences under the direction of an instructor whereby they can be involved in the process of planning and conducting learning activities. Instructors are, in reality, most effective when they are able to help learners become independent. Ultimately, learners must "go it on their own." As individuals leave the formal school setting and become involved in their careers, there are many opportunities to be involved in group activities in which there are participatory planning and decision-making. Examples of these types of activies are role playing, brainstorming, the nominal group process and quality circles (see Figure 4-2).

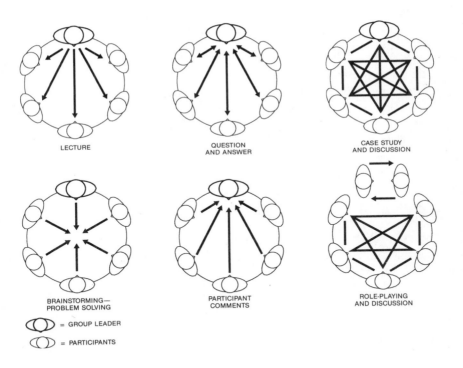

Figure 4-2. Group interaction methods can be used to increase student participation in the classroom.

Role Playing

Role-playing requires participants to act as though they are involved in a real-life situation. Role-playing is effective because it gives students a better understanding of others' emotions and behaviors in similar situations. This teaching method helps students to better understand their own behavior and respond in positive ways to various human relationship situations.

Students often find it difficult to role-play and, consequently, gain little in the way of new insights from the experience. This is especially true when the roles played are artificial, or when the materials are prepared hastily. Many situations can, however, be acted out in a way that increases human relations skills.

In a typical role-playing session, each participant is given a descriptive situation to be improvised. This may be achieved through a written assignment or by orally briefing each participant. With oral briefing all students in the class should hear the directions. The role-players are then brought into contact with each other and play their parts.

Brainstorming

Brainstorming requires a group of students to suggest as many solutions to a problem as they can in a limited time period. No ideas are evaluated during the exercise, and unusual ideas are welcomed. The objective of brainstorming is to stimulate imagination and to encourage creative approaches.

Nominal Group Process

The nominal group process involves structured group participation that seeks to tap the experiences, skills and feelings of group members. The primary objective of the nominal group process is to (1) increase the creative productivity of individuals participating as a group, (2) enhance group decision-making, (3) stimulate critical ideas, (4) provide guidance as individual judgments are aggregated, and (5) provide participants with a sense of satisfaction. The technique is designed to be non-threatening as it focuses on the generation of ideas rather than personalities. The process allows group members who may or may not know each other very well to be able to generate ideas that focus on a common problem. The nominal group process assumes that individuals wish to participate, and it works best when participants are willing to think and work through the problem at hand.

Even though the nominal group process occurs in a group setting, each person, in fact, acts individually throughout the entire process of reaching a group consensus about a specific problem or question. One of the real advantages of the process is that it can be used with any size group, and its written format does enable unanimous participation which prevents domination by one or two individuals. The process is time consuming; however, if the problem to be solved or the decision to be reached is real and the best possible judgment from among the group of individuals is desired, the nominal group process works.

The *first step* is to present the question or problem to the group in written form. Then ask each of the participants to write down their ideas separately and independently in brief statements or phrases. Don't be too anxious to hurry this process since you want all individuals to give thoughtful concern to the question or problem and have a few moments of thoughtful consideration as they write down their ideas related to the problem or the decision to be reached.

The *second step* is to ask each member of the group to present one idea from his/her list. The group leader then records each idea on a sheet of newsprint or chart paper visible to everyone. This is not a time to discuss individual items but rather to get the ideas written down. After the leader has secured input from everyone in the group, and it is possible that some individuals will pass because someone else has already given their idea, the leader may then spend a few moments accepting additional ideas that may not have been generated. When one sheet of paper has been filled, it should be taped to the wall or chalkboard so that the entire yield of "idea generation" can be viewed by all.

In the *third step*, the leader asks members of the group to explain their reasons for agreeing or disagreeing with items listed. This step provides an opportunity for participants to explain the reasoning behind their ideas. This step allows refinement of the list and rewording to clarify the meaning of all items.

The *fourth step* requires the leader to distribute (5) three by five inch cards to each group member. Each individual is instructed to write the number and title of their five highest priority items on the cards. Each item goes on a separate card. After the group members have written the title of one item on each of the five cards, they are asked to rank the items by placing five points on the card that is the "best," "highest priority," or other adjective that is appropriate to the problem to be solved or decision to be reached. The other items then get four points, three points, two points, and one point in order from top to bottom. The leader then collects the cards and records the votes on the flip chart in front of the group.

The *fifth step* requires the leader to ask participants to discuss any new concerns about the items chosen or the voting pattern. This step is a clarifying step which may, again, result in a slight alteration of the wording.

The *sixth and last step* is a repeat of step four as individuals again select three to five items, depending on the total length of the list. Prioritize the items, as before, numbering them three, two, one, or five, four, three, two, one, as appropriate. The votes are tallied and a list is made of the items as ranked ordered by the group.

The nominal group process has unlimited potential for involving individuals in a meaningful decision-making process. The simplicity of the technique makes it easy to implement, and it does generate learner involvement in the decision-making process. In the strictest sense, it is not a teaching method although it is clearly a process by which individuals can learn and through which a group can arrive at a better decision than might be made by any one individual acting alone. This process would most often be used with mature learners or students who are at advanced levels in their subject area since it requires a substantial amount of prerequisite information and experience whereby the opinions and ideas of the individuals in the group would have validity.

Quality Circles

Quality circles are group participation activities, but they were not developed as an educational methodology. They are included in this chapter because they involve group participation, and there are educational implications for the process that should be understood by instructors and leaders of groups.

Quality circles are typically used in the workplace as opposed to an educational setting. A quality circle involves a group of individuals who meet together on a regular basis to identify, analyze and solve problems related to quality production or service in their area of the workplace. Quality circles are typically voluntary in terms of the involvement of any one individual is concerned. The organization or company may make a policy decision that the firm will introduce quality circles; however, the involvement of a given individual is typically not forced. The ideal size of a quality circle is typically seven to ten members. Obviously, if there are too few or too many, the interaction of individuals could not occur at an optimal level.

It is important for instructors to understand the nature of quality circles and to recognize the educational implications of this form of group participation. Quality circles are a creation of business and industry, in which many of the elements of discussion methodology and brainstorming are utilized. The purposes of a quality circle are to (1) bring about improvements in the quality of products or services, (2) increase productivity, and (3) increase motivation of group members. Quality circles were conceived in Japan in the early 1960's under the leadership of Dr. Kaoru Ishikawa, a professor of engineering at Tokyo University. In recent years, hundreds of western world companies have installed quality circle activities to increase quality and productivity through increased worker motivation.

The process by which a quality circle operates is based on the following four fundamental steps. *Step one* involves the idenfication of problems by the group members. Typically, several problems are identified that are interfering with quality productivity and/or morale. *Step two* involves a group decision about the specific problem that the group will attempt to solve or minimize. *Step three* is referred to as problem analysis whereby the group begins to dissect the problem into its component parts or subproblems. At this point, a resource person or technical expert may need to be called in to provide additional information or otherwise help group members gain greater insight. *Step four* requires a group judgment regarding the appropriate solution to the problem and the formulation of a recommendation for problem solution and/or reduction.

The four steps in the quality circle process involve the various techniques of discussion and other group participation methods previously discussed in this chapter. In fact, the quality circle must have a leader who keeps the discussion on track, who summarizes and makes note of the progress, just as the group leader functions in any other group participation process.

An organization that engages in quality circles makes an investment in morale enhancement through involvement that has long-term payoffs in terms of increased productivity and quality. It must be recognized that an investment is essential if the process is to be effective. Leaders must be trained, and an organization must be established for quality circles to function effectively. Even though participation by individual employees is typically voluntary, there are costs related to (1) the preparation of leaders, (2) the coordination of the process, and (3) time to participate in meetings (which may be from 30 minutes to an hour each week). As individuals are involved in quality circles, they feel more a part of the organization, and this concept of team building is very important to the success of quality circles. The entire concept of quality circles is based upon trust, respect and caring. These are very important human characteristics essential to the development of self-reliance, confidence and cooperation in others. Organizations that are serious about human development must make an investment in their members if they are to maximize both productivity and quality.

Again, it should be emphasized that quality circles are not an educational methodology. It is a process developed by business and industry to improve quality and productivity through increased employee morale. The process has been adopted and adapted by other organizations for similar purposes. The educational and human development implications are numerous as the process employs discussion and other group participation techniques that are used in the educational enterprise.

CONCLUSION

An effective presentation begins with a good plan. As suggested previously, the instructor's presentation is within the context of an overall plan for the lesson in which the presentation is a vital component. Nevertheless, it must be realized that the presentation component cannot be maximized unless the other elements of the lesson plan are carried out effectively. It is vitally important that the instructor clearly establish and articulate the objective or objectives to be accomplished. Likewise, it is essential that an appropriate introduction be planned whereby the interest and attention of the students will be directed appropriately to the instructor's presentation. After the "big picture" for the lesson has been established, the instructor's presentation itself needs to be carefully outlined in order that the scope and sequence is determined purposefully rather than left to chance.

Seldom is an oral presentation made in isolation. Typically, the instructor uses some type of visual aid, involves students in an activity, or utilizes questioning techniques to check on student learning, or to increase the amount of student involvement in the teaching/learning process.

As indicated previously, lesson planning involves the identification of interaction items that are used by the instructor to increase student participation. Interaction items are often questions, however, as suggested on page 110, there are alternatives to questions that will bring about interaction between instructor and students.

As important as planning is to effective presentation, planning alone cannot ensure a successful presentation. The manner in which the instructor behaves does affect the way in which students listen and learn. Several types of behavior were reviewed such as movement, attending, focusing, pausing and pacing. The effectiveness and the impact of the instructor's behavior is dependent somewhat upon the instructor's personality and the rapport that has been established with the class. Regardless of the personality limitations that may exist, the effective instructor must be concerned about the structure and clarity of the presentation. The words that are used, the instructor's articulation and the manner in which sentences are composed does affect the manner in which an idea is transmitted. These techniques can be learned with practice, and the instructor can become increasingly effective by giving careful attention to his/her "stage presence" as well as the tone, volume and pacing of the oral delivery.

In some subjects, the demonstration method of teaching is a predominant means of teaching procedures as well as concepts and principles. The sense of sight is added to the sense of hearing as a major means of communication between the instructor and the students. This method is characterized by showing on the part of the instructor and observing by the student.

It is important for the instructor to recognize that the demonstration method involves several elements in addition to showing. The instructor must explain the steps of procedure in order that these can be identified clearly as the student observes the instructor's performance. The instructor must use questioning and response to questions during and following the showing step in an effort to clarify as well as reinforce key elements of the process including factors of safety and equipment or instrument usage. The key component to any method is the application stage whereby students not only gain additional insight through the process of "doing," but the students also have opportunities to test themselves by seeing whether or not they can perform the procedures as shown by the instructor.

Much of the emphasis in the demonstration method relates to skill development on the part of the student. When the objective to be met is skill development, there not only must be an application stage in the demonstration lesson, but there must also be opportunities for the individual to practice until the process becomes automatic and the student performs the task in the most efficient and effective manner. Nevertheless, it should be understood that the demonstration method also applies to instruction other than skill development. There are numerous instances in which cognitive development is enhanced through the demonstration method. Often students can understand a concept or principle better through a demonstration than they would be able to gain understanding through words alone. Principles such as magnetism, specific gravity, deflection, and elasticity may be difficult for students to understand through the use of abstract verbal symbols. However, clarity may be enhanced through observing the demonstration of the concept or principle.

The demonstration is one of the most rewarding types of instruction because of the feeling of satisfaction that comes as students demonstrate through their performance that they have learned. This is direct proof that the instruction has been effective and that students have profited from the instructional process. The skillful instructor will find many opportunities to utilize the demonstration method.

As a given class period will include several different instructor and student activities and interactions, it is important that most of these interactions be anticipated and planned. In most class settings, it is important that students participate and have an opportunity to express themselves. Oral expression by students allows the instructor to assess the student's level of understanding and thus identify points that need additional clarification or emphasis. One of the better ways to stimulate student interaction is through effective questioning. It is important for the instructor to realize that there are several types of questions that assess learning at various levels of cognition. Too frequently, the instructor is satisfied with student responses at the knowledge level when the objectives of the lesson require the student to be able to apply, synthesize or evaluate knowledge. Although some questions will occur spontaneously, either from the student or from the instructor, it is important that the instructor pre-plan a number of questions in advance so that he/she can systematically assess the level of understanding resulting from the presentation.

In addition to the tendency to ask questions that require only recall, there is also a tendency for instructors to be unwilling to wait for a thoughtful answer on the part of the students. Instructors are too frequently uneasy with a pause in the action and feel a need to "fill the void" with the sound of their voice. As the instructor focuses upon higher levels of learning with questions that require the student to analyze, synthesize or evaluate, more time must be allowed for the student to consider alternatives and provide a thoughtful response. Care must be taken by the instructor to respond properly to student responses in order to encourage continued participation rather than to inadvertently discourage students from participation. Not only must the instructor be careful with regard to the words or phrases that are used in response to student questioning, but he/she must also be concerned with the non-verbal communication related to student responses. The instructor's posture or expression may communicate more than the instructor's words. The teaching/learning process requires careful planning and execution. The effective instructor must give attention to the various elements of classroom interaction in order to maximize the student's time as the student seeks to achieve the objectives that are specified for the lesson.

Discussion methodology has numerous general and specific applications through which individuals participate actively to gain greater insight, increase their level of understanding and participate with others in decision-making. The instructor is not as much at "center stage" as is the case with other methods such as the lecture or demonstration. Nevertheless, the instructor plays a substantial role in the planning process and sometimes in leading the group participation process. Under certain circumstances, the instructor may utilize other individuals as discussion leaders. However, in many instances, the instructor will utilize discussion methodology for only short periods of time as he/she moves from one form of methodology to another in an effort to achieve a variety of objectives during a given class period.

After the instructor understands the advantages and limitations of discussion methodology, it will be easier to make decisions regarding the appropriateness of discussion methodology under certain conditions and with certain groups of learners. Knowing the appropriate time to use a given instructional method is just as important as being able to carry out the methodology effectively. Even though the discussion methodology requires less direct talking by the instructor, the discussion method does not require any less advanced planning.

If group discussion is to proceed efficiently and result in the achievement of certain objectives, the process must be planned and conducted with care. As an indication of the care that must be exercised in the planning process as well as in the actual discussion itself, it is important to recognize that the instructor provides the direction. In fact, the term "directed discussion" is often used in educational methodology to indicate that there are planned outcomes and that the leader must continually summarize and point the group in the direction that will lead to closure. The discussion may appear to an outsider to be "free wheeling;" however, the skillful group leader directs the process to successful conclusion.

Some of the specific uses of discussion and group participation methodology are identified in various ways through the professional literature. Several of these variations have been included in this chapter, e.g., *role playing, brainstorming, the nominal group process,* and *quality circles.* These specific forms of group participation which typically involve some elements of group discussion have certain unique features that dictate their appropriateness under a given set of circumstances and for the achievement of specific objectives.

It is important for instructors to recognize the value of the discussion methodology as well as group participation for a variety of purposes that may be only indirectly related to the instructional process. Most group participation procedures are not viewed as efficient means of transmitting information; however, they are valuable for the achievement of other objectives such as group decision-making, application of knowledge, problem solving, increasing understanding, and learning to interact effectively with others.

Leading groups effectively is a skill that instructors can acquire, but it takes knowledge of the process and practice in the application of the process. As with any other type of skill, competence in discussion leading cannot be acquired by reading or observation without participation. To become an effective discussion leader one must practice and develop the skills over a period of time.

REFERENCES ————————————————————— 4

Bloom, B.S. (1956). *Taxonomy of educational objectives: Cognitive domain.* New York: David McKay Company, Inc.

Brock, S.C. (comp). (1976). *Practitioner views on teaching the large introductory college course.* Center for Faculty Evaluation and Development, Kansas State University, Manhattan, KS.

Brookfield, S.D. (1987). *Developing critical thinkers.* San Francisco: Jossey–Bass, Inc.

Cooper, J.M., et al. (1986). *Classroom teaching skills.* Lexington, MA: D.C. Heath Co.

Davis, R., & Alexander, L. (1977). *The lecture method.* East Lansing: Instructional Media Center, Michigan State University.

Delberg, A., Van der Vern, A.H., & Gustafson, D.H. (1975). *Group techniques for program planning: A guide to nominal group and delphi processes.* Glenview, IL: Scott Foresman & Company.

Dewar, D.L. (1980). *The quality circle handbook.* Redbluff, CA: Quality Circle Institute.

Dillon, J. (1984). Research on questioning and discussion. *Educational Leadership, 42* (3), 50–56.

Draves, W.A. (1984). *How to teach adults.* Manhattan, KS: The Learning Resources Network.

Edwards, B. (1984). *Case studies and critical incidents for trainers.* New York: Training By Design, Inc.

Flanders, N. (1970). *Analyzing teacher behavior.* Reading, MA: Addison–Wesley.

Gage, N.L. (Ed.) (1976). The psychology of teaching methods. *75th Yearbook of the National Society for the Study of Education,* Chicago: University of Chicago Press.

Gage, N., & Berlinger, D. (1986). *Educational psychology.* Boston: Houghton–Mifflin.

Good, T., & Brophy, J. (1986). *Educational psychology: A realistic approach.* New York: Longman, Inc.

Good, T., & Brophy, J. (1984). *Looking in classrooms.* New York: Harper & Row.

Kennedy, J., et al. (1978). Additional investigation into the nature of teacher clarity. *Journal of Educational Research, 72* (1), 3–10.

Knox, A.B. (Ed.) (1980). Small group instruction. *Teaching Adults Effectively.* San Francisco: Jossey–Bass, Inc.

Land, M., & Smith, L. (1979). Effect of a teacher clarity variable on student achievement. *Journal of Educational Research, 72* (4), 196–197.

Lewis, K.G. (1982). *Taming the pedagogical monster.* A handbook for large class instructors. Center for Teaching Effectiveness, University of Texas–Austin.

McKeachie, W., & Kulik, J. (1975). Affective college training, In F. Kirlinger (Ed.) *Review of Research in Education.* Itasca, IL: Peacock.

McMann, F. (1979). In defense of lecture. *Social Studies, 70,* 270–274.

Meyers, Chet. (1986). *Teaching students to think critically.* San Francisco, CA: Jossey–Bass, Inc.

Rosenblum, S.H. (Ed.) (1985). Discussion as an effective educational method. *Involving Adults in the Educational Process.* San Francisco: Jossey–Bass, Inc.

Rosenblum, S.H., & Darkenwald, G.C. (1983). Effects of adult learner participation in course planning on achievement and satisfaction. *Adult Education Quarterly. 33* (3), 147–153.

Tikunoff, W., Berlinger, B., & Rist, R. (1975). *An ethnographic study of 40 classrooms of the beginning teacher evaluation study.* Technical Report #75–10–5, San Francisco: Far West Regional Education Laboratory.

Van der Vern, A.H, & Delbecq, A.L. (1974). *Group decision–making effectiveness.* Kent, OH: Kent State University Press.

Rowe, E.M. (1974). Wait–time and rewards as instructional variables: Part I. Wait–time. *Journal of Research in Science Teaching, 11,* 81–94.

Weimer, M.G. (Ed.). (1987). *Teaching large classes well.* San Francisco: Jossey–Bass.

5

FACILITATING TEACHING AND LEARNING WITH TECHNOLOGY

The often quoted phrase, "a picture is worth a thousand words," indicates the power of communication techniques that go beyond the word symbols that are used by humans to convey thoughts and ideas as well as descriptions from one person to another. Primitive man drew pictures in the sand and on the walls of caves. Illustrations have always helped to convey ideas and describe people, things and events.

Effective instruction requires a variety of media to help convey meaning and increase learning. Systematic and effective instruction relies heavily upon instructional media. In the broad sense, instructional media refer to anything that establishes conditions which enable learners to acquire knowledge, skills and attitudes. In this broad context, the teacher, the textbook and the school environment are media. However, in the context of this chapter, media refer to the graphic, photographic, electronic or mechanical means for enhancing the transmission and reception of visual or verbal information.

During the last quarter of the 20th century, the United States definitely entered the information age. The explosion of knowledge and the means by which that knowledge is processed, stored and communicated has been revolutionized by a remarkable element called a microprocessor. This increasingly tiny piece or "chip" of material is, as its name suggests, a tiny processor of information. Microprocessors are found in microwave ovens, hand-held calculators, cameras, robots, appliances, automobiles, games and toys. However, the application of the microprocessor in the development of the microcomputer has brought about a revolutionary change in information processing. Not since the invention of the printing press has a technological device held such implications for the lPearning process.

Adults and children are surrounded by audio and visual impressions. These impressions are created by combinations of pictures, words and sounds that evoke emotions, change attitudes, communicate information and motivate action. The power of media can be observed by television commercials and numerous examples of print and non-print materials that motivate people to buy products, vote for candidates or donate to charities. The impressions created through combinations of media have been shown to be retained significantly longer than when the same messages were communicated through only the written or spoken word. It is important for the instructor to understand the advantages as well as the limitations of each type of media for instructional purposes. The use of media for its own sake is of questionable value. The medium chosen must relate directly to the message to be communicated. Any subject matter can be enhanced through the appropriate use of media, but the wrong medium or poor timing in the use of media can be a waste of time and effort for both the instructor and the student. Instructional media must be viewed as aids to teaching and learning. An inappropriately chosen medium or a medium used at the wrong time may contribute little or nothing to student learning. There are, indeed, times when "one picture is worth a thousand words" but not always. For example, one word may be as good as a thousand pictures. For example, the word "yes" to a proposal of marriage needs no picture to be understood. The effective instructor uses all the tools available in an effective manner at the time when they can best facilitate learning.

INSTRUCTIONAL MEDIA TECHNOLOGY

The term "media" as used in the instructional context refers to a variety of means available to the instructor that will improve the communication of information, ideas, concepts or relationships in order that individuals can learn more efficiently and effectively. Instructional media technology makes use of the power of pictures, words and sounds to stimulate interest, compel attention and enhance the understanding of ideas that may be too complex for verbal explanation alone. Media help overcome the limitations of time, space and size.

Impact of Media on Learning

In previous chapters, the instructor has received information about learning, selecting and organizing subject matter, lesson planning, and instructional methodology. Another fundamental component of a systematic approach to teaching and learning is the selection and/or development of instructional media. The golden rule related to media selection or development is that "the selection of media is based on its potential for facilitating the achievement of a given objective." There is no medium that is best for every student, subject or instructor. The real challenge to the effective instructor is to choose the medium that best establishes the conditions that will facilitate the learning of a given body of content at a given point in time under a given set of circumstances. The effective instructor recognizes that the selection of media follows the identification of content and the specification of objectives. Decisions related to media selection are an inherent part of the instructional planning process and should be reflected in the instructor's lesson plans.

The Need for Instructional Media

For obvious reasons, the real object under discussion may be the very best "aid for learning." However, there are times when the real object is not best and some form of media and related technology would be more appropriate. For example, when:

1. The real object is either too big, too small or not sufficiently compact to be viewed effectively.

2. The object is not available to the students except through some form of media. Newly developed and unavailable products or those objects too distant to be visited may be brought to the classroom through some form of media.

3. The real object or process is too expensive, dangerous or delicate for the students to manipulate.

4. The process is too slow moving as in the case of plant growth or chemical changes. Motion pictures employing animation or time-lapse photography are useful.

5. The rapidity of human or mechanical movement prohibits perception of detail. Slow motion photography or video tape may be an excellent aid to learning in such cases.

6. The process or phenomenon is invisible. The flow of electricity, chemical processes and the action of many gases are invisible to the learner. In such cases, some form of media must be substituted for the real thing.

Classification of Media

There are numerous ways or means by which verbal and visual information is gathered, processed and reconstituted. An analysis of this spectrum of instructional media allows a description of (1) the characteristics of each medium, e.g., color, motion, sound; (2) the manner in which each medium is presented, e.g., a still picture can be projected, displayed or incorporated in a book; and (3) the effective process of utilizing each medium. Because media materials are so commonplace in our lives, their classification may appear to be somewhat unnecessary. However, an orderly classification of media may enable the prospective instructor to review, in a systematic way and from a new perspective, the materials that are available. This review could provide information essential to the selection of media for specific purposes in the instructional process. As one considers instructional media, distinctions must be made between the materials and the equipment although both are involved in the instructional process. The media material is often useless without some type of technology to facilitate its use.

The terms "software" and "hardware" are used with increasing frequency. In more recent years, the manufacturers of computers have amplified the use of these two terms in their reference to the computer and its associated equipment as "hardware" and to the programs written for the computer as "software." However, in the more general usage related to instructional media, "hardware" refers to equipment which stores and/or transmits instructional content or stimuli, e.g., projectors, video tape playback units, television screens (cathode ray tubes). In this broader context, software refers to the medium materials that are stored and transmitted. In essence, the software contains the imbedded message, e.g., content or stimuli.

For the sake of convenience and simplicity, instructional media are often classified as follows:

1. *Graphic materials* include all flat pictures, posters, graphs, charts, diagrams and chalkboard illustrations.

2. *Projected materials* include motion pictures, transparencies for overhead projection, slides and strip film.

3. *Mechanical and electrical materials* include models (reductions or enlargements), actual objects, cutaways, computer controlled stimuli, electronic trainers and other types of teaching machines.

Types of Media and Related Technology

Once the content has been identified and the objectives are specified, the instructor begins the process of designing instructional strategies whereby the learner experiences the content and learning takes place. The selection of materials to facilitate learning is a primary responsibility of the instructor. Therefore, it is important for the instructor to be knowledgeable of the various media available, their unique or special characteristics and the variety of ways in which each medium may be presented. This section provides a brief description of the types of media materials and associated equipment. It is important to realize that a given medium may be utilized in a variety of ways, e.g., a still picture may be presented as a slide, a film strip frame, an overhead projection transparency, or in a textbook.

Real Things. Real things, as contrasted with other media, are not substitutes for real people, events or objects. When people, objects or events are readily and economically available; and when they facilitate the attainment of a given objective, they should be used. Instructors often overlook the obvious when reality is available. The actual object or "thing" is more meaningful than a re-creation in the form of some other medium. However, it is recognized that sometimes real things are not available or the real thing is too small, too dangerous, too expensive, or too time consuming to utilize in the instructional setting.

Verbal Representations. Printed materials place words in a visual context to preserve those spoken words that disappear so quickly. For the visually impaired, the words may be placed into tactal context through Braille. Obviously, for the hearing impaired, something other than the auditory context is essential for learning. Printed words may also be projected by the overhead projector and the film projector. This, of course, adds other media and increases the potential for enhancing learning.

Graphic Representation. Although similar to verbal representations, graphic representation attempts to place data and information into a two dimensional context for the purpose of communicating relationships. The typical forms which graphic representation take are charts, graphs, maps, diagrams and drawings. Often, these graphic representations are used directly in textbooks, self-instructional programs, or as handouts to students. However, they may also be combined with other media through which they appear as overhead projection transparencies, slides or filmstrips.

Still Pictures. A photograph of any object, person or event constitutes a picture. A still picture is a copy or record of a real object, person or event that may be enlarged or reduced. The still picture may be in color or black and white. As the term indicates, there is no motion although motion may be suggested. Photographs may be used directly or as textbook illustrations. However, they may be projected through slides, filmstrips or transparencies.

Motion Pictures. A moving image in color or black and white produced from live action or from graphic representations may be packaged in the format of an 8, 16 or 35 millimeter film or a video tape recording. The video unit, including camera, recorder and playback unit, is being used increasingly in instructional settings because of the control that can be exercised over the medium by the instructor. Objects or events may be recorded, the tape edited and played back in a relatively short period of time by the instructor or an assistant. Motion pictures used for instructional purposes are typically professionally prepared and have many positive attributes. However, the video cassette recorder technology has enhanced the flexibility and capability of instructor produced motion pictures.

Objects, people or events may be photographed in normal motion, in slow motion with time lapse or stop motion. The film can be edited for purposes of highlighting or abbreviating the presentation. The motion picture may be combined with sound and narration can be added.

Audio Recordings. Audio recordings may be made on magnetic tape, disc or on a soundtrack for motion picture. Audio recordings allow the reproduction of actual events or they can be used to provide sound effects for other types of presentations. Sound can provide reality to instruction as it can bring people and events into the classroom. Audio recordings permit oral presentations to be captured for later listening or repeated listening for reinforcement or for clarification.

Simulations. Simulation is the replication of real situations that are designed to represent an actual process or set of conditions. Many forms of media, including the computer, can be used to enhance simulation. For example, the "simulator" has been used for pilot training for many years where a rather complete environment is provided to present the trainee with a variety of circumstances and situations. Computer technology is often used to provide simulated settings for the learner who has a number of different options from which to choose as decisions are made. The entertainment industry has capitalized on this new technology to involve the individual in simulated economic or geographic conditions which demand active participation and decision making.

Models. Models are a means of representing reality with some form of replica. The model may be the exact size, although, it is typically either a reduction or an enlargement in size depending on the size of the original. A modification of the model is referred to as a "mock-up" which also represents the real object, but it is constructed in a manner which allows emphasis of a particular part or function. The model or mock-up may be made so that the parts can be manipulated. Models are made of tiny objects such as an atom which could not be viewed without some form of visual representation. Likewise, a model of a building might be constructed to allow detailed study of various features that would be impractical if students had to deal with the actual object.

Television. This type of media technology refers to the presentation of an image on a television monitor (cathode ray tube). The source of the image may be "live" from a studio, from a video tape or from a motion picture film and still be viewed on a television screen. The origin or the method of transmission is not important to the classification, although, it is very important to its classroom use. The source may be directly from a single camera, from a central transmitter, a cable distribution center or from a satellite, but the image on the screen is the important result.

Programmed and Computer-Assisted Instruction. Programmed instruction refers to prepackaged sequences of information designed to lead a student through a learning process in which there are predetermined and predictable responses. This type of instruction may take the form of programmed textbooks or instructional programs prepared for use with computers. The information may be presented through one medium or a combination of media. For example, the learner may be presented with information through printed words, audio tape, film, slides or images on a cathode ray tube. The learner is required to respond to the information as it appears, and the learner's response will activate the presentation of other information through images. The learner's response is typically reinforced immediately in terms of success or failure. Some programs build in remedial units for responses that are incorrect.

Using Media Technology Effectively

The process of teaching and learning is, indeed, complex as it requires the interaction of many variables. While the learner is the central point of focus in the teaching/learning interface, the instructor has the responsibility for planning, delivering and evaluating teaching and learning. Therefore, it is important for the instructor to recognize the complexity of the teaching/learning process and be able to take into account the many interrelated factors that impact on learner outcomes. The selection and use of instructional media, although isolated for purposes of discussion in this chapter, must be viewed within the total context of instructional planning, delivery and evaluation.

Instructional media of any type should be selected or produced carefully, whether they are to be a part of the instructor's presentation or whether they are to be used directly by students working independently. Well developed media materials not only communicate "messages" in terms of information, but they also impact in a substantial way upon student interest, attention and motivation.

The primary value of instructional media materials lies in (1) their appeal to the senses, (2) their ability to attract and hold attention, and (3) their ability to highlight or focus on key elements to be learned. For instructional purposes, the reproduction of a device or process is often much more effective than an oral or verbal description alone. As one instructor said, "It saves a lot of hand waving."

It would be nice if there were a single formula that could enable an instructor to select the best medium for each teaching situation. However, educators recognize that no single medium has properties that make it best for all purposes. Many instructors select media for use on the basis of familiarity and convenience. These are certainly important factors, but instructors need to be sensitive to other factors in making decisions about media materials and strategies for specific instructional applications. Educational technology scholars have given considerable attention to the matter of selecting and utilizing instructional media. A publication entitled "Selecting Instructional Strategies and Media: A Place to Begin" by the University Consortium for Instructional Development and Technology, summarizes much of the research and experience related to the characteristics of effective media materials and criteria for selecting media for various types of learning outcomes.

The process of selecting media materials is subjective and depends upon the instructor's knowledge, insight and experience. A review of a few of the factors that are involved in the instructor's decision may be helpful in this decision making process.

Appropriateness. Once the objective to be achieved has been clearly delineated, it should be possible to select a medium which helps the students acquire the specified behavior. If it is judged that a picture of an actual object would be desirable, decisions must be made regarding the size of the photograph, whether it is in color or black and white, whether the photograph needs to be of the actual object or a facsimile which leaves out some of the detail which could interfere with the learner's attention to major components and other factors. Likewise, if the objectives require detailed information about a manufacturing process, should one show a film that describes the process, take a field trip to see the product being manufactured, or listen to an audio tape from the foreman of the production line? In the process of selecting appropriate media, the instructor will often find that different forms of media will be available and that any one might be appropriate. Therefore, selection of the medium cannot be based on appropriateness alone. Once a medium has been identified as appropriate, it should be subjected to other criteria such as technical quality, cost, availability, simplicity, flexibility, and level of sophistication.

Technical Quality. The physical characteristics of the specific media material chosen to use in a given lesson may impact significantly on its instructional effectiveness. The overhead projection transparency may be an appropriate medium to facilitate learning on the part of the student. However, if the lettering used is too small, too crowded, contains too much prose or contains errors, its use may have an adverse effect upon student learning. Likewise, a filmstrip may be appropriate to help students achieve a given objective. However, the filmstrip may be blurred, torn or contain frames that show out-of-date equipment which may distract student attention or cause them to miss the "message" because of other distractions within the media material itself. Unless the technical quality of a particular instructional aid is relatively good, it probably should not be used. Poor quality media materials may be more detrimental to effective learning than supportive.

Cost. As media materials are considered, the instructor must give consideration to the monetary as well as the time costs involved in the acquisition or development of a specific item of media for a given lesson. The instructor must ask the question, "Is the cost in either time or actual money worth the potential learning gain or efficiency that can be derived from a particular item of media?" For example, a large chart which depicts items in enlarged form so that they can be viewed by students from the back of the classroom may not be necessary if the same chart is available in the student's textbook whereby all students can look at the illustrations simultaneously during the lesson. However, the economic argument should not constrain the instructor from identifying and specifying the optimum medium to accomplish a given educational objective. Cost should be considered since there are times when two items may be equally effective in terms of their impact on the achievement of objectives, but one is much more expensive or it takes more instructor time than the other. The decisions may not always be clear-cut and compromises may need to be made on the basis of cost.

Availability. On occasion, an instructor might identify a specific item of media that would be "just right" to use in a lesson but not be able to acquire the item for use at the appropriate time. In other instances, the particular item is in a format that cannot be used. For example, the specific item might be in video cassette form that is incompatible with the projection system available to the instructor. Acquiring materials that cannot be used or that cannot be used at the appropriate time is pointless. Media materials used "out of step" with the presentation of the content tends to lose their effectiveness. Films shown "when the film or auditorium is available" are often useless in terms of achieving specified educational objectives.

Simplicity. Too often complex media materials are utilized which actually provide a stimulus "overload" to the learner and obscure the specific content to be learned. The learner cannot assimilate a large number of facts presented at one time. A variety of ideas presented simultaneously tend to confuse the student. Many instructional films are prepared with no specific objectives in mind, and as a result, they often "cloud the issue" and interfere with the achievement of specific objectives. Short films on specific phases of the subject are typically much more effective since they can target on specific content or objectives. The effective instructor does not obscure the message with the media.

Flexibility. Selection of media materials that allows use at the appropriate time and for the length of time that is both necessary and desirable is an important factor. The medium should not control the lesson but should be chosen to facilitate the achievement of objectives specified for the lesson. The instructor's ability to control and utilize the medium to fit his/her needs is important. Overhead projection transparencies would be an example of a medium that has a high degree of flexibility whereas an educational film in the form of a motion picture would have a low level of flexibility. The effective instructor seldom teaches the same lesson twice in exactly the same way. No two groups of students have exactly the same needs; therefore, the use of a given item of media may need to be used at a different time or in a different context. Therefore, flexibility is an important factor to consider as one invests either time or money in the acquisition or development of a given item.

Level of Sophistication. The level of sophistication of a given item of media refers to the vocabulary used, the rate at which the content is presented, the type of visualization, and the approach to the subject. Often times, commercially prepared materials are aimed at a wide age level of audience in order to increase the marketing potential of the product. Therefore, it is especially important for the instructor to determine the appropriateness of each item of media in terms of its level of sophistication for the group with whom it is to be used. The level of sophistication may be too advanced or at too low a level for a given group of learners.

To illustrate this point, consider the medium of programmed instruction which is designed in a step-by-step progression as the learner moves through the process of learning concepts or principles. Frequently, the steps are small and minute, and the advanced learner finds the process laborious since by virtue of intelligence, maturity and/or experience, the learner could move more rapidly. In this case, the level of sophistication is too low for the learner and leads to boredom and lack of interest. When this occurs, another medium such as a well-selected textbook or reference might provide a better learning experience than the "programmed" material.

Factors Affecting Use of Media Technology

It should be obvious that an instructional medium cannot be selected without a clear view of its use. Selection must be based on a consideration of the manner in which the medium will be used in the instructional setting. The factors related to effective utilization depend on the assumption that the medium has been appropriately selected. There are no absolutes or formulas which will tell the instructor, in advance, the specific impact that a given media material will have on the attainment of a specified objective. However, there are guidelines which do help the instructor to select the most appropriate medium once objectives have been defined in performance terms.

The effective instructor reviews the lesson content to identify areas that need illustration, amplification or clarification. No instructional aid takes place of an instructor nor does it necessarily make the instructor's job easier. Media materials may assist an instructor to teach more effectively, to save time and to facilitate student learning. As these decisions are made, the following guidelines may be helpful:

1. To the extent that the content and procedures within the medium bring about responses that are very similar or identical to the desired terminal behavior, a high degree of transfer from the learning situation to actual practice will occur.

2. When facts and concepts are presented with visual cues, the potential for learning is enhanced.

3. The process of learning is facilitated when media present examples of the concept to be learned.

4. Visuals typically provide the learner with an opportunity to identify relationships that may not be as easily discovered when presented in written form.

5. The use of media helps the instructor to "change the pace" within the classroom, and this factor in and of itself attracts attention and focuses student learning.

MEDIA MATERIALS AND DEVICES

Instructors should be knowledgeable about the various media materials and devices available so that appropriate materials and devices can be selected to increase the effectiveness of teaching and learning. After the instructor has identified the content to be taught and the objectives to be achieved by learners, consideration must be given to media materials and devices that will maximize instructional effectiveness.

Overhead Projector

The overhead projector is the most versatile projection device for general classroom use. See Figure 5-1. The following are major advantages of an overhead projector:

1. The room need not be darkened.

Eastman Kodak

Figure 5-1. The overhead porjector is the most versatile projection device for general classroom use.

2. The projector can be operated from the front of the room so the instructor can maintain eye contact with students.

3. Numerous methods are available for producing and storing overhead transparencies.

4. It is possible to use transparent overlays to show (1) steps of procedures, (2) stages of construction, or (3) the internal assembly of equipment. In addition, the overhead projector can be used with working models to show moving parts of equipment. It is even possible to give the effect of movement, such as a heartbeat or the flow of liquids, by using special attachments to the overhead projector.

Overhead projectors are often equipped with a roll of transparency film, which is wound across the machine and makes it possible to project a considerable amount of material that has been prepared in advance or that is developed through discussion in the class.

Instructors often prefer to use the overhead projector as they would use the chalkboard, by writing directly on the transparency at the same time that it is projected.

Transparencies can be used in conjunction with the chalkboard. Diagrams and equations may be projected on the board and then altered or developed with white or colored chalks. Green background transparencies projected on a green chalkboard give the best line contrast.

Thermal and plain paper copier transparencies can be made in a few seconds. The process is completely electric and requires no chemicals. Material can be edited by blanking unwanted items with a sheet of plain paper while the transparency is being made. Transparency stock is available in several colors.

The suggested procedure for using the overhead projector is as follows:

1. Arrange transparencies in proper order for showing.

2. Plan an outline of commentary for each transparency.

3. Plan additional comments or symbols that are to be added to the transparencies.

4. Indicate on the lesson plan when each transparency is to be used.

5. Set up and focus the projection on the screen. See Figure 5-2.

6. Show each transparency at the proper time and with appropriate comment.

7. Be prepared to show transparencies a second time for review and emphasis.

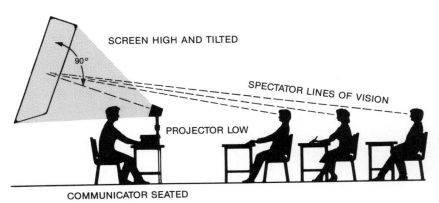

Figure 5-2. Proper projection techniques are essential when using an overhead projector.

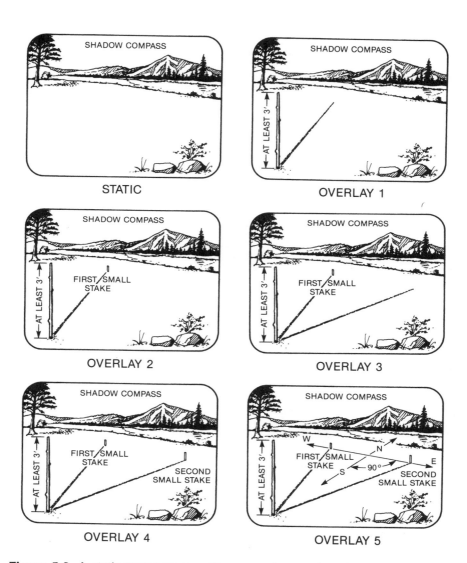

Figure 5-3. A static transparency with successive overlays is used to develop complex items in a series of steps.

Overlays. A distinct advantage of the overhead projector comes through the use of a static transparency with one or more overlays. A static transparency is one transparency sheet displaying graphics and/or data. Successive overlays present additional information one step at a time. Successive overlays may be used when the instructor wishes to develop a complex idea in a series of steps. The following shadow compass technique for finding directions when lost in the woods was developed by Robert Owendoff, a boy scout from Falls Church, Virginia. See Figure 5-3.

1. In an open area (static frame) a stake is driven into the ground with at least 3' of its length above the ground (overlay 1). The tip of the shadow cast by this stake is marked with the first small stake (overlay 2).

2. After a wait or not less than 10 minutes a second shadow is cast and is marked with a second small stake (overlays 3 and 4).

3. A line is drawn to join the two small stakes (overlay 5). This line always points east and west, regardless of time of day or year. A line drawn at 90° to the first will point north and south. Under some conditions, this method of finding directions is more accurate than a compass. The average error is 8°.

Recent technology makes it possible to project computer images through the overhead projector to produce large images for audiences. See Figure 5-4.

Eastman Kodak

Figure 5-4. A projection pad used in conjuction with an overhead projector enables an instructor to project computer-generated images onto a screen without a video projection system.

Slide Projector

A slide projector is instructional hardware used to project an image from a slide to a screen. See Figure 5-5. Slides have an advantage over filmstrips in that the order in which the pictures are used can be changed, and slides can be eliminated or added.

Eastman Kodak

Figure 5-5. A slide projector provides flexibility in the number and sequence of slides shown.

The flexibility of slides provides relatively low-cost individualized instruction. Frequently, a set of slides is prepared with an accompanying audiocassette tape, which can be used by a student as a self-instructional package. This means of packaging instruction brings together both a visual and audio stimulus.

The technology involved in bringing the learner in contact with the message through a variety of media materials ranges from a slide projector and an audio recording to a device having the capability of electronically controlling the visual and audio message as the learner pushes the appropriate button. Modern technology allows the time and pace of the learning experience to be selected and controlled.

Filmstrip Projector

A filmstrip projector is instructional hardware designed to project an image from filmstrips frames to a screen. See Figure 5-6. Some filmstrip projectors are used with audiocassette tape so instructions can be heard by students as the filmstrip is viewed. The following procedures for using a filmstrip projector are suggested.

Dukane Corporation

Figure 5-6. A filmstrip projector is used to project still illustrations of people, events, or objects.

1. Preview the filmstrip and determine comments that should be made during the showing.

2. List the filmstrip's title and key points on the chalkboard.

3. Prepare the room and equipment. Adjust the projector so the proper image size is obtained on screen. Arrange seats so everyone can see.

4. Introduce the filmstrip by indicating key ideas to obtain from the showing. Explain procedures to be used in assessing student understanding of the content presented.

5. Show the filmstrip. Allow time for students to read the printed explanations on each frame. Answer questions as needed.

6. Consider reshowing the filmstrip to emphasize main points and to clear up misconceptions.

7. Evaluate student learning by using oral or written questions or performance tests.

Opaque Projector

An opaque projector is instructional hardware that projects an image of a printed picture, photograph, or flat illustration. The room must be dark when the opaque projector is used. Some opaque projectors are equipped with electronic pointers, which are useful in placing an arrow of light at any point on the projected image. Small illustrations should be mounted on uniform paper or cardboard. Suggested procedures for using the opaque projector include:

1. Arrange illustrations in the proper order for showing.

2. Plan comments to be made for each illustration.

3. Set up equipment (if pictures vary in size, move the projector to change the size of the projected image) and arrange student seating.

4. Use a pointer to illustrate key ideas.

Motion Pictures

Motion pictures are available on many subjects and from many sources. Films are designed to provide facts, steps of procedure, and an understanding of complex problems. Films often provide an excellent variation in the teaching process. Most films are general in nature and are more useful for orientation than for instruction in specific areas.

Care should be taken in the selection of films to be used in the classroom. Obtaining information about films for a course is an important, but time-consuming task. Local audiovisual suppliers and universities and other educational institutions have film catalogs available. Film libraries are also available in many locations through commercial loan and rental agencies and the military and other government services.

The following procedures are suggested for using motion pictures in the classroom:

1. Preview the film and take notes about content. Ask the following questions: Does the content meet the objective of the lesson? Which points need to be emphasized or clarified?

2. Set up the film projector prior to the class session and check focus and sound levels. Prepare the room for showing the film. See Figure 5-7.

3. List the film's title and the key points on the chalkboard. Provide a brief overview of the film in order to set the tone for better student learning.

4. Inform students if they will be tested on the film's content.

Eastman Kodak

Figure 5-7. Films provide excellent instruction when illustrating the motion of an operation or process.

5. Discuss the pertinent material shown in the film. This may be done by asking leading questions and listing key points on the chalkboard.

6. Evaluate what students have learned by oral, written, or performance tests.

Motion pictures provide valuable instruction, especially where motion such as that found in any operation or process is to be shown. When properly used, films can increase learning, save time, and provide variety in the course.

Television and Video Monitors

Television is a powerful means of mass communication. Educational television stations broadcast hundreds of cultural and educational programs. Vocational and technical programs are being added to the programming on several stations. Television can be used to present instruction about a variety of subject areas. As an educational aid, television has demonstrated its usefulness for mass orientation and for reaching those at home.

A major disadvantage of television is that the instructor cannot see or hear a student. The instructor has no way of observing the student's reaction.

Closed-Circuit Television. Closed-circuit television is being used in a number of situations, including medical and military service schools. The image is sent to receiving monitors in one or more classrooms. The following are advantages of closed-circuit television:

1. One demonstration can be sent to several classrooms at the same time.

2. Magnification of small and hard-to-see demonstrations is possible.

3. Dangerous, distant, or current phenomena can be transmitted back to viewers by the television camera.

4. An important procedure may be shown repeatedly to many students through television. For example, medical students may repeatedly watch a skilled surgeon perform an operation.

Television Playback. Instant television playback can be used for instruction. For example, the University of Missouri-Columbia has used closed-circuit television to show trainees how an experienced school guidance counselor works with a group of young people. The instant replay makes it possible to go back over important phases of the counseling process immediately following first-time observation. Videotapes of such sessions can also be used for more intensive study of counseling behavior. Teacher education programs are using portable television equipment to capture teacher and student behaviors for analysis and improvement. Methods courses in education often videotape small group instructional settings as a means of providing the prospective teacher with immediate feedback.

Within the individual classroom or laboratory, television can be used to magnify people, events, or objects. For example, a television camera can be mounted on equipment in motion, which makes it possible for students as a group to see the action. A television camera can also be mounted on a microscope, thereby making it possible for a large group to see individual slides.

Portable Television. Advancements in the production of portable video cameras, VCRs, and compact video cameras (camcorders) have increased the use of television for instructional purposes. These technological advances have allowed education to move out of an era that required specialized studios, large capital investments, and technical specialists.

Television, like chalkboards, motion pictures, or working models, has limitations, strengths, and weaknesses. An instructor must decide which materials, methods and aids contribute most to the teaching-learning process.

Audio Recordings

Audio recordings are used in schools, particularly in music, language, and speech training. Sound can be recorded on discs or reproduced magnetically on plastic tape.

The electronics industry has succeeded in making recording equipment compact, lighter in weight, and less complex to operate, while increasing sound quality. The audiocassette player/recorder uses a self-contained tape cartridge that is easy to load or remove. The audiocassettes are relatively inexpensive and can be erased and reused indefinitely.

Recording equipment can be most useful for individual or self-instruction or for practice in speech, language, or music training. Recordings can be used to aid students in the recognition of sounds, such as the sounds of an improperly operating cutting tool, a worn bearing, or an overloaded motor. The following are suggestions for recording and use:

1. Set up the recorder according to the manufacturer's instructions.

2. Record a period of live sound.

3. Rewind and play back for quality.

4. Record a second time with different microphone placements.

5. Include notations that record the length and any questions about the recording if it is to be part of a lesson.

Simulators

A simulator is a device that is similar to, but not identical with, the real equipment in operation. The degree of similarity required depends on the way the device is to be used in an instructional program.

Simulators are designed to provide instruction on critical skills, which are required on the actual equipment. Simulators are often superior to actual equipment during the initial phases of instruction.

The need for simulators in educational programs increases as complex human-machine relationships are involved. High fidelity simulation is common in military training and on critical skills required to operate complex equipment. Simulators are also useful in less complex instructional programs.

A simulator provides systematic practice of critical skills that may not be feasible when the actual equipment is in operation. For example, a portion of a complex machine can be simulated so that the student can gain experience under the most favorable conditions. This is important with such skills as engine troubleshooting, production line work, and work to be done under hazardous conditions. The simulator need not duplicate the whole task, but it must truly simulate whatever the student must transfer to the operating situation.

Simulator training that produces habits that are not the same as those required in the operating situation may result in negative transfer and can be dangerous. For example, a target simulator used to train military personnel to fire on a moving target must truly represent the real situation.

The last phase of simulation instruction usually consists of training on the actual equipment. This instructional phase bridges the gap between the simulator and the actual equipment under true operating conditions. Generally, this live operation is provided on the job by the supervisor responsible for the work or by a highly skilled employee, who reports to the supervisor. Simulators have their greatest value in the following situations:

1. The actual equipment is so complex that the trainee cannot be given adequate experience and practice on specific procedures before total integrated performance is required.

2. The actual equipment is dangerous in the hands of a trainee until the ability to adjust quickly to emergency conditions has been developed.

3. The emergency situation does not occur often enough on operating equipment to maintain the degree of skill required for such situations.

4. The actual equipment is too expensive to be used exclusively for instructional purposes.

In making decisions regarding the selection and use of simulators, it is important to

1. determine the critical skills for which instruction is required,

2. compare costs of simulator and actual equipment,

3. analyze the degree of positive transfer required, and

4. consider the possibility and danger of negative transfer.

Driving Simulators. One of the most effective simulators used is in driver training. A complete installation consists of stationary mock-up automobiles equipped with normal controls. Students operate these automobiles in response to a motion picture projected on a screen at the front of a special room. Although the simulators are stationary, the effect of movement provided by the motion picture is fairly realistic.

The action taken by each student driver, in response to the simulated driving condition, is recorded by a machine at the rear of the classroom. The instructor can use this information to evaluate each student's progress.

The driving simulator provides standard instruction on basic driving skills and shortens the time required for actual driving on the road. It has been estimated that 12 hours of simulator instruction when combined with three hours of actual driving are equivalent to six hours of actual driving. Other factors, including safety, instructor time, and standardization of instruction make the driving simulator a desirable instructional device.

Nonprojected Graphics

Graphics in the form of large pictures, diagrams, posters, and charts are practical for instructional use. Graphics can be drawn or constructed by the instructor to fit a specific teaching situation. The characteristics of a good graphic are

1. all unnecessary details are omitted,

2. lettering is simple and easy to read from any seat in the room,

3. color is used to identify related parts and to direct attention toward main ideas, and

4. technical details and symbols are correct.

Graphics may be placed on the bulletin board or wall for further examination by students. Graphics must be changed frequently. The following is a suggested procedure for using posters and charts:

1. Select and prepare graphics that help emphasize or illustrate points in a lesson. Many ideas can be illustrated by sketches drawn on paper using grease pencils, colored chalk, or crayons.

2. Mount illustrations where they will be seen and used by students.

3. Plan how and when the graphics will be used in a lesson.

Chalkboard

The chalkboard is one of the most flexible and practical aids used by teachers. The chalkboard can be used to list important points in a lesson, solve problems, and illustrate ideas. The chalkboard should never be used as a means of conveying large amounts of written information that can be provided to each student on a handout. Suggested procedures for using the chalkboard include the following:

1. Plan all chalkboard illustrations before class.

2. Prepare complicated drawings before class by reproducing light lines on the chalkboard, clearly visible to the instructor but not to the class. By tracing over these lines with chalk, a neat and accurate drawing may be made quickly while the class observes.

3. When the same basic outline of a drawing is needed several times, it may be transferred to the board by using a stencil.

4. When the outline of an object such as a tool, chemistry flask, map outline, or machine is needed repeatedly, it may be desirable to construct a template.

5. Illustrations may be placed on the board by projecting an image with the opaque or overhead projector, and then tracing the important parts of the image. This is also an excellent technique for increasing the size of an illustration. A large sheet of paper may be taped to the wall or chalkboard if a permanent illustration is desired.

Flannel Board

The flannel board has several distinct advantages for the presentation of material where one idea must be added at a time. The flannel board permits the adding of prepared graphics and words as the lesson is presented. The technique is useful in explaining organizational structures, parts of equipment, and abstract ideas.

Suggested procedures for using a flannel board include the following:

1. Lay out the total illustration for the lesson. Be sure important parts are emphasized by size and color.

2. Have each element or part of the total illustration prepared as a separate piece.

3. Complete a trial run of the lesson and add each illustration as needed.

4. Stack the illustrations in the order needed for logical development.

5. As the lesson progresses place each illustration on the flannel board firmly.

Models

Models may be examined and handled by students, and they show relationships and shapes better than any other instructional aid. Mock-ups, cut-away models, and exploded models are used chiefly to show location and movement of internal parts and unique equipment features. Working models are valuable when demonstrating the operation of tools or machines. The following is a suggested procedure for using models:

1. Select or construct the models needed. Many models are made from common construction materials.

2. Display models to be seen and used continuously.

3. Plan to use models in instructional lessons.

4. Allow students the opportunity to examine the model.

Programmed Instruction

Programmed Instruction is a systematic approach to individualized instruction. While many instructional materials and methods can be individualized, programmed instruction is designed specifically for use with the individual learner.

One step at a time is the way people have learned to swim, read, drive an automobile, and solve mathematical problems. In learning, students must proceed from simple acts to more complex acts as they gain confidence and increase judgment on the way.

Generally, programmed instruction must have the following characteristics:

1. Material to be learned is presented in relatively small steps, or frames. A frame is instruction that consists of information plus questions.

2. Material is carefully sequenced so that the student is led from one frame to the next by questions, illustrations, or clues.

3. The student responds to the information contained in each frame by writing a response, manipulating equipment, or making a computation.

4. Immediate feedback is provided to the student to indicate whether or not the response was satisfactory.

5. The rate of progress through the course is determined by the individual's ability to master the materials. The learner sets the pace of learning.

6. Each unit of material is prepared so students may proceed with little or no help from an instructor.

LINEAR PROGRAMMING

SERIES AND PARALLEL AC CIRCUITS

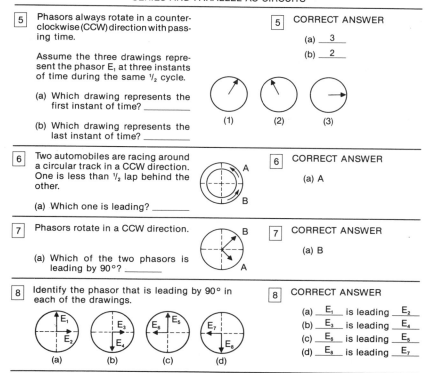

Figure 5-8. Linear programs present information and require responses that provide meaningul practice.

The recent history of programmed instruction and teaching machines dates back to the 1920s and the work of Sidney Pressey at The Ohio State University. Pressey invented several devices intended to provide a mechanical grading method for testing students.

Renewed interest in what is now called programmed instruction came from the work of B.F. Skinner at Harvard University Psychological Laboratories. Skinner's 1958 article, "Teaching Machines," generated a renewed interest in programmed instruction.

Although there are many variations and combinations of programming, there are two distinct types used with written materials. These are linear and branching.

Linear Program. In a linear program, the content of the program is arranged from simple to complex. The information is presented by brief statements in which a single idea is emphasized. In preparing the program, the idea is presented in a direct and complete written statement. The statement is then rewritten and a key word or other information is left out and indicated by a blank space. The student fills in the blank. The response is checked by uncovering the correct answer as supplied in the program. After observing the correct response, the learner proceeds to the next step.

Linear programs present information and require responses that provide meaningful practice. Linear programs may also use illustrations and diagrams to convey concepts. See Figure 5-8.

Branching Program. A branching program is characterized by presenting several paragraphs of information at a time. Each unit of information is followed by a multiple choice question. The student must select an answer. This is done in machine programs by pressing a button. In a programmed text the student's selected answer then refers to another page in the text. Such pages tell the student whether or not the answer is correct. If correct, the student is referred to the next unit in the program. If incorrect, reasons are provided as to why the response was wrong, and additional information is provided. The learner is then referred to the next appropriate unit in the program. See Figure 5-9.

Adjunct Programmed Material. A practical approach to programming is to use available material as a well-written textbook and programmed questions. Several advantages to this approach include the following:

1. The text material may be used for programmed learning and also for review and reference. Adjunct programs have a distinct advantage over

programmed materials, which are self-contained. Adjunct programmed materials allow an overall view of the content for review and serve as a ready source of specific information.

2. An adjunct program is relatively easy to prepare and to modify.

3. The student has all the advantages of the textbook, including the table of contents and an index that provide for quick review and the location of specific information.

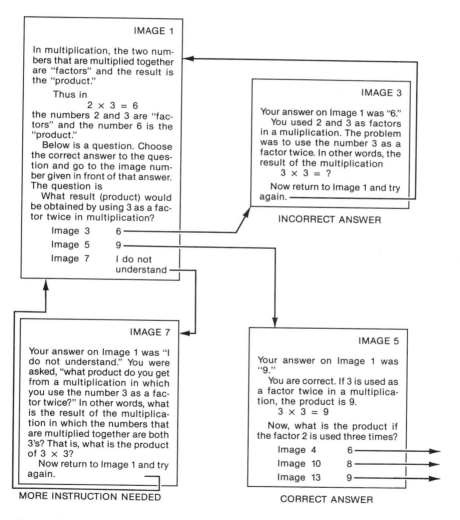

Figure 5-9. A branching program is characterized by presenting information followed by a multiple choice question.

4. The rapid and experienced learner is not held back by having to read and respond to a large number of small and relatively simple steps as found in linear programs.

Dividends from Programmed Instruction. Programmed instruction has helped to improve instruction by requiring objectives that specify outcomes in terms of behavior. Programmed instruction emphasizes the need for an analysis of what the student must know and be able to do. With a thorough and accurate content analysis, the job of programming a course of instruction is half complete.

Programmed instruction should be built on sound principles of learning, such as

1. students should work and learn at their own rate,

2. one-student-to-one-instructor learning is ideal,

3. students should be informed of progress, and

4. programmed texts may be used advantageously for out-of-class study so class time can be used for creative thinking and the use of tools and equipment.

An appropriate and skillfully designed unit of programmed instruction may provide for individual student practice and drill, thus saving the instructor's time for more creative work.

Programmed instruction is often highly effective in those instructional programs that have precise standards of performance specified as an objective. Instruction of this type has been used successfully for training that has exact and standardized procedures.

Educational specialists who use programmed instruction have always

1. required specific objectives for each course and lesson,

2. analyzed tasks as a basis for designing instructional programs,

3. taught through a series of properly sequenced steps,

4. provided for practice and drill on key elements of the program, and

5. evaluated instruction in terms of the student's performance as defined by the objectives.

Instructional technology provides a means for translating instructional materials into visual and/or audio formats, which can be presented to the learner on an individualized basis through the use of a variety of devices. At this time, no one device has proven to be most effective for individualized instruction. Increasingly, computer technology is being used to deliver and control programmed instruction. The effectiveness of the instructional equipment is closely linked with the quality of instructional materials being presented to the learner, as well as the nature of the content being presented.

Microcomputer Technology

Although computers have been commonplace in the business and research arenas during the second half of the 20th century, the significant breakthrough in computing for teaching and learning came in the late 1970s with the introduction of microcomputers at an affordable price, e.g., Apple, Radioshack, Commodore Pet, Atari, IBM. Like any other technical device that can be used to facilitate instruction, the microcomputer is not a magical panacea; it is a tool that requires the same careful use as any other educational device. (See Figure 5-10.)

Figure 5-10. Computers are an integral part of education and training.

The purpose of this section is to provide prospective instructors with an orientation to the microcomputer and its implications for assisting learners and instructors in carrying out their respective roles. The microcomputer, as an aid to learning of certain types of content under certain conditions, is emphasized. Likewise, attention is given to the microcomputer as an aid to instructors as they carry out their managerial and administrative responsibilities. The focus is upon the instructor as a user of "packaged programs" or software for the classroom and the office. There is no attempt to provide the instructor with the skills needed to use specific software to carry out specified functions with the microcomputer. These applications are best learned through specific instruction, application and practice sessions with the software and hardware available to the instructor. Nevertheless, it is essential for the instructor to become familiar with and knowledgeable of the educational applications of microcomputer technology. This technology coupled with others such as satellites and fiber optics are rapidly transforming the ways in which data and information are transmitted, processed, stored, retrieved and transformed in the communications process. Even though there is ongoing research in the area of "artificial intelligence," it is important to remember that computers can only follow the instructions they are given. Simply stated, the computer is a machine that processes information electronically. The key component of the microcomputer is a microprocessor which can be "programmed" to send the necessary signals to the microcomputer's electronic components to carry out the instructions that are provided.

Microcomputer Hardware

The microcomputer and its associated parts and auxillary devices are referred to as "hardware." The microcomputer itself is a machine with mechanical and electrical parts that processes, stores, manipulates, retrieves, displays and prints out information. The hardware components are typically a *keyboard console,* which is used to interact with the internal or microprocessor activated electronic components. The heart of the computer system is the *central processing unit* (CPU). (See Figure 5-11.) The CPU controls all the computer's functions since it is made up of electronic circuits that interpret and carry out instructions written into the software. The CPU also retrieves software instructions before decoding and executing them. The components of the CPU are the memory, the control unit and the arithmetic/logic unit (ALU). The latter component of the central processing unit performs mathematical calculations required for many data processing applications. This component performs these calculations with greater speed

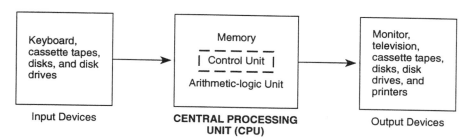

Figure 5-11. The central processing unit (CPU) is the electronic control center that translates input into output.

and accuracy than is possible for the human mind. Another important piece of hardware is the *screen* on which information and directions are displayed. This screen is a cathode ray tube (CRT) similar to that found in a regular television set. Another significant piece of hardware is the *disk drive unit*, which holds the thin plastic diskettes (floppy disks) or the more stable compact disks that may contain some predetermined commands or instructions for the microcomputer or may serve as a medium for the storage of information. Some units have information stored on a more permanent device referred to as a "hard drive." When a printed record of the information displayed on a screen or stored on the plastic disk is desired, a *printer* is connected to the microcomputer and letters or other graphic symbols are produced on paper perforated for easy removal.

Microcomputer Software

As previously indicated, the microcomputer is a machine that can receive, process, store and reproduce information that it receives directly from input by a person through a keyboard or by directions supplied by "software" in symbolic or coded form transmitted electronically. Basically there are two types of software. The systems software is imbedded within the computer to carry out its basic operations. A second type of software is referred to as application software which contains instructions or "programs" for the microcomputer. These disks (diskettes), ranging in sizes from 1 1/2 up to 8 inches in diameter, may be preprogrammed and read by the computer through the disk drive mechanism. In addition, blank disks are used as secondary or auxillary storage for information that is generated within the microcomputer. These disks can be removed and reinserted in the disk drive mechanism.

Most computer users rely on disks that are programmed to provide instructions to the microprocessor within the computer to carry out certain functions on command. The program on the disk allows the operator to input certain information through the keyboard console and move the information around in certain predetermined ways, and then move that information at the desired point in time to the blank disk for storage and retrieval. Some instructors may want to learn a programming language which is composed of an alphabet of symbols, codes and rules through which instructions in the form of a computer program are written electronically on a blank disk. Others will be content to let specialists develop the programs that can be used to carry out the many and varied functions associated with the role of the instructor in managing and facilitating learning. Nevertheless, these "floppy disks" represent the software component of a microcomputer system.

A variety of extensions beyond the basic microcomputer system have been made possible by electronic technology. For example, microcomputers can shift from their basic computer language to another language by the addition of electronic cards or use of programmed diskettes that aid the computer in making the transition from one language to another. In addition, microcomputers can converse with larger computers by the insertion of another type of electronic card and the addition of a "modulator-demodulator unit" called a "modem." When the modem is connected to the microcomputer and the user's telephone, the device converts digital pulses from the microcomputer to analogue wave forms suitable for transmission over the telephone line. Retranslation is needed at the receiving end via a modem link to the host computer system. Then after the information is processed by the larger computer, the modulation/demodulation is repeated.

As the technology advances, microcomputers become increasingly flexible and extend the capabilities of the system to an increasing number of home, business and educational uses. For example, a printing attachment provides for the retrieval of information placed in memory and printed directly on paper rather than to be merely output on a screen for the user's viewing. The printed copy can be produced in several different qualities depending on the sophistication and cost of the output accessory used.

Computer Literacy

Microprocessor technology surrounds each of us in our daily lives. We do, in fact, live in a computer age; and adults in our society, who are unaware or uncomfortable with computers, are at a distinct disadvantage.

Through the widespread use of computer games and toys, children of the 80s and 90s are relatively free of unfounded fears and prejudices about computers. This allows them to become more willing to participate in computer related activities. There are, however, many adults in our society who are unaware of microprocessor technology and lack the fundamental knowledge of the implications that microcomputers have for their daily lives.

Computer literacy, while originally defined as "learning about computers through reading and study," is currently understood to refer to both knowledge of and experience with computing. In addition to knowing many of the functions that the microcomputer can carry out in school, at home or in the work place, computer literacy also includes an awareness of the potential that computer technology has for the future—for jobs and for everyday living. Although definitions of computer literacy vary, the term does not refer to a sophisticated or professional level of computer capabilities. An individual can be computer literate without being able to program a computer.

As microcomputer systems have become more affordable, they have become more feasible for both school and home use. Even though the cost of microcomputers has decreased markedly in the past several years, some traditional educators have been very reluctant to adopt a computer literacy curriculum. Part of this reluctance may be the result of teachers and administrators who lack knowledge about computers and computing. Setting up a microcomputer system in a school and introducing students to the system requires some level of computer literacy on the part of instructors and administrators. However, the alternative to developing computer literacy may certainly be more costly in the long run for our society. If a society relies on computers to accomplish much of its work, members of that society must become computer literate in order to participate.

In the business world of today, computers have become standard equipment. Data processing is perhaps the most familiar application of computers in business. The amount of accounting and bookkeeping procedures that must be performed in business is overwhelming. The computer is able to perform mathematical calculations quickly and accurately. Computers also have the ability to expedite the staggering amount of paperwork necessary to keep a business operating. Computers are used to perform inventory, record keeping, payroll, billing, and a number of other functions that are essential to most businesses. Word processing technology has changed the nature of secretarial work and the preparation of reports and manuscripts can be accomplished in less than one-half the time that typing second and third drafts previously required.

Obviously, computers are with us to stay. Personal computers keep their users aware and informed in an information rich society. The number and range of computer applications in our society can only increase; and more than likely, the increase will be at an astonishing rate. For individuals to participate fully in the information age, they must be computer literate and prepared to take advantage of the many benefits offered by computer technology. The computer literate individual will have increased job potential and earning power in the years ahead. The U.S. Bureau of Labor Statistics predicts that the demand for trained computer professionals will double in the next decade. Even those who work in fields not immediately connected with computers are likely to find themselves working with computers in some capacity. Computer literacy is fast becoming a vital job skill as basic as reading.

Microcomputer-Based Instruction

The development of computer technologies has led to the emergence of computer-based instruction or CBI. CBI is a generic identification which encompasses the entire range of ways in which the computer can be utilized in the instructional process. The basic fundamentals of teaching and learning are applied through computer technology. The methodology and principles involved in teaching and learning must be observed just as carefully when using the microcomputer as with any other media material and associated equipment. In reality, the computer is just another tool for helping the instructor facilitate learning on the part of students.

Computer-Assisted Instruction. The most popular term used to describe the use of computers for instructional tasks is computer-assisted instruction (CAI). Computer-assisted instruction can take many forms as the instructional material is presented by a display unit (TV monitor) such as a cathode ray tube (CRT). Typically, the student scans the presentation by means of a switch or key and indicates readiness to proceed. The computer then may give further information, or it may present questions whose answers are to be recorded in a notebook or maintained on file in the computer's memory. CAI is a general category that includes several forms of instruction, each with unique features and formats. *Drill and practice* is the simplest form of CAI and involves the provision of computer practice of skills already learned. *Tutorial* CAI is a more sophisticated form through which information is provided in relatively small segments which gives the student an opportunity to manipulate the information and then tests the student's mastery of that information. Some tutorial programs provide for reteaching through additional information when the students give the wrong response as they proceed through the program. Other interesting and attractive forms of CAI involve *simulation* and *problem solving*. Simulations allow the student to assume a role in a situation in which a number of options are provided so that the student can experience the results of the choice of several options.

Computer Managed Instruction. Another approach to the application of microcomputer technology to instruction is referred to as computer-managed instruction (CMI). In reality, CMI does not provide instruction. Instead, it manages instruction in a classroom or school through computer-assisted testing and record keeping, which monitors student mastery or the absence of mastery of specified objectives. Instructional management systems (IMS) must rely upon computer technology to handle the record keeping that is required for competency-based programs where large numbers of behavioral objectives are involved for each student. Each CMI program has its own design and capabilities. Some systems will provide reports for teachers and parents that list the objectives mastered by each learner over a given period of time. The CMI software automates the record keeping process and is a computerized version of a criterion-referenced system for instructional management. It is possible to customize a CMI program for the unique needs of a given institution or for the learning objectives of a given subject area. While the computer can manage certain elements of instruction, such a system should never be used as a complete instructional plan for all students. Many other instructional strategies and learning experiences such as discussions, experiments, discovery, peer learning, and manipulation of concrete objects, play important roles in the educational process. The computer is a tool to use in the process, but it does not absolve the instructor of the responsibility for planning instruction, delivering and evaluating instruction. However, the microcomputer can assist the instructor and the learner as they carry out their respective roles.

Drill and Practice. The easiest and most common form of computer-assisted instruction or computer-assisted learning is the provision of practice to reinforce a concept or skill. The microcomputer is programmed to provide the learner with a series of questions or exercises similar to those that might be found in a workbook. The problems or exercises that provide the learner with practice could include mathematics problems, estimating the size of an angle, identifying geometric shapes, identification codes, or diagramming sentences. Many of these "drill and practice" routines are available as commercially developed programs. However, the programming skills necessary to develop drill and practice routines is relatively simple for one who has learned a programming language and wishes to prepare their own drill and practice programs. Typically, the program begins with posing a problem, soliciting a response; the response is judged and feedback is given before the next problem is posed. More elaborate programs may begin with questions or a pretest to assess the prerequisite knowledge of the learner and then use that information to provide practice at the most appropriate level of complexity. Some programs maintain a record of student responses which are reported to the student and instructor at the end of the program. This record of performance serves as a basis for prescribing additional instruction.

For as long as there have been educational programs, there have been routines for memorizing. It is necessary for the learner to commit some things to memory, and repetition with understanding is an essential means by which associations can be strengthened and stored in long term memory. Teachers have long used mimeographed sheets of exercises, flash cards and memorization rituals which were quite difficult to individualize and provide in the proper amount to meet the needs of each student. Computer-based instruction, however, has the potential to identify through pretesting the areas in which students need practice.

The best drill and practice software possesses an interesting format which will encourage reuse by students. This reuse ensures mastery of the skill or the establishment of the stimulus-response association required for effective memorization. Any subject area can take advantage of drill and practice software. For example, computers can provide for vocabulary development wherein the computer displays a definition and the student types in the appropriate word. This process can be repeated until the association between words and the definitions are complete.

As drill and practice programs are selected or developed, the instructor should judge their appropriateness in terms of (1) their ease of use, (2) their adaptability to a variety of learner levels, (3) their level of interest for the learner, and (4) their educational validity.

Tutorial. Tutorial CAI functions much like a "private tutor" as it utilizes written explanations, descriptions, questions, problems and graphic illustrations. Effective tutorial programs resemble a dialogue between an experienced teacher and the student. In this regard, the program accomplishes the learning goals by guiding the student through questions from one concept to another until the student grasps the whole meaning of the lesson.

In the tutorial program, a question or problem is posed for the learner.

As the student responds, the computer provides the next learning experience based on the nature of the student's response. If the response is correct, the computer may move on to the next block of instruction. However, if the response is incorrect, the computer may select one of several possible remedial sets of instruction depending on the nature of the error made by the student. (See Figure 5-12.)

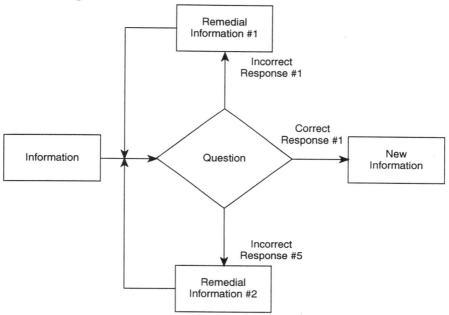

Figure 5-12. Tutorial CAI programs must anticipate all possible student responses.

As one might suspect, software of the tutorial type requires more complicated instructional design and programming techniques. The author of the tutorial program must predict all possible correct responses. The program must also respond intelligently to incorrect answers and offer specially tailored explanations and learning experiences for the most common incorrect answers. Many tutorial programs closely resemble programmed instruction with its frame-to-frame approach. Tutorial CAI usually breaks the material down into small digestible bits which require the student to make regular responses, checks those responses to be sure the student understands, and then customizes the next stage of instruction to meet the needs of the student.

Even though tutorial CAI does resemble the dialogue between an experienced teacher and the student, such programs can never replace the teacher. Tutorial programs are best considered as aids rather than teacher replacements. A good tutorial program requires an effective instructor if it is to be used properly. The effective instructor will identify those situations in which tutorial CAI can be most effective for a given learner involved with specific content and objectives to be achieved. Other factors to be considered are (1) student interest, (2) cost, (3) efficiency, and (4) appropriateness for learners of differing abilities.

Simulation and Problem Solving. Simulations for educational purposes allow students to experience situations which would be difficult or impossible to duplicate in a classroom setting. Specially designed simulators for flight training and for driver education have been available for years. However, the advent of the microcomputer provides a quick and economical means of providing students with variable sets of data from which the student may select certain options or risks and then witness the result of the decision. In some of the common examples, simulation programs for microcomputers allow the learner to describe the results of combining two or more variables and extending the potential results as the value of these variables is altered. For example, the program "Lemonade Stand," a famous simulation geared toward elementary school students, involves each child in decisions such as (1) what price to charge per glass of lemonade, (2) how many advertising signs should be made, and (3) how many glasses of lemonade should be prepared. In this simulation, each child begins with a small amount of money and supplies (assets). If too much is charged for the lemonade or too much lemonade is made, the lemonade stand owner will not sell enough lemonade to make a profit. Also, certain factors are beyond the learner's control. For example, the computer decides (by randomly selected number) whether the day will be clear, cloudy or rainy. The weather, therefore, is a chance variable which will influence the sale of lemonade. Perhaps the most beneficial aspect of such a simulation is involvement and participation of the learner. Even though the lemonade stand is imaginery, students do experience some of the feelings and problems associated with owning a business. They see the reasons for developing good business strategies, and as a result, they begin to think in a more organized fashion.

Simulations for the social sciences, natural science, and vocational subjects can be valuable learning devices when properly integrated into the curriculum at appropriate times. Simulations are most effective when they are used to illustrate and use certain skills, ideas and experiences that may have been first explored through other methods such as lectures, questioning, discussion, reading, etc.

Simulation programs offer the opportunity to experience "real world" problems without the associated risks such as a fatal crash, bankruptcy, or broken equipment. In addition, a well designed simulation can reduce radically the cost of instruction as well as compress the time needed for learning. Simulation aids transfer of learning as students who acquire a skill through simulation find it easier to transfer that skill to the real world than when training consists only of the traditional lecture and demonstration. The programs that teach procedures and processes have high transfer value.

Simulations are one of the most powerful instructional applications of computers, but they are also one of the most difficult to achieve. The programming is complex and time consuming, and as a result, a limited amount of effective simulation software is available. To be effective for instructional purposes, these programs must reflect accurately the processes they seek to simulate. As with any other type of instructional aid, the advantages and limitations must be considered. The factors which must be considered are (1) student interest, (2) economy, (3) safety, (4) realism, (5) effect on transfer, (6) development costs, (7) learning time, and (8) learner anxiety.

Microcomputers as an Instructor's Aide

One substantial part of an instructor's role is the management of data. Just as the personal computer has many home applications such as balancing checkbooks, keeping financial records, preparing tax forms, generating letters and other textual material, such as lists, appointments, etc., the microcomputer can assist the instructor in managing the professional world of words and numbers of which they are a part. While it is not the purpose of this section to enable the instructor to apply microcomputer technology to the several managerial and administrative functions carried out by instructors, this section is designed to acquaint instructors with the applicability of microcomputer technology as an aid in carrying out administrative and managerial functions such as (1) testing and grading, (2) filing, retrieving, and reporting, (3) attendance, (4) record keeping, (5) graphics, and (6) word processing.

Because of the time demands of the process, any instructor would like to have an aide who compiles and duplicates tests, scores them, records grades, and provides reports as needed. Unfortunately, most instructors do not have access to an assistant who can take care of many of the labor intensive tasks associated with testing and grading. However, the microcomputer can provide the needed assistance. Software is available to assist the instructor in managing these chores and many others.

Test Development. The development of achievement tests is a difficult and time consuming task. Effective instructors realize that they cannot give the same test items time after time and that it is desirable to have a number of different test items to assess the same content or objective. Over a period of time, a number of systems have been developed for instructors to accumulate test items that are evaluated in terms of their effectiveness, modified and combined in different ways to create several different test forms. Computer software is now available that allows an instructor to create a bank of test items classified under specified objectives within various units of the course. Likewise, the directions for different types of test items can be stored in the bank. The software program allows the selection and grouping of items by test category with the appropriate directions in order that a different form of the test can be generated. This ability to manipulate items and directions can save several hours each time the instructor develops a new test. In addition, the computer facilitates the systematic assessment of items and the recording of information relative to each item's strengths and limitations as discussed in Chapter 6.

Test Scoring and Analysis. Even though individual students can be tested via the computer as the student can respond to items displayed on the screen, most testing procedures require the test instrument to be in a paper format. Nevertheless, through the use of prepared answer sheets or cards, these answer sheets can be scored for the instructor. In addition, the items can be analyzed and appropriate information regarding the difficulty and the discrimination power of each item can be recorded for future use. In addition to indicating the number of right or wrong answers, the software program can provide for the calculation of the percent of correct responses or even the assignment of letter grades if these parameters are provided in the instructions.

Managing Grades. One of the more popular uses of microcomputers by instructors is to manage the grades assigned to students in each class. One primary advantage of maintaining an electronic record of each student's grades is that the stored data can be easily manipulated. Programs are available which provide the instructor quick access to the information needed to fill out reports and generate lists of students that are requested in the school setting. Programs of this type simulate an actual grade book, but the microcomputer provides far more flexible and useful capabilities than the traditional grade book. The instructor would begin by entering the names of students in each class. When entering a set of grades for a test, a quiz, homework, etc., the grades would be stored along with the appropriate student name. Weight values are usually assigned to each type of score so that a quiz, for example, might have a smaller weight in the final grade than a regular examination. With a special computational formula, the microcomputer can provide grade averages at any time during the year when the instructor or student might need to determine the achievement level. Other program features may include a report generating capability that summarizes the performance of individuals, a small group or the entire class. Statistical summaries are also available which show the mean, the standard deviation, and perhaps even a graphical representation of performance. As students enter or leave the class, the list can be alphabetized within the microcomputer so that the report that is generated can be realphabetized in seconds. Effective grade book programs will also allow the teacher to correct the data entering mistakes, enter grades for late assignments, and assign letter grades if the numerical parameters are provided in the instructions to the computer.

For the instructor who may have 4 to 6 groups of students with 25 to 50 students in a group, and 5 to 10 scores for each student, the number of entries and calculations needed to arrive at a grade for a given grading period is extremely time consuming. Therefore, microcomputer technology can be a real time saving for the instructor and the accuracy of the calculation functions can greatly reduce the number of errors and the necessity to verify calculations.

Filing, Retrieving and Reporting. A number of software programs are available which will enable the microcomputer to file information electronically on a diskette just as one might place pieces of paper in a file folder and store these folders in a filing cabinet. One such system, produced with the trade name PFS:FILE distributed by Software Publishing Corporation, works very much like a standard filing system but without the use of paper. The program permits the instructor to record, file and retrieve information in ways that are not really possible with the traditional system. Instructors can design forms to meet their own needs and then enter the specific information. The information can be retrieved from the format electronically in a matter of seconds. In addition to the PFS:FILE program, the system also has a PFS:REPORT program that permits the production of reports in the form of tables using the information stored in files. The PFS:REPORT program permits sorting on any information category in the file. For example, an alphabetical list of names and addresses could be sorted by zip code order. In addition, numeric data stored in the records could be manipulated to provide averages, totals and percents. Since this technology is changing rapidly, instructors should be alert to the availability of software packages that can best meet their needs.

Attendance. Attendance can be kept and reported through the use of grade book programs previously mentioned or the instructor may be a part of an entire school's computerized attendance reporting system. If, however, the instructor wishes to keep a separate attendance record, microcomputer programs are available for this purpose. If the school system requires that students provide excused absence forms signed by parents or physicians, this additional record keeping can be facilitated through the microcomputer with appropriate software. The real time saving feature is in the production of attendance reports for each class with categories of absences, excused absences, tardies, etc., which would be very laborious to produce by other means. The primary limitation to this type of system is the time involved to "input" the information to the microcomputer system in order to have it available to organize and report via the software program.

Resource Circulation. Many instructors have books, magazines, audio visual materials, tools, instruments or equipment that they loan to students or other staff members. A microcomputer can facilitate the record keeping of these kinds of items by using software, which keeps track of borrowed items, listing student or faculty member's name, title, author, catalog number or other descriptive information and the date when the item should be returned. Not only does this type of program simplify the record keeping arrangements, but it can print lists of materials that are overdue or any other type of list by item, by individual or by classification. Any instructor can benefit from this type of record keeping arrangement because it allows easy day-to-day tracking of the whereabouts of all borrowed material.

Graphics. Software programs are available which allow the display of data in the form of bar graphs, line graphs and pie charts in color or black and white. One such software program under the trade name PFS:GRAPH, allows the display of data in graph or chart form thus eliminating the tedious and time consuming drawing and labeling that one typically does to display data in two dimensional format. The PFS:GRAPH software enables the instructor to prepare graphs and charts and add labels or shift from one graph option to another easily and quickly. In addition to setting the format scaling, legend labeling automatically, PSF:GRAPH will also read data files from PFS:FILE or VisiCalc without reentry of data. There are a number of other graphic software packages available which should be investigated thoroughly in order to select the software that best meets the instructor's needs.

Word Processing. Word processing involves the generation of words on a computer screen which can be proofed, revised, printed and stored on a diskette. These word processing functions can involve a specific device referred to as a word processor which is a specialized set of hardware including a computer (mini, micro or mainframe), a screen or cathode ray tube, a keyboard, and a long-term memory device (usually a disk), and a printer. However, in most educational settings, the word processing functions are carried out on a standard microcomputer with specialized software. The microcomputer with one or two disk drives, the software package and printer can carry out the word processing functions and still be available for other instructional management/administrative functions.

When using the microcomputer as a word processor, the computer screen serves as the blank sheet of paper and the text is entered using the microcomputer keyboard. The first draft of a letter or report can take as much time to enter as it would take to type it on an electric typewriter. However, mistakes are corrected with the touch of a key rather than with an eraser, which, in and of itself, saves time and results in a better quality finished product. Most word processing programs allow for the insertion and deletion of letters, words, lines and even paragraphs with the touch of a few keys. This permits even those mistakes uncorrectable by normal typing methods to be easily accomplished with the microcomputer. Most word processing programs have a *word wrap* feature whereby the typist can enter long paragraphs without ever pressing the return key. The computer makes certain that no word exceeds the right hand margin and automatically brings words that are too lengthy down to the next line. This is a great time saver because hyphenation decisions need not be made, and the touch typist can concentrate on reading the material being typed. At intervals in the typing process, the user can save the copy by special command that places the copy on a diskette from which it can be recalled whenever needed in the future.

A word processing system is of little value unless a printer is available because the natural outcome has to be words printed on paper so that others can read the written material. For most applications, the dot matrix printer will serve adequately. However, when the output should resemble that provided by a regular electric typewriter, a letter quality printer is necessary. The real time saving with the word processing system results after an initial draft is prepared and the author wishes to make substantial revisions. No laborious retyping is required as the operator calls the original draft from the storage diskette and makes the appropriate deletions, insertions, or paragraph shifts as necessary. A second or third draft of a report can be generated where the only input required is for new information that is to be added to the report or substituted for lines or paragraphs that ought to be deleted.

Word processing allows letters to be personalized by changing the greeting and even some of the lines or paragraphs within a standard letter. The resulting letter generated for each individual will look as though it has been individually typed by a skilled typist. In addition to reports and letters, files of students' names, addresses or parents' names and addresses can be kept up-to-date quickly and easily. Labels can be printed which reduces much laborious typing or writing. As the instructor gains proficiency with the word processing operation, many different applications will come to mind as various needs become apparent to the instructor.

Just as word processing programs increase the value of the microcomputer to instructors, these programs would be equally beneficial to students as they prepare papers, reports, homework assignments, etc. With the increasing availability of personal computers in the home, their use by students for school work is increasing. Of course, there would be a considerable advantage if the home computer and that available at school are compatible so that the students can carry their work to school on a diskette and use the school printer to produce final copy. One final word of caution. If the instructor does not type by the touch system, it would be advisable to learn keyboarding skills before trying to use the word processing capabilities of the microcomputer. In the long run, the investment of the time to become proficient with the touch system of typing will pay substantial dividends.

Teacher Educator's Application

Many of the preceding applications of the microcomputer's application to the instructor's role would be applicable to the role and responsibility of an individual faculty member in a teacher education program. However, there are several role responsibilities that are somewhat unique to members of the faculty of a teacher education program for which the microcomputer can be especially helpful. To illustrate the applicability of a variety of software formats to the major categories of faculty responsibilities, Drs. Michael Dyrenfurth and F. M. Miller of the University of Missouri-Columbia developed the chart shown in Figure 5-13.

Computer Operations	Faculty Work Categories				
	Research	Service	Managing	Advising	Instructing

Word Processing
 	
• PFS: Write
• MP: Wordstar
    Spellstar
    Mailmerge
• MS: Word
	Proposal boilerplate, Articles	Transcription of dictation and letters	Transcription of dictation and letters	Standard letters	Updating of handouts, schedules and syllabi

Filing/Retrieving
 	
• PFS: File/Report
• MP: Infostar
    Datastar
    Reportstar
• FileMaker
	Bibliographic references	Committee rosters	Address file, Mailing lists	Student program records	Handouts, Test item banks

Calculating • Visi-Calc • Lotus 123 • Excel • Stat Pro	Proposal budgeting, Analyzing data		Completing travel form calculations, Budgeting	Projecting GPAs	Grade calculation and recording
Scheduling • LISA: Project • MacProject • Harvard Project Manager	Project planning		Project tracking and controlling	Charting degree program sequence	
Graphics • PFS: Graph • SuperPaint • FreeHand	Displaying results		Analyzing and presenting information		
Communication • ASCI-II Express • Z-Pro • White Knight	Entering data and control programs, Searching data bases	Electronic mail	Electronic mail		

Figure 5-13. Valuable microcomputer contributions to faculty productivity.

Beyond those major responsibilities for which microcomputer programs can be applied, the following list of responsibilities suggest other responsibilities of teacher educators for which the microcomputer can be of assistance.

- networking
- communications
- instruction
- electronic mail
- scheduling personal calendars
- PERT charting
- filing advisee records
- entering research data to mainframe computer
- prepare manuscripts
- tracking budgets
- organizing and indexing bibliographies
- assembling and accessing test item banks
- keeping address files
- generating customized form letters
- searching data bases
- checking spelling
- merging address and letter files
- transcribing, editing and final typing correspondence
- developing budget for proposals
- recording and grading student achievement
- updating syllabi and course handouts
- dialing telephone numbers
- presenting video-slide program visuals
- printing out from mainframe computer
- scheduling appointments
- presenting data in graphic format

As Professors Miller and Dyrenfurth have applied microcomputer technology to their work as faculty members, the following observations are offered to facilitate the work of anyone seeking to apply microcomputer technology to the job of the instructor.

1. Don't be concerned about having the latest hardware and software. Instead, be most concerned with utility and getting the most out of the hardware and software available to you.

2. Where two or more individuals within the same unit are utilizing microcomputer technology, there is great value in standardization of hardware

and software families. This will result in a considerable amount of savings in both time and fiscal resources.

3. Develop a microcomputer network that includes a local dealer, specialist in the campus computer center, and other microcomputer users outside your immediate technical specialty.

4. Software and hardware prices vary; therefore, whenever possible bundle software items with hardware purchases and realize savings in the process. Be a comparative shopper as prices are soft and negotiable.

5. Whenever possible, prepare a copy of a program so the master disk is retained on file.

CONCLUSION

Effective instruction requires the management of time, people, ideas, materials, and equipment. Instructors are called upon to make hundreds of decisions each day as they plan, deliver and evaluate instruction. Some of these decisions relate to the selection or development and use of instructional media technology to facilitate learning.

As revealed in this chapter, instructional media refer to the graphic, photographic, electronic or mechanical means for enhancing the transmission and reception of visual or verbal information. It is essential that instructors are knowledgeable of the various media materials available in order that appropriate materials can be selected to increase the effectiveness of teaching and learning. After the instructor has identified the content to be taught and the objectives to be achieved by learners, consideration can be given to media materials and associated technology which will maximize instructional effectiveness.

The media materials contain the essence of the content to be taught or the stimuli to be presented, e.g., words in audio or print form and visual images in photographic or illustration format. Although some instructional software is used directly with learners, e.g., photographs, posters, charts, books, most media materials require equipment, e.g., projectors, video tape playback units, audio cassette players, to make the software usable for instructional purposes. This equipment is often referred to as "hardware." The primary focus of media materials and associated equipment relates to the impact that they have upon student learning. In fact, the primary criterion for selecting media materials relates directly to the impact of a given medium upon the achievement of a given objective by the learner. However, it is important to recognize the value of media materials in attracting and holding attention and stimulating interest which also impacts significantly on the efficiency and effectiveness of learning. Even though the impact of a given medium upon student learning is the primary criterion, it is also important for the instructor to consider other criteria such as *appropriateness, technical quality, cost, availability, simplicity, flexibility,* and the *material's level of sophistication.* Although suggestions have been made regarding the appropriate use of each of the types of media materials presented in this chapter, there is no substitute for good judgment exhibited by the instructor. Only the instructor can know the variables involved in a given teaching/learning situation. The use of media materials must be consistent with content, the objectives, the background and experience of learners as well as the instructor's level of skill and experience. Not every technique can be used with equal effectiveness in all settings and by all instructors. However, effective decision making does depend upon an instructor who is knowledgeable of media materials and their potential for influencing learning as decisions are made in the instructional planning process.

Instructors have a continuing responsibility for their own professional development. As new developments occur in their fields of specialization, professional instructors should be quick to consider the implications for instructional content as well as the means through which instruction is delivered. Microcomputer technology and its applications to education are examples of the types of rapid technological advance of which instructors must keep abreast.

The innovative and effective instructor must look continuously for ways in which microcomputer technology can make teaching and learning more efficient and effective. There are many implications of microcomputer technology for the improvement of teaching and learning as well as the management of a myriad of job functions that must be carried out by the instructor. The purpose of this chapter is to broaden the instructor's horizon by increasing the level of sensitivity to microcomputer applications. To become competent in·the application of this technology to the various roles of the instructor will take an investment of time and energy. Because of the long term benefits in increased efficiency, the initial investment will pay substantial dividends. While it is not essential for instructors to become microcomputer programmers, there is much to be learned in terms of the proper utilization of existing program software in order to gain the maximum benefit from available software programs.

While the literature related to microcomputers focuses upon the application of microcomputer technology to instruction and student learning, it must be recognized that this technology has very limited use for large group instruction. Like other devices, there are strengths and limitations which must be taken into account. By understanding the strengths and limitations of microcomputer technology, the instructor can make appropriate decisions regarding the application of this technology to a given set of circumstances. The microcomputer is an especially effective tool for individualized instruction. At the present time, the primary limitation on microcomputer utilization is the limited availability of software programs in many subject areas and/or grade levels.

In addition to teaching/learning applications of microcomputers, this technology can be used very effectively to manage many of the information related functions that are inherent in the job of the instructor, e.g., testing, grading, filing, keeping attendance, preparing reports.

REFERENCES _____ 5

Atkinson, F. T., & Locatis, C. N. (1984). *Media and technology for education and training*. Columbus, OH: Charles E. Merrill Publishing Company.

Bittner, G., & Camuse, R. (1984). *Using a microcomputer in the classroom*. Reston, VA: Reston Publishing Company.

Bork, A. (1985). *Personal computers for education*. New York: Harper & Row.

Bowker, R. R. (Ed.) (1986). *Audio visual marketplace: A multimedia guide*. New York: R. R. Bowker Company (1180 Avenue of Americas, 10036).

Bowker, R. R. (Ed.) (1986). *Index to overhead transparencies*. New York: R. R. Bowker Company (1180 Avenue of Americas, 10036).

Gerlach, V. S., & Ely, D. P. (1980). *Teaching and media: A systematic approach*. Englewood Cliffs, NJ: Prentice-Hall, Inc.

Green, L. (1983). *Use your overhead*. Wheaton, IL: Victor Books.

Kemp, J., & Dayton, D. (1985). *Planning and producing instructional media*. New York: Harper & Row.

Minor, E., & Frye, H. R. (1977). *Techniques for producing visual instructional media*. New York: McGraw-Hill.

NICEM (1986). *Index to overhead transparencies: NICEM media index.* University Park, CA: University of Southern California, National Information Center for Educational Media, 90007.

Radin, S., & Lee, F. (1984). *Computers in the classroom: A survival guide for teachers.* Chicago: Science Research Associates.

Simonson, M. R., & Volker, R. P. (1984). Media planning and production. Columbus: Charles E. Merrill Publishing Company.

Thomas, J. L. (1982). *Nonprint production for students, teachers and media specialists.* Littleton, CO: Libraries Unlimited, Inc.

3M Visual Products (1984). *Teaching your overhead projector some new tricks.* St. Paul: 3 M Company.

3M Visual Products (1984). *How to create overhead projection transparencies that get attention.* St. Paul: 3M Company

University Consortium for Instructional Development and Technology, *Selecting Instructional Strategies and Media: A Place to Begin.*

Willis, J. W., Johnson, D. L., & Dixon, P. N. (1983). *Computers, teaching and learning: A guide to using computers in schools.* Beaverton, OR: Dilithium Press.

Wittich, W. A., & Schuller, C. F. (1973). *Instructional technology: Its nature and use.* New York: Harper & Row.

6

TESTING AND
EVALUATION

Written achievement tests and other measures of achievement are used to help determine the extent to which the student has learned at any point in the instructional process. They also are valuable in determining the learner's level of knowledge acquired over a longer period of time or they may be used prior to the course to determine the level at which instruction should be initiated. Indirectly, tests can indicate the level of instructional effectiveness. Tests can be effective either as daily or weekly quizzes or at certain other points in the course wherein they provide for review and emphasis. Following completion of a course, tests may help to measure the amount of information that has been retained and can be applied.

Written tests are valuable tools in the learning process, and few programs would be complete without them. However, even the best tests can measure only part of an individual's achievement or performance level. They can provide valuable information, but they never tell the whole story of an individual's development. No written test is capable of measuring all of the student's developmental changes which occur as a result of an educational experience. Written tests must be supplemented with performance tests, behavioral observations, attitude scales, and interest inventories to gain a clearer picture of a student's development.

Instructors must learn to use achievement tests properly, weigh test results carefully and combine test results with other evidence of progress and achievement for the best possible evaluation of each student's development.

Measurement is the systematic assessment of the magnitude of a trait or characteristic in quantitative terms. For example, it can be reported that a student answered 8 of 10 questions or received a rating of 16 on a scale used to assess performance when 20 represents a perfect performance. *Evaluation*, on the other hand, is a broader concept through which an instructor may take measurement results that vary in precision and add subjective assessments to arrive at as fair and accurate appraisal as professional judgment permits.

As the instructor engages in course and lesson planning, the development of a systematic plan for determining student achievement must be a part of the process. As indicated in Chapter 2, the student syllabus, which reveals the results of the instructor's course planning efforts, should contain a section which describes the instructor's plan for assessing achievement and assigning the course grade. Numerous decisions must be made as the effective instructor develops and implements an evaluation plan. The quality of the decision making will depend in large part on the instructor's understanding of fundamental concepts of evaluation and associated principles of measurement.

Purposes of Evaluation

Evaluation requires professional judgment regarding the adequacy of a student's knowledge, understanding, skills or attitudes. The purpose of evaluation is to make decisions regarding the student's progression, placement and/or a course grade. As the instructor engages in the evaluative process, several procedures and/or techniques will be used to obtain the data and information necessary for a sound evaluative judgment. Some of the data and information involved will be secured through a more precise measurement process whereby quantitative descriptions of each student's performance or behavior are secured. Test scores, grades on term papers, research reports, project ratings, and performance test results are a few of the types of measurements that might be taken to provide data and information used by the instructor in the evaluation process. An increasing demand for accountability in educational programming will increase the emphasis on measurement and evaluation procedures used in educational programs. The effective instructor will recognize accountability as an opportunity to demonstrate that the instructional program was well planned and well delivered.

Although the primary purpose of achievement tests is to ascertain the extent to which learning has taken place, well-constructed achievement tests can serve several other purposes in the teaching/learning process. Several of the more important purposes are to:

1. **Emphasize important content.** A test and the discussion that should follow may be used to review, summarize and emphasize the importance of certain facts, principles and procedures.

2. **Reveal areas of student weakness.** A test may identify those parts of the course on which the student should spend more time in study or practice. The test that requires student performance reveals clearly the need for more preparation.

3. **Identify weaknesses in instruction.** A test may reveal to the instructor certain areas that were not well taught or where another approach or more emphasis might be needed.

4. **Hold students accountable.** Tests often cause students to feel more responsible for learning. As a general rule, students make greater progress in a course when they know they will be tested over the content presented.

5. **Provide a basis for grades and advancement.** Tests are used to measure the extent to which students have learned in comparison with known standards and/or the performance of others in the group. From these comparisons combined with other assessments of the student's performance, a fair and significant evaluation can be obtained from which a grade can be derived. Student performance records can serve as a basis for classifying students and placing them in a program at the appropriate level. Student progress is clearly impeded when students lack prerequisite knowledge and skill.

Types of Evaluation

The focal point for this chapter is the assessment of student achievement. As previously indicated, this assessment may take several forms, some of which seek to describe achievement in rather precise quantitative terms, while other means are more subjective and judgmental. Regardless of the level of objectivity or subjectivity involved, it is important to understand the point of reference from which one judges the level of achievement as well as the purpose of the assessment.

Criterion-referenced. When an instructional program is directed toward student achievement of specific behavioral objectives, a logical question to be asked at the conclusion of the instruction is: "To what extent does the student exhibit the behavior specified in the objective?" Another way of phrasing the question is: "To what extent does the student exhibit the competency implied or specified in the behavioral objective?" Tests of knowledge, skills or attitudes that are formulated to answer these questions must contain certain criteria by which judgments can be made. Therefore, the assessment of student performance that is directly interpretable in terms of criteria or standards of performance is referred to as *criterion-referenced*.

Tests or other evaluative instruments that are criterion-referenced require specific standards for acceptable performance. These standards are set in terms of specifying a performance that either is or is not acceptable. Students whose test scores indicate that they have the ability to perform at or above the established standard are judged to pass and those who fail to perform at or above the acceptable level do not pass. Using this point of reference for assessment could result in all students passing, some of the students passing or none of the students passing, since "passing" is determined by the student's performance in relationship to a set criterion or standard and not by the performance of other students in the class.

Norm-referenced. Unlike criterion-referenced testing, *norm-referenced* assessment compares the performance of each student with other students. Even though the instruments used in assessing student performance may involve the same elements of knowledge, skill or attitudes, the basis for determining whether a student has "passed" or "not passed" is substantially different when norm-referencing is used than when criterion-referencing is used. Most achievement tests, aptitude tests, teacher ratings and course grades are based upon a norm-referenced approach to assessment. The focus of this type of assessment is upon the relationship of an individual's performance in comparison with other students in the group or some external norm group that is used as a frame of reference. The primary objective of this type of assessment is to separate students within the group in terms of some variable such as achievement. Therefore, the students are ranked from the high score to the low score, and decisions are made in terms of a course grade or progression on the basis of the individual student's performance compared with the performance of the group of students.

Formative Evaluation. When students are assessed to secure diagnostic measures of performance and when the results of these measures are used to influence or formulate instructional methods, content or objectives, the process is referred to as *formative evaluation*. When formative procedures are used, the purpose of the assessment is to identify inadequacies in terms of student skill, knowledge or attitudes that may have implications for the nature and extent of the instructional program. Likewise, such procedures could also identify competencies that students have mastered thus allowing the instructional process to be altered, thereby eliminating needless duplication. Assessment can also be used in a formative manner during the instructional process. Questions interjected during the instructional sequence may serve to highlight certain content or give the student an opportunity to test themselves and, as a result, clarify their own level of understanding. Students who have successful experience with short quizzes during the instructional sequence feel more positive toward learning because of the positive reinforcement. The key to formative evaluation is that the purpose of the assessment is to provide assistance to the learner by influencing the amount of content learned or the depth of understanding of the content being learned.

Summative Evaluation. The most common role for measurement and evaluation related to student learning is for the purpose of assessment at the conclusion of a course or sequence of instruction. This type of assessment is referred to as *summative*. The real purpose of summative evaluation is to ascertain the extent to which all students have achieved the established objectives for which the instructional program was designed. Used in this manner, *summative evaluation* is the "bottom line" or accountability assessment. This is the level of evaluation that communicates the level of competence possessed by a learner at the end of the instructional program.

Descriptive Statistics

In an effort to provide information to the students, parents and school officials regarding performance on tests, a number of procedures have been developed which help to explain the nature of a given score within the array of scores made by all members of a group. These procedures are referred to as descriptive statistics. Therefore, descriptive statistics describe the distribution of scores in terms of the extent to which they cluster together as well as the extent to which they tend to be different. The statistics that describe the tendency of scores to cluster together are referred to as "measures of central tendency" and include the concepts of mean, median and mode. The statistics which describe the manner in which scores tend to be different are referred to as "measures of dispersion" and refer to the concepts of range, percent, percentile, variance and standard deviation.

Measures of Central Tendency. The measures of central tendency are as follows:

1. Mean—The average score made by the group taking a given test. The scores made by the students on a given test are added together and the sum of these scores is divided by the number of students who took the test.

2. Median—The median represents the middle score in an array of scores listed from the lowest to the highest.

3. Mode—In an array of scores on a given test, the score that is made by the largest number of students is referred to as the mode.

To illustrate the application of these measures of central tendency, a score distribution with some of the associated statistics is shown in Figure 6-1. This figure represents a frequency distribution of scores on a 30-item test. A review of the frequency distribution will reveal that 30 students took the test. In statistical terms, this is referred to as N = 30. The tallies shown under the "frequency" column reveal the number of students who earned each of the scores between 3 and 30. The distribution indicates that 2 students received scores of 30, 3 students had scores of 27, 3 students had scores of 24, and so on. This frequency distribution reveals the frequency with which each score appeared in the actual distribution. Since the mean score was only slightly above the mid point, it might be concluded that the test was too difficult. However, since five students scored 90 percent or better and the scores were spread well, it appears that the test did discriminate among the students. This means that the test items were at various difficulty levels.

Measures of Dispersion. While measures of central tendency tend to look at scores as they are clustered together, the measures of dispersion are used to study the distribution of scores. The simplest distribution statistic is

Scores	Tally	Frequency	
30	//	2	
27	///	3	
24	///	3	Mean $= \dfrac{\text{Sum of Scores}}{\text{Number of Scores}} = \dfrac{570}{30} = 19$
21	++++ ///	8	
18	////	4	
15	////	4	Median = Middle Score = 21
12	///	3	
9	//	2	Mode = Most Frequent Score = 21
3	/	1	
Σ = 570		N = 30	

Figure 6-1. The mean, median, and mode are measures of central tendency.

the *range* which describes the dispersion of scores from the lowest score through the highest score. Taken in conjunction with a measure of central tendency, the range provides important information for interpreting test results. For illustration purposes, consider the performance of students on a test with 150 possible points. The mean score for each class is 100. However, the classes are very different as one class had a range from 65 to 147 while the second class had a range from 89 to 108. In addition to the range, several other measures of dispersion used to describe test data are as follows:

1. Percentages—Raw scores can be converted into percent by dividing the number of points in the test into each student's score. If the instructor uses a standard percent as the basis for assigning letter grades, the percent may be more meaningful to the student than the raw score.

2. Percentile score—Conversion of raw scores into percentile scores involves computing the percent of scores in the total distribution that are lower than a given student's score. For example, the 50th percentile is roughly equivalent to the median score. Fifty percent of the scores in the distribution are higher than the median, and 49 percent are below the median. Therefore, a score that is at the 75th percentile is lower than only 25 percent of the scores in the distribution and higher than 74 percent of the scores. Therefore, percentile scores not only allow the ranking of students, but also provide more specific information about the exact placement of a given student relative to other students and to the range of scores as a whole.

3. Ranking— One of the simplest ways to differentiate students is to rank the students from lowest to highest.

4. Variance—The variance is the average of the squares of the differences between each of the individual scores and the mean of the distribution. The variance can be calculated by first figuring the mean score for the distribution of test scores. Then, each individual score must be compared with the mean. This difference between the mean and the individual score is then squared. The sum of all of these squared differences is divided by the number of scores in the group. Distributions that have many scores close to the mean will have a small amount of variance. Likewise, distributions with many scores that are considerably different from the mean would have a large variance. The size of the variance, therefore, depends directly on the percent of scores that differ from the mean and the magnitude of those differences.

5. Standard Deviation—Another measure of dispersion is the standard deviation which is calculated from the variance. In fact, the standard deviation, by definition, is the square root of the variance. Therefore, variance and standard deviation are both measures of the degree to which scores

are dispersed from the mean rather than similar to the mean. The larger the variance and the resulting standard deviation, the greater the degree of dispersion of scores from the mean.

Normal Distribution. As a result of a substantial amount of research and observation over a long period of time, it has been found that many human characteristics and traits follow a distribution pattern that has been called a "normal" or "bell-shaped" curve. For example, if one were to record the height or weight of a sample of 100 males or females, the distribution of results would reveal a pattern like Figure 6-2 in which the largest number of individuals with the same height would be at the midpoint of the distribution with about the same number of individuals who are either shorter or taller than the height of the largest group of individuals within this sample. As described in Chapter 3, the attribute of intelligence is distributed normally with the largest number of individuals having an IQ score of 100 and an equal number of individuals having scores less than or more than 100.

It is very important for instructors to understand that this phenomenon of "normality" holds true for characteristics, traits and attributes as they occur in nature; and when measures are taken from a large sample of indi-

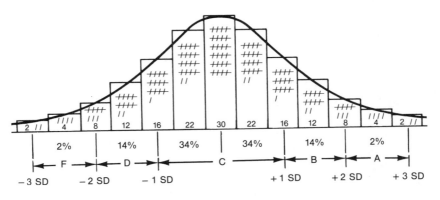

Figure 6-2. Test scores can be graphed as a histogram under a curve of normal distribution with pecentages and standard deviations.

viduals, that represents the total population. Most subgroups with which instructors deal are seldom large enough or sufficiently representative of a "normal" group to approximate a normal curve on any characteristic trait or attribute measured. This observation would be especially true for achievement test scores for groups of students at the post-secondary and adult levels since the educational process causes students at the upper levels to be increasingly homogeneous and less likely to be representative of the "normal" population.

Unfortunately, a little knowledge can be a dangerous thing, and as a result, instructors have applied the normal curve of distribution to achievement test scores. Such an inappropriate application would arbitrarily assign a C grade to 34 percent of the students who scored above the mean and 34 percent of the students who scored below the mean. The grade of B would be assigned to students who scored between 34 percent and 48 percent above the mean. Likewise, a D grade would be assigned to students who scored between 34 percent and 48 percent below the mean. This would leave the top 2 percent who would receive an A grade and the bottom 2 percent who would receive an F grade. While this mathematical approach to the assignment of grades may appear to be very objective, it is based on too many unwarranted assumptions that cannot be justified.

As difficult as it may be, the most defensible scheme of assigning grades from an array of scores is to decide on the level of performance or standard judged most appropriate for the different levels of grading and assign a letter grade to that standard. With this system, when the students achieve the standards, they receive the grade. It is theoretically possible for all students to achieve the highest standard; and, therefore, every student in the class could receive a grade of A. The system of assigning grades will be discussed in more detail later in this chapter.

ACHIEVEMENT TESTING

Good tests are valuable and necessary measuring instruments, but poor tests may be worse than none at all. Tests that measure the wrong things or that measure the right things inaccurately or inconsistently may actually detract from the instructional program and discourage students. The fundamental purpose of achievement tests is to ascertain the extent to which students have met the objectives of instruction. These objectives may be in terms of the cognitive domain, the psychomotor domain or the affective domain. Depending on the nature of the behavior to be observed, different types of instruments may be required to secure an assessment of the extent to which objectives have been met.

Since a given student's behavior cannot be observed on a continuous basis over a sustained period of time, the assessment of competence is usually done on a sampling basis. In other words, assessments are taken several times during the course, and it is assumed that the student's performance at each of those points in time, when averaged, represent the student's level of competence. Likewise, when achievement in the cognitive domain is being assessed, it is impractical to assess every item of content to which the student has been exposed. Therefore, a compromise is made and the instructor develops a test which, in reality, samples the knowledge or information that the student has acquired. If, indeed, the sample that is taken does represent the student's level of knowledge, the test is said to be a reasonable assessment of the student's knowledge. If the instructor does not do an effective job of sampling, the assumptions made about the student's level of knowledge or competence could be erroneous.

Hundreds of types of tests and other measuring instruments have been designed. These, however, can be grouped as follows:

1. *Oral questions* which are used primarily as a spot check of students' understanding of concepts at the time they are taught as a part of the formative evaluation process.

2. *Written tests* are most useful for measuring students' information about and understanding of facts, principles, and procedures. Written tests can be based on both knowing, doing, and attitudinal content. (Cognitive, psychomotor or affective).

3. *Performance tests* require students to demonstrate all or part of a procedure. Performance tests are based primarily on the doing or elements.

4. *Observation of students at work* is a vital part of the educational program wherever practical application of learning is an objective. Rating scales can be prepared that list the essential criteria to be used in making the judgments in a more objective way.

Evaluating Achievement by Observation

Direct observation of students as they carry out their assignments and work with other students in the class can provide an assessment of achievement not available by other means. It is rarely possible to evaluate student achievement on the basis of written and performance tests alone. This type of assessment can, at best, represent only samples of achievement. Certain attitudes, work habits and creative abilities can be assessed best by observing the students at work in typical situations. Such observations should not be done in a careless fashion. Both the instructor and the student should know the characteristics being observed and the standards being used to make judgments. When observing, the instructor should look for certain specific behaviors at each level of achievement. Figure 6–3 shows both sides of a 5" X 8" card designed to assist in evaluating students in a specific course.

	PARTICIPATION	CARE AND USE OF TOOLS	WORK PROCEDURE
ABOVE AVERAGE 3	Makes an effort to learn Always industrious Always prompt in starting to work Always cooperates with others Solves all problems	Repairs and replaces tools Conserves materials and supplies Excellent selection and use of tools for specific job	Always follows standard procedure Always follows safety precautions Always has organized plan for the work Always exceeds requirements
AVERAGE 2	Shows average effort to learn Works well with little special attention Usually prompt in starting to work Usually cooperates with others Solves some problems	Generally careful with tools Generally careful with materials and supplies Generally correct selection and use of tools for specific job	Usually follows standard procedure Usually follows safety precautions Shows some plan and organization for working Usually meets requirements
BELOW AVERAGE 1	Puts forth very little effort to learn Wastes time and bothers others Usually slow in starting to work Seldom cooperates with others Unable to solve problems	Continually misplaces and breaks or dulls tools Wasteful of materials and supplies Incorrect selection and use of tools for specific job	Seldom follows standard procedure Seldom follows safety precautions Disorganized Always behind in work Low quality of work Seldom meets requirements

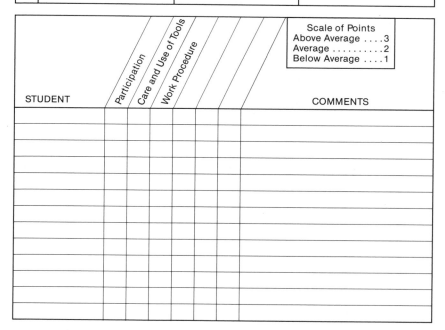

Front and Back of a Student Evaluation Card

Figure 6-3. Obseravation checklists are used by the instructor to make a fair and consistent evaluation of student progress.

Observation checklists are used to establish standards and as an aid to the instructor who seeks to make a fair and consistent appraisal of student progress. Observations should be made at predetermined points in the course, and a written record should be kept.

Characteristics of Performance Tests

If the objectives to be assessed relate to the student's performance of a task or the application of knowledge which involves some type of physical act, performance tests would be most appropriate. If the objective to be assessed were related to knowledge, basic concepts or information, some type of written test rather than a performance test would be used.

The performance test rates high in terms of its validity since it is a direct assessment of the individual's competence. If the performance test is constructed systematically and is properly administered, it also can have a high degree of reliability. Performance tests can be designed to measure a student's skill on such operations as:

1. Developing an outline.

2. Using proofreader notations.

3. Use of calculator for basic arithmatic functions.

4. Reciting a poem.

5. Reading a map.

In the development of a performance test, the instructor must identify and describe the standards or criteria against which the student's performance will be judged. There are a number of factors which the instructor must consider in developing and administering the performance test. Some of these factors are as follows:

1. Accuracy in following the proper steps of procedure.

2. Speed at which the task can be completed properly.

3. Quality of the completed task.

4. Consideration of safety precautions.

5. Written instructions should be available so that students will know exactly what they are to do and when they are to be observed. If a time limit exists, this should be known.

6. All necessary tools and materials must be available and in good condition. The student should be allowed to perform the operation or task without interruption except where the violation of a safety practice might be detrimental to the student, to others, or the equipment.

In developing the performance test, it is suggested that the instructor perform the operation or task and double check the appropriateness of the criteria, steps of procedure and standards by which judgments will be made.

Characteristics of Written Tests

The assessment of the extent to which students have achieved objectives that relate to cognitive behavior is typically accomplished through written achievement tests. Even though good judgment is at a premium in the development of effective tests, there are certain principles of test construction that need to be understood by instructors as they seek to develop effective achievement tests. For example, it is important that instructors recognize that they cannot test every possible element of content at any one point in time. As a result, a written test typically samples the content to which the student has been exposed. There is a practical limit to the number of test items that can be completed by students within a standard class period. Therefore, questions must be asked regarding the extent to which the sample of questions chosen will result in a true measure of the student's level of competence.

The instructor must ask the question "What skills and knowledges are essential for the student to meet the objectives of the lesson or course for which the examination is designed?" Each test item should be evaluated to make certain that it measures essential knowledge and skill. There is a tendency to measure those elements of content that are easy to measure. The effective instructor must be certain that all elements of important content are tested. In other words, does the test give the appropriate emphasis to the content covered in the course? Obviously, the greatest number of items in the test should be directed to the most important elements of the course. Tests should be neither too easy nor too difficult. Normally, some students should get a high score, but the test should not be so easy that everyone gets a high score. The mastery test is one exception to this general guide. If the test covers dangerous and critical operations on which no mistakes can be allowed, instructors are justified in "drilling" on this operation until everyone can pass the test with a perfect score. When teaching or testing for mastery, time must be a variable. The only appropriate grade would be pass or not yet pass. Because of individual differences, some learners may take much longer to reach the specified level of mastery than others.

As the instructor makes decisions related to the development of a test, it is important to consider such factors as validity, reliability, objectivity, comprehensiveness and practicality.

Validity

Validity, the most important characteristic of a good test, means the test measures what the instructor wants it to measure as determined by the course objectives. If the test measures elements other than those consistent with the objectives, instructors can never be sure what they have measured. Test validity can be increased by applying the following guidelines:

1. Include questions which cover important theories, facts, and procedures presented in class. Keep course objectives in mind.

2. Do not include questions that are so general in nature that students can determine the answer with little or no knowledge about the specific subject.

3. Make test items consistent with students' reading abilities. If a student knows the answer but fails to respond properly because of an inability to read and understand the question, the validity of the test question is weakened. Test items using illustrations and photographs may be more valid for certain technical content depending on the student's reading level.

4. Keep tests free of insignificant information.

5. Avoid tests overemphasizing a learner's ability to memorize facts. This is a common weakness in many tests. The ability to use and apply facts and principles gives a more valid measure of achievement.

The most practical approach to determine validity is to analyze and judge each test item or question to ensure that it reveals a student's actual achievement in the course. After the test has been administered, validity can be judged by comparing the test results with other indications of the student's progress. If a student is an outstanding performer in class, but does poorly on a written test, perhaps the test contains items of questionable validity.

Reliability

Reliability is the consistency of a test as a measuring instrument. In developing a test, reliability can be increased by using the following guidelines:

1. Provide clear test directions for answering each type of item in the test.

2. Reduce or eliminate complicated, ambiguous, vague, and confusing questions that encourage guessing.

3. Increase the length of the test, thus reducing the chance of students guessing correct answers. Students have a better chance of guessing all items correct on a 5-item test than they have on guessing all items correct on a 50-item test.

Objectivity

Objectivity refers to tests that can be scored by different instructors with equal results. When creative achievement is to be measured, for example, in writing and design courses, objective tests must be supplemented by other more subjective assessment procedures. When subjectivity enters into the assessment process, the instructor must use written criteria and a numerical scale to record judgments.

Comprehensiveness

A good test samples all parts of a lesson, unit, or course for which the test is designed. A test is *comprehensive* if a proportionate number of test items are developed from several areas of study being assessed. The more comprehensive the test, the greater its content validity and reliability.

Practicality

A test is practical if it is easy to administer, read, understand and score objectively. A test is easy to administer if the instructions to students are clear and concise. Type size and legibility, quality of paper, arrangement of the items, and use of illustrations are all contributing factors. In addition, the test must provide students with adequate time to consider each item.

Test Construction

As previously indicated, written tests are developed primarily to assess the extent to which students have achieved in relation to cognitive objectives specified for the lesson, unit or course. Even when instructors do not specify student objectives in precise terms, there is still a delineation of course content that the student is expected to learn. In addition to the direct assessment of cognitive behaviors or content, written tests also serve as indirect indicators of the extent to which the students have acquired selected psychomotor and affective behaviors.

Test Length and Coverage. As a practical matter, the instructor is constrained in the development of written tests by the length of the class period in which the test is to be administered. There are a number of variables that must be considered as one attempts to match test length to the period of time available. For example, a student can respond more quickly to single sentence true/false items than multiple choice items. Completion items that include long sentences with several omitted words are much more time consuming than short sentences with a single word omitted. Short answer items that require two or three sentences or a short paragraph as a response require more time on the part of the student than most other objective test items. In addition, such factors as student reading ability and intelligence will also affect the length of time required for students to respond to test items. The inexperienced instructor might use the generalization of "two objective items per minute" and then vary this generalization as other factors are considered such as sentence length, use of short essay items, ability level of group, etc. After the instructor gives several examinations, experience will provide a substantial amount of insight regarding test length.

Regardless of the time available for testing, a test will typically include items that only sample the content and objectives of the unit covered. Therefore, decisions have to be made about the nature of the test sample. This problem is most obvious for mid-term and final examinations, but it is also a significant factor for unit and periodic examinations as well.

If all of the unit or course objectives are important, the test should sample from the full range of objectives and content covered. Even though the number of items in each area will, by necessity, have to be limited, it is important that the test be comprehensive. There should also be a relationship between the number of test items and the various areas of content being tested. Those areas considered to be most important should have more test items than those elements of content judged to be of lesser importance.

Effective instructors plan tests just as they plan for instruction. Even though testing is acknowledged to be a sampling process, it is important that the sampling is done systematically with as many items as possible within the time constraints of the testing period.

In addition to the factors of time and the distribution of test items appropriately among the objectives and/or course content, instructors must also give attention to the levels of learning expected of students in the course. For example, if the test deals with cognitive content, it is important for the instructor to decide on the levels of cognition included in the instructional program in order to make the test parallel to the levels of cognition emphasized in instruction. It might be helpful to refer to Chapter 2 where Bloom's Taxonomy of Educational Objectives emphasizes the levels of knowledge, comprehension, application, analysis, synthesis, and evaluation. If the unit or course emphasized psychomotor learning and affective learning, the instructor might also want to be certain that the written test gives some indirect attention to the psychomotor and affective areas of learning as well.

Tables of Specifications. A systematic method of developing a test that is comprehensive, representative of the various content areas or objectives, and emphasizes the desired levels of learning established by the instructor involves the use of a *table of specifications*. This device provides a way for the instructor to structure the decision making that is involved in developing an appropriate examination. Decisions related to the inclusion of test items

CONTENT AREA TO BE TESTED	(1) Emphasis in Percent	(2) Number of Items	Recall of Facts 10%	Recognition 30%	Application 40%	Synthesis 20%	Actual Number of Items	Total Percent
1. Principles of learning	10%	8	1	3	3	2	9	11.25
2. Selecting and organizing content	30%	24	3	8	9	5	25	31.25
3. Instructional aids and devices	15%	12	1	3	4	2	10	12.50
4. Developing and using instructional material	20%	16	2	4	6	3	15	18.75
5. Measuring and evaluating achievement	25%	20	2	6	9	4	21	26.25
TOTAL	100%	80	9	24	31	16	80	100.00
PERCENT	—	—	11.25	30.0	38.75	20.0	—	100.00

Figure 6-4. A table of specifications provides a systematic method of developing a test that is representative of the course objectives.

are made by all instructors, either on purpose or by default. The effective instructor makes these decisions on purpose in a systematic and rational way. The table of specifications is a means of accomplishing this end. Even though there is no absolute format, an example is provided in Figure 6-4, which is a typical example with objectives or content areas written on the left-hand side of the table. The first column marked (1) provides an opportunity for the instructor to decide the percent of emphasis or the amount of weight to be given to each objective or content area. The second column marked (2) can be used to specify the number of items needed to provide the amount of emphasis desired. For example, if an 80-point examination is planned and 10 percent emphasis is desired for a given objective or content area, the number of items entered in column (2) would be 8. The next three or more columns are used to specify the extent to which the items chosen should measure the student's ability to recall, recognize, synthesize, apply or any other level of learning desired.

The last two columns are not completed until all selections have been made. In essence, they are the "reality" columns and reveal the decisions that have been made on the basis of the guidelines provided by the other columns in the table. As a result of the fact that some items may yield more than a single point, and the use of percents may yield parts of some items, the examination will not always yield the exact percent and number of items initially planned in the specifications, thus the need for the last two columns.

Application of the Table of Specifications. Developing the written test based on the parameters established in a table of specifications requires that test items be developed or will be developed before the test can be prepared from a table of specifications. The process will be described as if test items have been prepared for the instructor's use. The next section of this chapter will present detailed information about the construction of test items and the establishment of an item bank from which selections can be made. Each item may be recorded on an index card.

The following steps are suggested in constructing a written achievement test after the *table of specifications* has been prepared:

1. Take all multiple choice item cards that relate to a given objective, content area or unit and select those that are appropriate for the test.

2. Review the selected cards and eliminate the least desirable questions in order to get the proper or desired number of questions.

3. Repeat this process for the other types of items to be used.

4. Arrange the cards at random, in the order of difficulty or in any way desired.

5. Add a heading card for the test and a direction card for each type of item.

6. Have the test typed, if possible; make out the answer sheet; and refile the cards. The fact that the items are already typed and in good order will aid in the final preparation of the test.

The method of selecting and filing questions facilitates keeping tests up to date. As they can be changed easily, there is less tendency to use tests which do not fit the lesson, unit or course. As a result of the relatively large number of items on file, the cards may be used for review purposes and special on-the-spot examinations without repeating the use of an item in later tests. As new test material becomes available, the file can easily be improved by the addition of new items. Here are some further suggestions in constructing the written achievement test:

1. Use no more than four or five different types of items.

2. Include some reasonably easy items and some more difficult ones.

3. Arrange the items of each type together in the order of difficulty, starting with the easier items.

4. Organize the items so that scoring is simple, rapid and accurate.

5. Consider using answer sheets.

6. Prepare clear and precise directions for the student.

7. If at all possible, try out the test on other instructors before giving it in its final form to the group for whom the test was constructed.

8. Check with other instructors and specialists on every phase of test construction.

Developing Test Items

For written achievement tests, the types of items that have common and useful applications are the (1) true/false, (2) completion, (3) multiple choice, (4) identification, (5) matching, and (6) short answer essay. To assist the instructor in preparing appropriate items, a section with examples and instructions for each type of item has been developed. It should be observed that the term "question" is not to be used indiscriminately since the more appropriate term is *test item*. The term *question* is appropriate only when it is a direct interrogative expression followed by a "question mark".

True-False. A *true-false item* is a single statement that is either true or false. True-false items are useful when large amounts of information should be tested in a short period of time. True-false items are less reliable than other test items because there is more chance for student guessing. True-false items also tend to measure memory rather than understanding or application. A test composed entirely of true-false items should contain at least 50 items. The more items in the instrument the less chance the student has of guessing a high percentage of the answers. The following are suggestions for writing true-false items:

1. Be sure statements are either completely true or completely false. Do not include items that are part true and part false unless the directions specify that the item must be entirely true to be marked true.

2. Make approximately 50% of the items true and 50% false. Randomly mix items so no pattern of response exists.

3. Keep the language simple.

4. Make the test items as short as possible.

5. Use only test items covering important material emphasized in the objectives.

6. Avoid words that may help students guess the right answer. Words such as always, usually, none, and only should be used with caution.

7. Do not write the true statements consistently longer or shorter than false statements.

8. Avoid using sentences directly from the text. See Figure 6-5.

Advantages of using true-false test items are that they (1) can be used to assess a wide range of content, (2) are easy to score, and (3) are simple to develop. Disadvantages of using true-false test items are (1) students have a 50% chance of guessing correct answers, (2) they may measure students' reading abilities rather than knowledge of subject matter, and (3) the items may be low in reliability.

Directions: The following statements are true or false. If a statement is true, circle the T at the left. If the statement is false, circle the F at the left and explain why it is false.

T   Ⓕ   Istanbul is the capital city of Türkiye.

Explanation:_____

_____

_____

Ⓣ   F   The present perfect tense is used to express an action or state which began in the past and continues in the present.

Explanation: _____

_____

_____

Ⓣ   F   There is no gender in the Türkish language.

Explanation: _____

_____

_____

Figure 6-5. Some true-false test items require an explanation for all false responses.

Completion. *Completion test items* measure the student's ability to recall exact words or facts, such as technical terms, dates, formulas, or exact specifications. A completion item is a true statement in which blank spaces are inserted in place of one or two important words that have been omitted. The student must write the proper word in the blank or on an answer sheet.

The following are suggestions for writing completion items:

1. Write a number of short statements covering the most important information in the unit or course.

2. Review these statements and omit one or two important words. Make sure the meaning of the sentence is clear after the words are omitted.

3. Omit only words that call for specific information. Make sure only one word is correct; if there is more than one possible word, give credit for all correct answers.

4. Make all blanks the same length to avoid clues regarding the length of correct answers.

5. Omit only those words that test the student's knowledge of specific content learned during instruction, not items of general knowledge. Do not omit the statement's verb and do not provide clues by using articles such as *a, an,* or *the.*

6. Number each blank space and provide a space for answers on a separate answer sheet that has corresponding numbers or in blank spaces along the left margin of the test sheet. See Figure 6-6.

Completion test items may be in the form of a question as well as an incomplete statement.

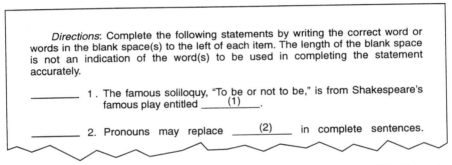

Figure 6-6. Completion test items measure a student's ability to recall facts, such as technical terms, dates, formulas, or exact specifications.

Advantages of using completion test items are (1) there is little chance to guess correct answers, and (2) they are good when students must remember specific facts, words, or symbols. Disadvantages of completion test items are (1) they measure memory rather than judgment, and (2) it is difficult to develop items that call for only one correct answer.

Multiple Choice. A *multiple choice test item* is a statement followed by a series of alternatives, all of which are plausible but only one of which is correct. The multiple choice item is designed to test for facts. See Figure 6-7. The following are suggestions for writing multiple choice test items:

1. Include the correct response and at least three alternatives (distractors) for each test item.

2. Include only plausible alternatives.

3. Provide appropriate space for responses on the test or on a separate response sheet.

4. Include as much of the test item as possible in the first part of the statement. Make the alternatives as short as possible.

5. Avoid test items on trivial facts.

6. Measure only content that has been taught.

7. Use diagrams, drawings, and pictures when necessary.

8. Avoid the use of *a* or *an* as the final word in the introductory statement.

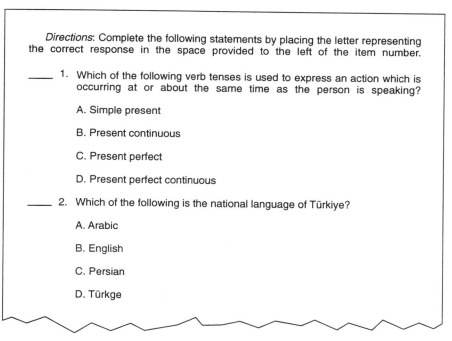

Directions: Complete the following statements by placing the letter representing the correct response in the space provided to the left of the item number.

_____ 1. Which of the following verb tenses is used to express an action which is occurring at or about the same time as the person is speaking?

    A. Simple present

    B. Present continuous

    C. Present perfect

    D. Present perfect continuous

_____ 2. Which of the following is the national language of Türkiye?

    A. Arabic

    B. English

    C. Persian

    D. Türkge

Figure 6-7. A multiple choice test item is a statement followed by a series of plausible alternatifves and one correct response.

The advantages of using multiple choice items include (1) there is little chance of guessing correct answers, however, if plausible alternatives are not provided, a multiple choice item is easily reduced to a true–false item, (2) objective scoring is facilitated, (3) they may be designed to measure judgment as well as memory, (4) they can be altered to test many types of subject matter, and (5) they can test for a lot of material in minimum time.

Disadvantages of using multiple choice items include (1) it is difficult to construct items that measure judgment, (2) an instructor may be measuring a student's reading ability rather than knowledge, (3) the questions often provide trivial distractors, and (4) multiple choice are the most difficult and time consuming items to write.

Matching. *Matching test items* consist of two columns of related information. For example, one column may be names of famous poets and the second column may be titles of poems or famous lines from the poems. The student matches the name with the appropriate title or line. This type of item is highly discriminating where exact information is required. See Figure 6-8.

The following are suggestions for writing matching items:

1. Use at least five, but no more than 15 items in each matching set.

2. Include no more than three items in the column of alternatives (second column) than in the column of statements.

3. Include homogenous information in matching lists. Place numbers and dates in ascending or descending order, and arrange names in alphabetical order.

4. Each item should be used only once.

5. Place the entire matching list on the same page.

Directions: Select the correct response from Column II and place the corresponding letter in the appropriate blank in Column I.

Column I   Column II

Abbreviation   *Complete Title or Phrase*
_D_ 1. AAUP   A.   Better Business Commerce
                         B.   British Broadcasting Corporation
_B_ 2. BBC   C.   Federal Deposit Insurance Corporation
                         D.   American Association of University Professors
_G_ 3. COD   E.   American Association Union Pacific
                         F.   Certified Public Accountant
_F_ 4. CPA   G.   Cash on Delivery
                         H.   Federal Directorate Industry Claims
_C_ 5. FDIC

Figure 6-8. Matching test items require students to match one set of information with a corresponding set of information.

Advantages of selecting matching test items are that large numbers of responses can be obtained in a short period of time and with minimum student writing. Matching items are objective and discriminating. Disadvantages result because matching test items are not the best method for measuring complete understanding of information, and they are difficult to construct properly.

Short Answer Essay. A *short answer essay item* requires a student to respond to a test item in sentence and paragraph form. See Figure 6-9. Short answer essay items have value in measuring a student's general understanding of a subject. Like full-length essay items, short answer essay items are difficult to grade objectively, time-consuming for instructors to read, and may encourage excessive verbalizing on the student's part. Therefore, an instructor seldom prepares an entire test composed of essay items.

The following are suggestions for preparing and scoring essay items:

1. Ask for specific information that can be given in a short paragraph. Decide what will be accepted as a correct response and determine the value for full or partial responses.

2. Make sure the item is clear and that the student knows what is expected.

3. Require the student to explain, describe, or provide reasons for the response.

Directions: Respond to the following items as briefly as possible. Use complete sentences and make your replies clear and direct.

1. Describe the conditions that spawn tornadoes.

Figure 6-9. An essay test item measures a student's comprehension of a subject.

Advantages of the short answer essay test item include that they (1) are easy to develop, (2) provide students with an opportunity to organize and express ideas, (3) provide the best indication of students' overall knowledge of certain subjects, and (4) measure written communication skills. The disadvantages of the short answer essay item are that they (1) may measure students' communication skills rather than knowledge of the subject, (2) are difficult to grade objectively, (3) measure a limited number of objectives in a specific time period, and (4) may encourage excessive verbalizing.

Before scoring essay examinations, conceal students' names so their identity is unknown during the grading process. Read and grade one item on all test papers before proceeding to the next item. This process gives the instructor an overview of the average quality of responses and provides a basis for assigning scores. Some instructors write the expected response for each test item prior to scoring, and assign a proper weight to each response by giving points for significant subject matter described properly by the student.

Item Bank. Use index cards of different colors for the various types of items; for example, salmon for true-false, yellow for completion, blue for multiple choice, and so on. Use 3X5" cards for those items which do not require large drawings, etc., and 5X8" cards for those items which require more space.

Use a *standard heading* for each card so that the card may be replaced properly when removed from the file. The heading makes it possible for others to use the file intelligently and keep it in order.

The sources and page number(s) provide a record of instructional materials being covered. This is valuable as a reference when the test item is being discussed by students.

Write out items of each type on cards of the color selected. For items that make use of drawings, use the 5X8" cards, allowing a margin of one-half inch on each side of the drawing as a seven-inch space is the effective width of stencils or masters used for reproduction on 8 1/2X11" paper. As new test items become available or are written for a course, add them to the file.

Several methods of filing the cards have been found practical. That shown in Figure 6-10 is perhaps best for the individual teacher, since all of the types of questions for one course are located in one box or drawer. The 5X8" cards should be filed separately. Standard sets of general directions to the student on each type of item should be typed on colored cards that distinguish them from the cards on which individual items have been typed. A card for directions should be prepared for each type of item. Other cards carrying standard information can be added.

Microcomputer technology can provide the instructor with valuable assistance in the establishment of an electronic item bank. By filing the items electronically, the items can be edited, information can be added such as the difficulty index and discrimination index, the date on which the items were used in a test instrument can be recorded, and a group of items can be

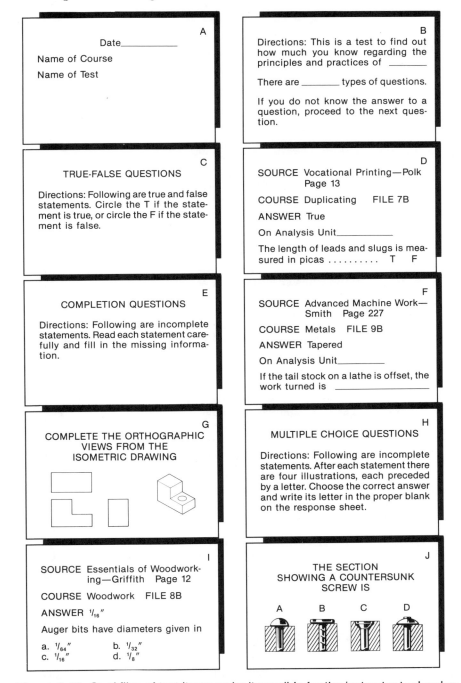

A

Date_____

Name of Course

Name of Test

B

Directions: This is a test to find out how much you know regarding the principles and practices of _____

There are _____ types of questions.

If you do not know the answer to a question, proceed to the next question.

C

TRUE-FALSE QUESTIONS

Directions: Following are true and false statements. Circle the T if the statement is true, or circle the F if the statement is false.

D

SOURCE Vocational Printing—Polk
          Page 13

COURSE Duplicating   FILE 7B

ANSWER True

On Analysis Unit_____

The length of leads and slugs is measured in picas .... T   F

E

COMPLETION QUESTIONS

Directions: Following are incomplete statements. Read each statement carefully and fill in the missing information.

F

SOURCE Advanced Machine Work—
          Smith   Page 227

COURSE Metals   FILE 9B

ANSWER Tapered

On Analysis Unit_____

If the tail stock on a lathe is offset, the work turned is _____

G

COMPLETE THE ORTHOGRAPHIC
VIEWS FROM THE
ISOMETRIC DRAWING

H

MULTIPLE CHOICE QUESTIONS

Directions: Following are incomplete statements. After each statement there are four illustrations, each preceded by a letter. Choose the correct answer and write its letter in the proper blank on the response sheet.

I

SOURCE Essentials of Woodwork-
          ing—Griffith   Page 12

COURSE Woodwork   FILE 8B

ANSWER $1/_{16}''$

Auger bits have diameters given in

a. $1/_{64}''$ b. $1/_{32}''$
c. $1/_{16}''$ d. $1/_8''$

J

THE SECTION
SHOWING A COUNTERSUNK
SCREW IS

A   B   C   D

Figure 6-10. Card files of test items make it possible for the instructor to develop a comprehensive test.

selected for use and printed out section by section as a new form of the test is desired. Obviously, the key concept relates to the instructor's development of an item bank with proper documentation. However, the manner in which it is organized is up to the instructor's preference.

Test Evaluation and Scoring

An instructor should keep a record of the times each test item is missed. This record provides information necessary for decisions regarding the validity, reliability, and usability of each test item. This information can also be used to identify content that was not learned by students and should be taught a second time.

If an item is missed many times, the following type of analysis should be made:

1. If the test item is missed by both high achievers and low achievers, it probably contains information that is ambiguous and should be rewritten or discarded. If the item is missed by the least capable students, but answered correctly by the most capable students in the class, the item is valid, reliable, and discriminating. If an item is generally answered correctly by both high achievers and low achievers, it may mean that the item is too easy.

2. Tests can be used for teaching as well as evaluating. The instructor and students can learn much from studying the results of a good test. Time should be provided in class for a thorough review of the test. Discussion helps to clear up misunderstandings and provides valuable information to the instructor and students.

Beyond the preceding general assessment of the adequacy of a teacher-made test, there is a substantial body of knowledge related to the analysis and evaluation of test items as well as the entire test instrument. References which provide more detail in this area are listed at the end of Chapter 6; however, for the beginning instructor's purposes, a brief review of a systematic way for assessing item difficulty and item discrimination is provided in the following section.

Item Analysis. As mentioned previously, the instructor should make a careful analysis of student responses to the various items on an examination. It is also important to secure student input regarding the thinking processes used to arrive at both correct and incorrect responses. This may provide the instructor with clues regarding both test item construction as well as modifications that might be made in the instructional process itself.

In addition to the more general review and analysis, two basic statistical procedures have been developed that enable the instructor to make systematic observations and comparisons of items. The first of these procedures is referred to as a *difficulty index*. The difficulty index represents the percent of students tested who respond correctly to an item. Therefore, a difficulty index of .75 for an item indicates that 75 percent of the students responded correctly to a given item. A high or low difficulty index does not, in and of itself, tell the instructor that the item should or should not be included. Obviously, the instructor will want some items that all or nearly all of the students get correctly. However, the instructor wants the students to answer correctly because they know the content rather than because of the manner in which the item is worded. Likewise, an item with a low numerical difficulty index, indicating that a small percent responded to the item correctly, does not, in and of itself, tell the instructor that the item is either "good" or "bad." Upon examination of the item, the instructor may decide that the item is a good item but that there needs to be a better instructional strategy in order for more students to learn the content being tested. On the other hand, the item may be worded poorly; and, as a result, even students who know the content miss the test item. If the instructor keeps a pool of items for future use, either in a card file or on a microcomputer disk, it is valuable to record the difficulty index for the item each time it is used. This allows a historical record of the way in which students respond to the item.

Another systematic means by which items can be analyzed involves a comparison of the performance on a given item by students who did well on the entire test and those who did poorly on the test. This statistical comparison is referred to as a *discrimination index*. The discrimination index is based on the assumption that student performance on the entire test provides a reasonable expectation for the way in which a student will respond to any given item. In reality, the discrimination index indicates the extent to which student performance on any given item correlates with the performance by students on the test as a whole. The following procedure is suggested for the calculation of a difficulty index and a discrimination index for a given test item.

Difficulty Index

1. Separate the test papers into an upper third, a middle third, and a lower third. Set aside the middle third and work with only the top and bottom third.

2. However, for small classes of 30 or less, it would be just as appropriate to use the top and bottom half; therefore, our example uses a class of 30 with 9 students answering item #1 correctly.

3. Record the responses for each group for each item.

4. After all correct responses have been recorded for all items, the responses and place them into the following formula to determine the difficulty index for each item:

$$\text{Difficulty Index} = \frac{\overset{(6)}{\text{(high correct}} + \overset{(3)}{\text{low correct)}}}{\underset{(15)}{\text{(N of high group}} + \underset{(15)}{\text{N of low group)}}} = \frac{9}{30} \text{ or } .30$$

Discrimination Index

1. For each item, subtract the number of correct responses made by students in the low group from the number of correct responses made by students in the high group. For example, on item 1 of the test, 6 students from the high group answered the item correctly and 3 students from the low group answered the item correctly. Therefore, the mathematical process would be 6 - 3 = 3.

2. For each item, the numerical difference between the high and low groups would be divided by the number of students in one of the subgroups being used. The formula, therefore, would be:

$$\text{Discrimination Index} = \frac{\overset{(6)}{\text{(high correct}} + \overset{(3)}{\text{low correct)}}}{\underset{(15)\quad(15)}{\text{high or low N}}} = \frac{3}{15} \text{ or } .20$$

There is no absolute value that one should seek for each item. In theory, one should expect students who do well on the entire test to do well on each item. Therefore, the larger the discrimination index the better. An item which discriminates perfectly would have all students in the upper group to answer the item correctly and all students in the lower group to answer incorrectly. Obviously, if you had a negative discrimination and more students in the lower group answered the item correctly than in the higher group, the instructor would need to review the item carefully to identify the reason that students who theoretically knew more about the subject responded incorrectly.

As mentioned previously, the results of the item analysis process do not give absolute answers regarding the decisions that an instructor needs to make. However, they do provide information that suggests to an instructor that test items or instructional strategies need to be reviewed.

ASSIGNING GRADES

Grades are an inherent part of the educational process. Like most anything in life, grades have advantages and disadvantages. The effective instructor learns to maximize the advantages of grades and minimize the disadvantages.

Most instructors expect grades to serve as part of the motivation/reward system as well as provide a documentation of performance or achievement. As indicated earlier in the chapter, the evaluation process may involve a number of factors that must be considered as a student's course grade is determined. Typically, there will be scores on tests, scores on written reports, scores from projects or other student activities, performance test scores and observational ratings made by the instructor. The number of points on the various assessments will probably be different. For example, one test may have 80 total points possible while another might have 120 points possible. A student report may be worth 75 points and the teacher may assign 40 points for class participation, cooperation with other students and other attitudinal factors. Even though students like to know what kind of letter grade they are getting at any given point in the course, it is best to report the actual score earned on a given instrument for the various measures taken during the course. Of course, the instructor or the student can calculate a simple percent by dividing the number of points possible into the student's raw score. If you have announced your grading standards in advance, e.g., 90-100 percent equals A; 78-89 percent equals B; 60-77 percent equals C; 48-59 percent equals D; and 59-0 equal F, students will be able to gain an approximation of their grade by translating the raw score to a percent.

Translating Scores Into Grades

Whenever possible, only raw scores should be reported to students during the course since letter grades on measures of different weight can be misleading. If you accumulate the student's raw scores on several measures during the course, you make only one translation to a letter grade at the end of the course. The instructor should not get trapped into trying to average a dozen or so As, Bs, Cs, Ds and Fs for a course to arrive at a defensible course grade. Most students and parents can understand the translation of raw scores into percents and most will understand the concept of using a percent standard to arrive at a grade. Not everyone will be in agreement with the breakpoint between A and B or between C and B, etc., but there is no substitute for the instructor's judgment based on experience. Over time, the instructor will be able to arrive at the expectation levels for students and course grading will be regarded as fair and reasonable.

In reality, this means of arriving at course grades is somewhat of a compromise between norm-referenced and criterion-referenced grading. With this method, the achievement of one student has no bearing upon the grade received by other students. In fact, all students could receive the grade of A if they all had raw scores that could be converted to 90 percent or higher. Beginning instructors often have difficulty in establishing expected standards of performance, and, as a result, may find a "flexible" standard to be advantageous. With a flexible standard, the instructor would announce that students who receive a grade of 92 percent or higher would receive an A and that students who scored between 80 and 91 percent would receive *at least* a grade of B. In this way, the inexperienced instructor would provide a degree of freedom to allow the "norm-referencing" concept to be brought into play. For example, if the natural break between a group of high achieving students revealed that the *lowest* of the high scores was 89 with the next highest score being an 85, the instructor might assign the grade of A to all scores 89 and higher. The B scores might then begin at 88, even though no student received an 88 and the B range might be dropped down to 77 or 78, again depending on the natural break in scores within the class. As previously described in the section on *statistical concepts*, norm-referencing has some value in grading. Especially with a new instructor who is uncertain regarding the performance standards that should be established for grades. This allows an appropriate use of norm-referencing without the inappropriate and arbitrary use of the normal curve for assigning grades.

Many schemes are available to assist in the translation of numerical scores (raw scores) into letter grades. However, it must be emphasized that there is no substitute for the instructor's judgment based on experience. As previously mentioned, the simplest and perhaps the approach which is easiest to communicate to students and others is the translation of raw scores into percents. With the development of microcomputer software, much of the laborious calculation of percents from raw scores can be handled quickly and accurately. Likewise, the use of a *gradebook* program allows the entry of scores of the various evaluation items throughout the course. (See Chapter 5.)

CONCLUSION

The primary purpose of an instructional program is to facilitate learning on the part of students. Instruction is planned and executed to facilitate learning. Evaluation procedures are designed and applied in an effort to assess the extent to which learning has taken place and indirectly to assess the effectiveness of the instructional process.

Evaluation is a broad concept which takes into account numerous types of measurements, observations, and judgments that provide the instructor with input as decisions are made regarding the extent to which students have learned. Measurement is a more limited concept in which the magnitude of a given attribute or characteristic is determined quantitatively.

As instructors make decisions regarding the extent to which students have learned, they must give careful consideration to the criteria or standards by which achievement is to be judged. An understanding of fundamental statistical procedures will enable the instructor to analyze test data and draw meaningful conclusions related to student achievement and instructional effectiveness.

Although many human traits and attributes distribute themselves in a pattern that has been referred to as a curve of normal distribution, which is "bell-shaped," there are a number of assumptions that would have to be met in order for this concept to be applied to the assignment of achievement test grades. Unfortunately, many instructors have learned about the "curve of normal distribution" without understanding its limitations. As a result, the device has been used inappropriately to arbitrarily assign grades that have little relationship to the student achievement of course objectives.

Student achievement occurs in the cognitive, psychomotor and affective domains, and these areas of development require differing techniques of assessment. The three typical ways in which achievement is judged across these domains are performance tests, observational ratings and written tests. The characteristics of validity, reliability, objectivity, comprehensiveness and practicality can be applied to any of the several achievement measures, although they are most often discussed in terms of written tests. As tests are constructed, instructors will make numerous decisions regarding the length of the test, the amount of content to be covered, and the levels of learning to be assessed. These decisions can be made in a systematic and organized manner through the use of *tables of specifications*. A table of specifications allows the instructor to make decisions regarding the length of the test and the nature of the test in terms of the content to be tested and the levels of learning to be assessed.

The most commonly used types of items for achievement testing are the (1) true/false, (2) completion, (3) multiple choice, (4) identification, (5) matching, and (6) short essay. A number of suggestions for constructing these various types of test items have been provided in an effort to maximize their value in written tests of achievement.

After test items have been developed and organized into a test according to a table of specifications, the test must be administered, scored and ultimately translated into grades. It is extremely important for the effective instructor to develop a systematic procedure for scoring examinations efficiently and accurately. Likewise, the translation of raw scores into course grades must be done in a manner that can be understood by students so that everyone is satisfied that the instructor has gone about the task in a professional manner with a minimum of error and a maximum of fairness and objectivity. Grades and grading practices are valuable in the educational process. However, when they are carried out in a manner which adversely affects student morale and motivation to continue learning, their positive benefits are undermined.

REFERENCES ———————————————————— 6

Bloom, B., Hastings, J., & Madaus, G. (1971). *Handbook on formative and summative evaluation of student learning.* New York: McGraw-Hill.

Bloom, B., et al. (1956). Taxonomy of educational objectives: The classification of educational goals. *Handbook One: Cognitive Domain.* New York: Longman.

Boyd, J., & Shimberg, B. (1971). *Handbook of Performance Testing.* Princeton: Educational Testing Service.

Erickson, R., & Wentling, T. (1976). *Measuring student growth.* Boston: Allyn & Bacon, Inc.

Gage, N., & Berliner, D. (1979). *Educational psychology.* Chicago: Rand-McNally.

Girod, G. (1973). *Writing and assessing attitudinal objectives.* Columbus, OH: Charles E. Merrill Publishing Company.

Green, J. (1975). *Teacher made tests.* New York: Harper & Row.

Gronlund, N. (1985). *Stating objectives for classroom instruction.* New York: The MacMillan Company.

Kubiszyn, T., & Boritch, G. (1984). *Educational testing and measurement.* Glenview, IL: Scott Foresman & Company.

Mitzel, H. (Ed.) (1984). *Encyclopedia of Educational Research.* New York: The Macmillan Company.

Natriello, G., & Dornbusch, S. (1985). *Teacher evaluative standard and student effort.* New York: Longman, Inc.

Popham, W. (1974). *Evaluation in education.* Berkley, CA: McCutchan Publishing.

Popham, W. (1971). *Criterion-referenced measurement.* Englewood Cliffs, NJ: Educational Technology Publications.

Rumors, H. (1963). Grading methods in research on teaching. *Handbook of Research in Teaching.* Chicago: Rand-McNally.

Thorndike, R., & Hagen, E. (1977). *Measurement and evaluation in psychology in education.* New York: Wiley.

Index